The Greatest Conspiracy Ever

SECOND EDITION

By Steven Speray

How Rome was usurped by the Modernists leaving a remnant underground Catholic Church

The Greatest Conspiracy Ever

Second Edition

ISBN: 978-0-578-03574-1

Published by Confiteor
P.O. Box 83
Versailles, KY 40383
www.catholictopgun.com

VERITAS

DEFENDING THE HISTORIC CATHOLIC CHURCH
2009

Dedicated to:

Our Lord, Our Lady, St. Michael, St. Stephen, St. Patrick and all of Heaven.

Table of Contents

(Covers the heresies of Vatican 2, definitions and statements from numerous Popes, Saints, and theologians from Canon Law to

Pope Pius XII's Apostolic Constitution *Vacantis Apostolicae Sedis* (December 8, 1945), which declares: "34. None of the cardinals may in any way, or by pretext of any excommunication, suspension, or interdict whatsoever, *or of any other ecclesiastical impediment*, be excluded in the active and passive election of the Supreme Pontiff. We hereby suspend such censures solely for the purposes of the said election; at other times they are to remain in vigor (AAS 38 [1946], p. 76)."

Active means they are allowed to vote, passive means they can be elected validly to the Papacy........................289

9. If sedevacantism is true, there could never be a true pope in the future. The interregnum period ends with the death of the last Cardinal since without Cardinals no future election is possible. No sedevacantist has ever come up with a theory as to how God could now restore the papacy in such a way that all faithful Catholics could join in recognizing the new pope as certainly valid..291

10. Church must be visible which it wouldn't be without a pope. Sedevacantists believe in a headless monster.........295

11. There are no bishops with ordinary jurisdiction therefore, no authority. Also, Matthew 18:17-18 cannot apply without a pope or bishops with supplied jurisdiction.......295

12. If they are doubtful, we must give them the benefit of the doubt. It is possible they are insane, therefore not true heretics...297

13. Look at the chaos of sedevacantism. There are so many types all rendering each other as non-Catholics. There is no unity and yet the Church is one faith. The chaos of not knowing what is valid or not is also present..................298

14. All laws and disciplines of the Vatican 2 Church are not infallible, therefore sedevacantists cannot use this argument against the Church....................................299

Part 1 of the Argument: If nothing is wrong with an approved discipline without spot or blemish, it needs no further improvement because it is complete, perfect, and lacking nothing, otherwise something is wrong with it. Changing it wouldn't be necessary. Webster's defines the word perfect: 1. excellent or complete beyond improvement. 2. without flaws or blemish. 3. accurate in every detail. 4. thorough, utter. 5. Some commentators object to the use of comparative terms such as most, more, and rather with perfect on the grounds that perfect describes an absolute condition that cannot exist in degrees...........................305

Part 2 of Argument: There is nothing wrong with having females serving and altar girls, lectors, acolytes. The previous condemnation was against the practice before it was approved because it was about disobedience not the practice itself..306

15. The harmful law and discipline doctrine applies only when they are universal. Females serving the altar was not a universal practice, therefore it does not apply. Altar girls are harmful but were not imposed on the whole church. Pope Pius XII in *Mystici Corporis*, 66 (1943) states: "Certainly the loving Mother is spotless in the Sacraments, by which she gives birth to and nourishes her children; in the faith which she has always preserved inviolate; in her sacred laws imposed on all; in the evangelical counsels which she recommends; in those heavenly gifts and extraordinary graces through which, with inexhaustible fecundity, she generates hosts of martyrs, virgins and confessors." Therefore, the church could issue harmful disciplines to part of the church as it has with altar girls..........................307

16. The *Novus Ordo* or new mass is not a new rite but a new form of old rite...309

Part 1 of Argument: First, if the pope were not allowed to change the rubrics of the Mass, then the Latin Mass that was created in the 5th century by Pope Gelasius or the seventh century by Pope Gregory, and confirmed by Pius V, would be the first candidate for the offense of "changing the rite," since the previous rite used in the 1-3 centuries was different than what was adopted later. Rest assured, if Pope Gelasius could change the rubrics of the Mass, then so can Paul.

Someone might argue that Gelasius and Gregory were permitted to change the rite because the Council of Trent did not come along until about a 1000 years later, but this argument is fallacious because, if Gelasius and Gregory changed the rite, then the Council of Trent, if Canon 13 applied to popes, would have never said that the rite could not be change, otherwise the council would have indicted Gelasius and Gregory..309

Part 2 of Argument: The definition of a new rite is the Church's to define, not the sedevacantists. Evidently, the Church understands a new rite other than what occurred in 1968 when Paul VI gave us the *Novus Ordo*, and that is because the *Novus Ordo* contains the same consecration formula as the previous mass. A new rite would be a mass that changed the consecration formula, or did away with it altogether..310

Part 3 of Argument: The language of Session 7, Canon 13, does not say "the pastor of THE CHURCH," but "any PASTORS (plural) of the CHURCHES" (plural). Hence, the universal church is not in view, otherwise "pastors" and "churches" would be in the singular..............................311

Part 4 of Argument: The original Latin of Canon 13 says *quemcumque ecclesiarum pastorem* which means whichever pastor of the churches. Because churches is in the

plural, Trent is first referring to the churches of the world under a particular bishop. Moreover, the fact that the pope has allowed various rites in the world (e.g., Latin rite, Byzantine rite, Melchite rite, etc) shows that he alone has the authority to allow or disallow them, and that the particular bishop of that church does not have the authority. It is granted, however, that the pope cannot change or eliminate the consecration formula of the Mass, for if he did, it would be a new rite. If Canon 13 is applicable to the pope, it is only applicable in that sense, but it is not Canon 13 that is the main obstacle to this limitation, but Session 13 and Session 22 on the Mass and Eucharist..........................311

Part 5 of Argument: The council's purpose was not to tie the hands of future popes in doing what the popes thought best for the dissemination of the Mass among the populace...312

Part 6 of Argument: The pope is the supreme authority, has the right to decide what is best for his people. The Council of Trent would have never said something to the effect: "We bind all future popes to the stipulation that they cannot change the rubrics or words of the Mass for any reason," but that's what the council would have had to say to prohibit future popes from doing so, but it would never have done so, and did not do so in Canon 13.....................312

Part 7 of Argument: The pope can be included by logical extension (although the language of Canon 13 applies mainly to pastors of the Churches in the plural). But the only entity that has the authority to define what a new rite is the Catholic Church, not any other sedevacantist. As such, Paul VI, Pope John Paul I, Pope John Paul II and Pope Benedict XVI have all agreed that the *Novus Ordo* is not a new rite under the definition of Session 7, Canon 13 of Trent. Because of that, (if you read about the development of the *Novus Ordo* wording) Paul VI was very careful to keep the

-All Scripture quotes come from one of the following sources:
Douay-Rheims,

Confraternity (Challoner Rheims),
Revised Standard Version Catholic Edition

-All papal or saint quotes come from one of the following sources unless otherwise noted:

-The Papal Encyclicals, Claudia Carlen, Raleigh: The Peirian Press, Vol. 1 (1740-1878), Vol. 2 (1878-1903), Vol. 3 (1903-1939), Vol. 4 (1939-1958)

-The Sources of Catholic Dogma, Denzinger "Enchiridion Symbolorum", Roy J. Deferrari, 13th Edition, Loreto Publications

-Decrees of the Ecumenical Councils, Norman P. Tanner SJ, Sheed & Ward and Georgetown University Press, 1990, Vol. 1 and 2, Tanner

-The Faith of the Early Fathers, William A. Jurgens, Collegeville, MN, The Liturgical Press, 1970, Vol. 1, 2, and 3,

Introductory Statement

I have observed over the years in all my talks, lectures, speeches, and debates that:

Most people hate or could care less about religion. Out of those, most of them find religion only remotely interesting. The few that actually find religion very interesting, only a few of them find religion as the most important thing in their lives. Out of the few that find religion the most important thing in their lives, very few of these care about how true their religion is. Out of those that care about the truth of their religion as the most important aspect of their lives, most of them will not see the truth because of the difficulty to actually accept it. All this in turn causes more people to hate religion because of the hypocrisy.

Now it is true that what will be presented will be very disturbing to the typical unknowing Catholic. As a matter of fact, when I finally came to the conclusion of what I will present to you, I could not sleep or eat properly for a week. My world was literally flipped upside down not knowing what to do next, except pray and find out more.

So I decided to let all my family and friends know what I had discovered. I also decided to let those whom I respected in the apologetic world on the same details. I found immediately that my newfound position was considered whacko, insane, illogical, and drastically incorrect.

Therefore I challenged them to answer the questions.

In every debate I've engaged in, I've cornered my opponents, proving them wrong covering every base lock, stock and barrel, and every single time they quit. These opponents include some of the best-known apologists in the world.

The most common reaction is completely dismissing the position of sedevacantism as the new wave of religious fanaticism.

But the facts speak for themselves. It is an illusion that modern day Rome is the same Catholic Church as that rock on which Christ built the Church. Catholics must be able to use their minds to think outside of the box created by the Vatican 2 illusionists.

Real and true Catholicism has been rejected by Rome, and it is up to Catholics to find out and accept that the Catholic Church is now a remnant.

Even now, I rarely encounter good-willed individuals. One would think that those who claim to love Christ and the His truth would want to know if he were in the wrong religion since doing so would create a false relationship with God. In fact, the opposite is true.

Most of these so-called Christians actually hate Christ and His truth precisely because of the pride they possess. It shouldn't matter how long one was in error unless he was so filled with pride to admit error; to be right regardless how wrong one is.

Speaking from personal experience, I attended the *Novus Ordo* mass 7 days a week for 15 years and defended the Vatican 2 Church giving lectures in high schools; a total of 33 years in the wrong religion, which I thought was the Catholic Church. Now I reject as valid the very mass that I attended and condemn the very religion I once defended. I became a real and true Catholic and found the rock on which Christ really built His Catholic Church. This is why my life was flipped upside down.

There is no glory, fame, or money in following this path. I do it because truth matters and apart from this truth is apart from Christ and ultimately salvation.

On top of all the new age nonsense coming out of Rome, there is a new wave of religious fervor among Evangelicals and it is spreading like wildfire. Because of the weird televangelists, Fundamentalists, Evangelicals, and even some sedevacantists, who all give Christianity a bad name, it's no wonder why many non-Christians such as the Jews have such a dislike for Christianity. It is a terrible scandal when Christianity is made to look ridiculous.

However, their form of "Christianity" is really a form of anti-Christianity. Their "Jesus" doesn't exist since the real Jesus, the Lord of History is found only in historic Christianity not found in the polluted landscape of churches found on every corner and TV programs on every satellite and cable programming.

Their form of religion is really a mockery of Christianity. It is satanic and keeps many people from seeing what historic Christianity is all about. There is only one form of Christianity, not thousands.

The best way to hide a tree is in a forest. The best way to find this particular tree is knowledge of its type and location.

With this in mind, we'll now shoot down the forest of defenses, so let's lock-n-load.

The following writing will be raw and unedited.

Bird's Eye View

In the Apocalypse, Rome becomes a harlot during the last days with Satan being released for one final assault on the Church. The universal testimony of the early Church Fathers prophesies that Rome will apostatize from the Catholic Faith.

In the nineteenth century, Freemasons boast about infiltrating the Catholic Church to the papacy, knowing Catholics will be *"blindly"* obedient to a Masonic *"pope."*

Pope Pius IX condemns liberalism in all its forms.

Pope Leo XIII condemns Freemasonry, composes prayer to St. Michael to protect papacy from the enemies (particularly Satan) of the Church to be said after Holy Mass.

Pope St. Pius X, the greatest pope in 500 years since Pope St. Pius V condemns Modernism as the *"synthesis of all heresies."*

Sister Lucia, from the famous Marian apparition of Fatima, says that a Great Chastisement will happen between 1957 and 1960. The Church approved apparition of Our Lady of Good Success gave prophesy of a popeless Church in 20th century.

In 1958, Angelo Roncalli was elected to the papacy taking the name John XXIII. He had previously been on Vatican record for many years for suspicion of modernism.

John XXIII called the Second Vatican Council. It was the first ecumenical council that was void of any anathemas, and reversed traditional Catholicism on several points. John refused to read the Third Secret of Fatima in 1960 as asked by Our Lady, he changed the mass and eliminated the St. Michael prayer from it, and he deleted several prayers and many feast days of the traditional calendar.

In 1963, Giovanni Battista Montini was elected to the papacy taking the name Paul VI. He had previously betrayed Pope Pius XII with his relations with the Soviets.

Paul VI sealed the Second Vatican Council and changed all seven sacraments. He suppressed the Mass of Pope St. Pius V and established his New Mass, which resembles the mass of Luther and Cramner.

After the first month reign of John Paul I, who took the name of his two predecessors, he died a mysterious death and John Paul II was elected.

John Paul II traveled the world visiting the world's pagan leaders sometimes participating in their worship services.

He beatifies John XXIII.

John Paul II is hailed by the whole world as a great leader, and praised by Protestants, Jews, Muslims, and Freemasons.

In his new Catechism of the Catholic Church, John Paul II never mentions or references Pope St. Pius X's documents against modernism.

After John Paul II's death, his right-hand man, Joseph Ratzinger is elected taking the name Benedict XVI.

Like John XXIII, Ratzinger was also on record for suspect of heresy.

He begins the canonization process of John Paul II.

Benedict XVI is on record saying that all papal documents against modernism are obsolete.

At present, a relatively small group of Catholics (called sedevacantists) condemn the last five claimants to the papacy as antipopes and claim that the prophecy of Rome apostatizing has come to pass.

The Purpose of this Writing

Truth matters or else there would be no point to religion whatsoever. Why practice any religion if it does not matter whether it is true or not?

If one religion is better than another but both are legitimate roads to Heaven, why would anyone practice the most difficult religion if only to have a greater place in Heaven but a greater chance of hell? Would Christ ask us to gamble with our souls?

All roads may lead to Rome but only one road leads to Heaven. The one and only road to Heaven is **Jesus Christ as He Himself states**, *"I am the way, and the truth, and the life; no one comes to the Father, but by me."* (John 14:6)

Christ implies that apart from the truth is apart from the way and life itself. The "Way" was how the Church was first known. The Way, Truth, and Life are so linked together, that you cannot have one without the others. You cannot have only one part of Christ. You either have Him totally or not at all.

Jesus replied to Pontius Pilate, *"You say that I am a king. For this I was born, and for this I have come into the world, to bear witness to the truth."* (John 18:37)

Christ bore witness to "the" truth. This means truth is not relative. If it is true for you, it must be true for me.

Jesus said He would build His [one] Church and it will never die.

"And I tell you, you are Peter, and on this rock I will build my church, and the gates of hell shall not prevail against it." (Matthew 16:18)

"I am with you all days, even unto the consummation of the world." (Matthew 28:20)

Notice, Christ built a church, not churches. The 20,000 plus denominations and non-denominations today, do not add up to "a" church. All have different ways, beliefs, teachings, and practices. They all do not make up a single religious church.

The Church of Christ is the Body of Christ because She is the Bride of Christ.

(Ephesians 5:22-32) "[22] Wives, be subject to your husbands, as to the Lord. [23] For the husband is the head of the wife as Christ is the head of the church, his body, and is himself its Savior. [24] As the church is subject to Christ, so let wives also be subject in everything to their husbands. [25] Husbands, love your wives, as Christ loved the church and gave himself up for her, [26] that he might sanctify her, having cleansed her by the washing of water with the word, [27] that he might present the church to himself in splendor, without spot or wrinkle or any such thing, that she might be holy and without blemish. [28] Even so husbands should love their wives as their own bodies. He who loves his wife loves himself. [29] For no man ever hates his own flesh, but nourishes and cherishes it, as Christ does the church, [30] because we are members of his body. [31] "For this reason a man shall leave his father and mother and be joined to his wife, and the two shall become one flesh." [32] This mystery is a profound one, and I am saying that it refers to Christ and the church;"

(Colossians 1:18, 24) "[18] He is the head of the body, the church; [24] his body, that is, the church,"

(I Corinthians 6:15) "Do you not know that your bodies are members of Christ? Shall I therefore take the members of Christ and make them members of a prostitute? Never!"

(I Corinthians 12:27) "Now you are the body of Christ and individually members of it."

(Romans 12:4-5) "For as in one body we have many members, and all the members do not have the same function, so we, though many, are one body in Christ, and individually members one of another."

The Church Christ founded is the Way.

(Acts 9:2) "so that if he found any belonging to the Way"

(Acts 19:9, 23) "[9] when some were stubborn and disbelieved, speaking evil of the Way before the congregation [23] About that time there arose no little stir concerning the Way."

(Acts 24:14, 22) "[14] that according to the Way, which they call a sect, worship the God of our fathers, believing everything laid down by the law or written in the prophets, [22] But Felix, having a rather accurate knowledge of the Way,"

If Christ is the Way and the Church is the Way, and the Church is the Body of Christ, then apart from Christ and the Church is apart from Life. Apart from life means apart from salvation, therefore, outside the church there is no salvation.

The Church is Christ's Flock.

"I am the good shepherd; I know my own and my own know me, as the Father knows me and I know the Father; and I lay down my life for the sheep. And I have other sheep that are not of this fold; I must bring them also, and they will heed my voice. So there shall be one flock, one shepherd." (John 10:14-16)

"Every one who is of the truth hears my voice." (John 18:37)

(I Peter 5:1-4) "So I exhort the elders among you, as a fellow elder and a witness of the sufferings of Christ as well as a partaker in the glory that is to be revealed. Tend the flock of God that is your charge, not by constraint but willingly, not for shameful gain but eagerly, not as domineering over those in your charge but being examples to the flock. And when the chief Shepherd is manifested you will obtain the unfading crown of glory."

The Church is "of the truth" because it hears the voice of Christ, who is the Head and Shepherd. Again, there is only "one flock" not different flocks. Those who are not of the one flock, Christ must bring into the fold. The implication again, is the flock will attain salvation with the "crown of glory", but outside the fold there will not be that crown of glory meaning no salvation.

The Church is a visible institution.

"You are the light of the world. A city set on a hill cannot be hid."(Matthew 5:14)

(I Corinthians 12:28) "And God has appointed in the church first apostles, second prophets, third teachers, and then workers of miracles, then healers, helpers, administrators, and speakers in various kinds of tongues."

(Colossians 1:24-25) "his body, that is, the church, of which I became a minister according to the divine office"

The Church is visible or else these passages are meaningless. If there are apostles and they are first, then the rest should follow them because Apostles are leaders, overseers, and the bishops of the Church. They did not appoint themselves but were appointed by Christ Himself or other Apostles after Him. They don't start their own churches (denominations and non-denominations) but spread the one Church already founded.

The Church is the household of God.

(Ephesians 2:19-22) "So then you are no longer strangers and sojourners, but you are fellow citizens with the saints and members of the household of God, built upon the foundation of the apostles and prophets, Christ Jesus himself being the cornerstone, in whom the whole structure is joined together and grows into a holy temple in the Lord; in whom you also are built into it for a dwelling place of God in the Spirit."

(I Timothy 3:15) "you may know how one ought to behave in the household of God, which is the church of the living God"

Notice, the Church is built upon Christ and the apostles and prophets, not men reinventing religion with a new foundation of enlightened thought such as the Protestant and Evangelical Reformers who started their own churches based on what they thought the church should be. Sola Scriptura (Bible Alone) is the myth, which became the justification to reject the foundation of the Apostles, and create a new foundation and just call it the foundation of the Apostles. Modernism is the enlightened thought of the new religion of Rome, which replaced historic Christianity and usurped the Catholic name.

The Church is the household of Faith.

(Galatians 6:10) "So then, as we have opportunity, let us do good to all men, and especially to those who are of the household of faith."

The Church equals Faith. If you have "the" Faith, you are of "the" Church.

The Church is the one Faith.

(Ephesians 4-6) "There is one body and one Spirit, just as you were called to the one hope that belongs to your call, one Lord, one faith, one baptism, one God and Father of us all, who is above all and through all and in all."

(I Timothy 6:20-21) "O Timothy, guard what has been entrusted to you. Avoid the godless chatter and contradictions of what is falsely called knowledge, for by professing it some have missed the mark as regards the faith. Grace be with you."

(Jude 1:20) "But you, beloved, build yourselves up on your most holy faith; pray in the Holy Spirit;"

Since there is only one Lord, it only follows that there is only one Faith. The Church is the Body of Christ. It equals the Faith, which equals the Way, the Truth, and the Life.

The Church has true authority.

"...tell it to the church; and if he refuses to listen even to the church, let him be to you as a Gentile and a tax collector. Truly, I say to you, whatever you bind on earth shall be bound in heaven, and whatever you loose on earth shall be loosed in heaven." (Matthew 18: 17-18)

(Galatians 1:8) "But even if we, or an angel from heaven, should preach to you a gospel contrary to that which we preached to you, let him be accursed (anathema or cut-off)."

(Titus 2:15) "Declare these things; exhort and reprove with all authority. Let no one disregard you."

If one has a disagreement about something of the Faith, which Church does he take it to? If the Faith is the Church, then there must be someone whom has the authority in the Church to say so. This someone is the one who has the authority to bind and loose. He is the one whom has the authority to anathematize. Although several persons could make certain decisions in the Church, it ultimately must come down to one person in the end. But the authority cannot be rejected or else you will automatically be cut-off from the Way. Thus, the rejection of this authority will be the rejection of salvation. *"Whoever hears you, hears me; and whoever rejects you, rejects me,"* says the Lord Jesus. (Luke 10:16)

The Church is immaculate and has no flaws or defections.

(Ephesians 5:25-27) "Christ loved the church and gave himself up for her, that he might sanctify her, having cleansed her by the washing of water with the word, that he might present the church to himself in splendor, without spot or wrinkle or any such thing, that she might be holy and without blemish."

This demonstrates how one cannot complain about anything the Church teaches or practices or else the implication would be the Church is not a spotless Bride, but rather a whore. He who rejects anything the Church teaches or practices, because he thinks them to be spots, wrinkles or blemishes of the Church, blasphemes Christ and His Church.

The Church is the pillar and bulwark of Truth and is infallible.

(I Timothy 3:14-15) "I am writing these instructions to you so that, if I am delayed, you may know how one ought to behave in the household of God, which is the church of the living God, the pillar and bulwark of the truth."

A pillar and bulwark is something that holds something else up. In this case, it is the Church who holds up the Truth. If something is not true, then it is a lie. The Church cannot lie. Everything the Church teaches must be true or this passage is meaningless.

"Every one who is of the truth hears my voice." (John 18:37)

"But the hour is coming, and now is, when the true worshipers will worship the Father in spirit and truth, for such the Father seeks to worship him. God is spirit, and those who worship him must worship in spirit and truth." (John 4:23-24)

The worship of the Church is of the spirit and truth. It is not apart from the spirit and truth, or else, it would not be the true Church doing the worshiping.

"[7] Nevertheless I tell you the truth: it is to your advantage that I go away, for if I do not go away, the Counselor will not come

to you; but if I go, I will send him to you. [13] When the Spirit of truth comes, he will guide you into all the truth; for he will not speak on his own authority, but whatever he hears he will speak, and he will declare to you the things that are to come." (John 16:7, 13)

"[17} Sanctify them in the truth; thy word is truth. [19] And for their sake I consecrate myself, that they also may be consecrated in truth." (John 17:17, 19)

"And I tell you, you are Peter, and on this rock I will build my church, and the gates of hell shall not prevail against it. I will give you the keys of the kingdom of heaven, and whatever you bind on earth shall be bound in heaven, and whatever you loose on earth shall be loosed in heaven." (Matthew 16:18-19)

What are the gates of hell but the lies of the devil and men. If the Church taught one lie, then the powers of hell would prevail. However, Christ promised this never to happen. The keys are given to one man, Peter. He is that someone whom Christ has given the power and the authority to bind and loose. He is the one whom has been given the authority to anathematize. The keys also denote succession. All this can be seen in Isaiah 22:22, from which Christ, the Eternal son of David, was drawing from, when He gave Peter the keys, just as Eli'akim was given the key to the house of David.

Therefore, Peter's true successors will have his same power, which ultimately comes from Christ. This has always been the belief and practice of the Church Christ founded. To reject Peter and his successors' authority is to reject the historic Christian faith. It also means the rejection of the Way, the Truth, and the Life who is Christ himself. Apart from this truth of Peter means apart from salvation. Salvation depends on this truth to make sense of the whole of the Scriptures about what the Church is, does, and means. Refusing to listen even to the Church, which must by necessity come down to the authority of one man, is to be as the Gentile and tax collector.

"tell it to the church; and if he refuses to listen even to the church, let him be to you as a Gentile and a tax collector. Truly, I say to you, whatever you bind on earth shall be bound in heaven, and whatever you loose on earth shall be loosed in heaven." (Matthew 18: 17-18)

The Church guards all truth and keeps out all false teachings out.

"Abide in me, and I in you. As the branch cannot bear fruit by itself, unless it abides in the vine, neither can you, unless you abide in me. I am the vine, you are the branches. He who abides in me, and I in him, he it is that bears much fruit, for apart from me you can do nothing. If a man does not abide in me, he is cast forth as a branch and withers; and the branches are gathered, thrown into the fire and burned. If you abide in me, and my words abide in you, ask whatever you will, and it shall be done for you. By this my Father is glorified, that you bear much fruit, and so prove to be my disciples. As the Father has loved me, so have I loved you; abide in my love. If you keep my commandments, you will abide in my love, just as I have kept my Father's commandments and abide in his love." (John 15:4-10)

(Galatians 1:8) "But even if we, or an angel from heaven, should preach to you a gospel contrary to that which we preached to you, let him be accursed (anathema or cut-off)."

(I Corinthians 16:21-23) "I, Paul, write this greeting with my own hand. If anyone has no love for the Lord, let him be accursed. Our Lord, come! The grace of the Lord Jesus be with you."

(II Timothy 4:3-4) "For the time is coming when people will not endure sound teaching, but having itching ears they will accumulate for themselves teachers to suit their own likings, and will turn away from listening to the truth and wander into myths."

(I Peter 5:8-9) "Be sober, be watchful. Your adversary the devil prowls around like a roaring lion, seeking someone to devour. Resist him, firm in your faith"

(Colossians 1:21-23) "And you, who once were estranged and hostile in mind, doing evil deeds, he has now reconciled in his body of flesh by his death, in order to present you holy and blameless and irreproachable before him, provided that you continue in the faith, stable and steadfast, not shifting from the hope of the gospel which you heard, which has been preached to every creature under heaven, and of which I, Paul, became a minister."

(I Timothy 1:3-11) "As I urged you when I was going to Macedonia, remain at Ephesus that you may charge certain persons not to teach any different doctrine, [4] nor to occupy themselves with myths and endless genealogies which promote speculations rather than the divine training that is in faith; [5] whereas the aim of our charge is love that issues from a pure heart and a good conscience and sincere faith. [6] Certain persons by swerving from these have wandered away into vain discussion, [7] desiring to be teachers of the law, without understanding either what they are saying or the things about which they make assertions. [8] Now we know that the law is good, if any one uses it lawfully, [9] understanding this, that the law is not laid down for the just but for the lawless and disobedient, for the ungodly and sinners, for the unholy and profane, for murderers of fathers and murderers of mothers, for manslayers, [10] immoral persons, sodomites, kidnapers, liars, perjurers, and whatever else is contrary to sound doctrine, [11] in accordance with the glorious gospel of the blessed God with which I have been entrusted."

(II Tim 1:14) "guard the truth that has been entrusted to you by the Holy Spirit who dwells within us."

CONCLUSION

According to the Holy Scriptures, the Church Christ founded is the household of God and Faith. It is a visible institution with divine offices. It has the full authority of Christ to teach, preach, sanctify, and anathematize. The Church is One, Holy, Catholic, and Apostolic. It is united in faith and perfected in truth. Outside this Church, there is no salvation. The Church of Christ can be found in all generations. Only one Church can claim to be this Church for only one has all the marks. One cannot claim to believe in Jesus, the Holy Bible, and Christianity without acknowledging it.

The TRUTH of religion matters for the salvation of men.

Truth is objective. The true religion must be perfect in every way. If one discrepancy can be found by way of doctrine in a particular religion, then the whole religion is corrupt. It must be rejected entirely.

Christ calls man to be perfect. (Matthew 5:48)

If God is to be worshiped in spirit and truth (John 4:24), then a false religion would not be in spirit and truth, but in contradiction and error.

To remain in a false religion as one picks and chooses out of the false religion what is good and what is bad, is not in spirit and truth.

The whole tree must be good. If it bears bad fruit, it should be cut down and thrown into the fire. (Luke 3:9, 13:7)

The Vatican 2 church is a massive tree that bears nothing but bad fruit. It is not the Catholic Church but a counterfeit church, an ape church that mocks Christ and everything that is holy.

Catholic Prophecies that Rome will lose the Faith

Sedevacantism is a position, not a religion, held by Catholics of the historic Catholic Faith. The word comes from the Latin - *Sede Vacant* (the Chair is Vacant). Catholics that hold this position believe Rome has lost the faith and the Chair of Peter has been vacant since the death of Pope Pius XII in 1958.

The reason for this belief is that the last five claimants to the papacy have demonstrated in the external forum that they are not Catholic in their beliefs, and have formally taught and promoted, as good, doctrines and disciplines that have been previously condemned by the Catholic Church as contrary to the Catholic Faith. These false claimants to the papacy will be referred to as the conciliar popes or antipopes.

In essence, the conciliar popes have not only usurped the papacy, but they have implanted a new religion altogether. This new religion of Rome began with the Second Vatican Council. Out of the council came novel teachings that contradict dogmas of the Catholic Faith. The conciliar popes have taught what the novel teachings of the council mean in order that the council is properly interpreted. Those novel teachings and interpretations will be covered in detail and in contrast to the dogmas of the Faith.

Also, the conciliar popes have introduced practices or disciplines that have been condemned by the historic Church as contrary to the Divine laws of God.

This study will cover the primary errors of the conciliar popes and will give the necessary answers to the objections against the position of sedevacantism.

A common misrepresentation for the reason of sedevacantism is the new mass (*novus ordo missae*) decreed by Antipope Paul VI. It is true that Catholics (sedevacantists) reject the once faulty consecration (*"For All"*) as invalidating the mass through reasonable doubt. However, sedevacantism is not based, nor has as its foundation the new mass of Paul VI. If the holy mass was never touched by Rome, sedevacantism would still exist today. However, the new mass of Paul VI is one of the bad fruits by which Christ tells His disciples that we'll know who the false prophets are. St. Peter writes that with false prophets, false teachers will be among them secretly bringing in destructive heresies.

Therefore, the foundation for sedevacantism is not the mass, nor is it the Second Vatican Council. The foundation which sedevacantism rests is Christ's promise that the gates of hell shall not prevail against His Church. The Second Council of Constantinople, in 553 AD, defined the gates of hell as the *"death-dealing tongues of heretics."*

If the papacy could be filled with a death-dealing tongue of a heretic, then the Head of the Church would be counted along with the devil, the father of lies. This is impossible since Christ with the pope is the Head of the Church. Christ is not in union with the devil, but a heretic is. Therefore, the pope cannot be a heretic nor formally teach heresy. This is what Christ meant when He said the gates of hell will not prevail, since the context of the biblical passage was with St. Peter's confession of Faith and Christ giving him the keys to the kingdom of heaven symbolizing both the power over the Church and dynastic succession.

Pope Leo XIII called the Roman Pontiffs *"the Gates of the Church"* in his 1894 encyclical letter *Praeclara Gratulationis Publicae.* Therefore, the gates of hell cannot be one and the same as the gates of the Church. If they could, then Christ's promise fails.

I submit that this argument alone debunks all theological speculation, theories, and opinions that the pope could be at the same time a heretic.

Also, the Catholic Church as dogmatically declared that She has no heretics.

Pope Innocent III, *Eius exemplo*, Dec. 18, 1208: *"By the heart we believe and by the mouth we confess the* ***one Church, not of heretics****, but the Holy Roman, Catholic, and Apostolic Church."*

Pope Eugene IV, Council of Florence, "*Cantate Domino*," 1441: *"The Holy Roman Church firmly believes, professes and preaches that all those who* ***are outside the Catholic Church****, not only pagans* ***but also*** *Jews or* ***heretics and schismatics****..."*

Pope Leo XIII, *Satis Cognitum* (# 9), June 29, 1896: "The practice of the Church has always been the same, as is shown by the unanimous teaching of the Fathers, who were wont to hold as outside Catholic communion, **and alien to the Church, whoever would recede in the least degree from any point of doctrine proposed by her authoritative Magisterium.** "...But he who dissents even in one point from divinely revealed truth absolutely rejects all faith, since he thereby refuses to honor God as the supreme truth and the formal motive of faith."

St. Vincent of Lerins (ca. 400-ca. 450): "What then should a Catholic do if some part of the Church were to separate itself from communion with the universal Faith? What other choice can he make but to prefer to the gangrenous and corrupted member the whole of the body that is sound. And if some new contagion were to try to poison no longer a small part of the Church, but all of the Church at the same time, then he will take the greatest care to attach himself to antiquity which, obviously, can no longer be seduced by any lying novelty." (*Commonitorium*)

This section on Catholic prophesies is an apologia for the position of sedevacantism by demonstrating the position is consistent with the teachings of the Catholic Church.

Such prophecies prove that sedevacantism isn't against Church teaching, since some of the following prophecies would create such a position. Many more prophecies could be added.

Also, the prophecies (especially the biblical ones) imply that Rome actually had the true Faith up until it loses it. This would necessarily indicate that any religion contrary to Rome before it apostatizes would prove that particular religion a false religion and not the true Faith. After all, the Holy Bible speaks about Rome losing the Faith and becoming a harlot which necessarily means that Rome had the Faith before losing it. That Faith found in Rome would be the true Faith. It wouldn't be an overboard statement to say that all those so-called Christian religions that oppose that Faith once found in Rome are really satanic religions since they oppose the Church founded by Christ.

The Holy Scriptures: The Great Apostasy and Counterfeit Church Prophesied

(Matthew 24:15-28) *"Therefore when you shall see "the abomination of desolation" which was spoken of by Daniel the Prophet (Daniel 9:27), standing in the holy place (he that readeth, let him understand) then they that are in Judea, let them flee to the mountains...."*

(Luke 18:8) *"But yet the Son of man, when he cometh, shall he find, think you, faith on earth?"*

(Matt. 24:21, Mark 13:19) *"For then there will be great tribulation, such as has not been from the beginning of the world until now, nor will be."*

Comment: Our Lord clearly implies the Faith may be in dire straits by the time He comes again. When uniting this statement with those found in Matthew 24, II Thessalonians 2, and the Apocalypse 17 and 18, we have a clearer picture what Christ was telling his followers. It will be worse than anything ever seen in history.

(Matthew 24:38-39) *"For, as in the days before the flood they were eating and drinking, marrying and giving in marriage, even till that day in which Noe entered into the ark, and they did not understand until the flood came and swept them all away; even so will be the coming of the Son of Man."*

(Luke 27: 26-30) *"And as it came to pass in the days of Noe, even so will it be in the days of the Son of Man. They were eating and drinking, they were marrying and giving in marriage, until the day when Noe entered the ark, and the flood came and destroyed them all. Or as it came to pass in the days of Lot: they were eating and drinking, they were buying and selling, they were planting and building; but on the day that Lot went out from Sodom, it rained fire and brimstone from heaven and destroyed them all. In the same wise will it be on the day that the Son of Man is revealed."*

Comment: The great flood of Noe (Noah) wiped out all but eight people in the world and only Lot's family survived the destruction of Sodom. It would appear that Great Apostasy will leave only a remnant of the faithful left on earth when Christ comes again.

Apostasies in History

"In the time of the Emperor Valens (4th century), Basil was virtually the only orthodox Bishop in all the East who succeeded in retaining charge of his see... If it has no other importance for modern man, a knowledge of the history of Arianism should demonstrate at least that the Catholic Church takes no account of popularity and numbers in shaping and maintaining doctrine: else, we should long since have had to abandon Basil and Hilary and Athanasius and Liberius and Ossius and call ourselves after Arius." (Fr. William Jurgens, *The Faith of the Early Fathers*, Vol. 2, p. 3)

"At one point in the Church's history, (approximately A.D. 380), perhaps the number of Catholic bishops in possession of sees, as opposed to Arian bishops in possession of sees, was no greater than something between 1% and 3% of the total. Had doctrine been determined by popularity, today we should all be deniers of Christ and opponents of the Spirit." (Fr. William Jurgens, The *Faith of the Early Fathers*, Vol. 2, p 39)

All of England fell in the apostasy of Anglicanism. If one country could so easily fall because of a corrupt king and continue through the succession of kings and queens, why not the whole world if deceived by several antipopes?

If nearly the whole world fell in the Arian heresy, and an entire country fell into the Anglican heresy, and these are not the Great Apostasy or Great Revolt prophesied in Scripture, how much worse could it be?

St. Athanasius stated: *"Even if Catholics faithful to tradition are reduced to a handful, they are the ones who are the true Church of Jesus Christ."* (*Coll. Selecta SS. Eccl. Patrum.* Caillu and Guillou, Vol. 32, pp. 411-412)

Rome admits in the 19th century that she will lose the faith:

Henry Edward Cardinal Manning

The Present Crisis of the Holy See, 1861, London: Burns and Lambert, pp. 88-90

"The apostasy of the city of Rome from the vicar of Christ and its destruction by Antichrist may be thoughts so new to many Catholics, that I think it well to recite the text of theologians of greatest repute. First Malvenda, who writes expressly on the subject, states as the opinion of Ribera, Gaspar Melus, Biegas, Suarrez, **Bellarmine** and Bosius that **Rome shall apostatize from the faith**, drive away the Vicar of Christ and return to its ancient paganism. ...Then the Church shall be scattered, driven into the wilderness, and shall be for a time, as it was in the beginning, invisible hidden in catacombs, in dens, in mountains, in lurking places; for a time it shall be swept, as it were from the face of the earth. **Such is the universal testimony of the Fathers of the early Church."**

Comment: Notice the date Cardinal Manning wrote this. It is not a novel position to hold that Rome will lose the faith but that it is the "universal testimony of the Fathers of the early Church."

St. Antony of the Desert (251-356):

"Men will surrender to the spirit of the age. They will say that if they had lived in our day, Faith would be simple and easy. But in their day, they will say, things are complex; the Church must be brought up to date and made meaningful to the day's problems. When the Church and the World are one, then those days are at hand. Because our Divine Master placed a barrier between His things and the things of the world." ([*Disquisition CXIV*] Quoted in Voice of Fatima, 23 January 1968)

The great St Athanasius wrote a biography on St Antony.

His life was filled with miracles, wisdom, and revelations. Satan and swarms of devils attacked Antony on a regular basis. He was nothing short of being one of the greatest saints who ever lived.

St. Francis of Assisi

No introduction is needed for this great saint. St Bonaventure said Francis took Lucifer's place in Heaven when he died.

Shortly before he died, St. Francis of Assisi called together his followers and warned them of the coming troubles, saying:

"1. The time is fast approaching in which there will be great trials and afflictions; perplexities and dissensions, both spiritual and temporal, will abound; the charity of many will grow cold, and the malice of the wicked will increase.

"2. The devils will have unusual power, the immaculate purity of our Order, and of others, will be so much obscured that there will be very few Christians who will obey the true Sovereign Pontiff and the Roman Church with loyal hearts and perfect charity. At the time of this tribulation a man, not canonically elected, will be raised to the Pontificate, who, by his cunning, will endeavour to draw many into error and death.

"3. Then scandals will be multiplied, our Order will be divided, and many others will be entirely destroyed, because they will consent to error instead of opposing it.

"4. There will be such diversity of opinions and schisms among the people, the religious and the clergy, that, except those days were shortened, according to the words of the Gospel, even the elect would be led into error, were they not specially guided, amid such great confusion, by the immense mercy of God.

"5. Then our Rule and manner of life will be violently opposed by some, and terrible trials will come upon us. Those who are found faithful will receive the crown of life; but woe to those who, trusting solely in their Order, shall fall into tepidity, for they will not be able to support the temptations permitted for the proving of the elect.

"6. Those who preserve their fervour and adhere to virtue with love and zeal for the truth, will suffer injuries and, persecutions as rebels and schismatics; for their persecutors, urged on by the evil spirits, will say they are rendering a great service to God by destroying such pestilent men from the face of the earth, but the Lord will be the refuge of the afflicted, and will save all who trust in Him. And in order to be like their Head, [Christ] these, the elect, will act with confidence, and by their death will purchase for themselves eternal life; choosing to obey God rather than man, they will fear nothing, and they will prefer to perish rather than consent to falsehood and perfidy.

"7. Some preachers will keep silence about the truth, and others will trample it under foot and deny it. Sanctity of life will be held in derision even by those who outwardly profess it, for in those days Jesus Christ will send them not a true Pastor, but a destroyer."

(Except for breaking up the narrative into numbered paragraphs and adding bold print for emphasis, the prophecy is presented without any alteration, as given in the *Works of the Seraphic Father St. Francis Of Assisi*, Washbourne, 1882, pp. 248-250)

Comment: We see many completely at odds with the teachings of the *Syllabus of Errors* of Pope Pius IX and *Pascendi Dominici Gregis* (On the Doctrine of the Modernists) by Pope St. Pius X.

The Franciscan Order is split, with one side sedevacantists and the other in union with Modernist Masonic Rome.

St. Nicholas of Flue (1417-1487) stated:

"The Church will be punished because the majority of her members, high and low, will become so perverted. **The Church will sink deeper and deeper until she will at last seem to be extinguished, and the succession of Peter and the other Apostles to have expired**. But, after this, she will be victoriously exalted in the sight of all doubters." (*Catholic Prophecy* by Yves Dupont, p. 30)

A short biography: St. Nicholas of Flue was born in Switzerland and later married to fill the desire of his pious parents. He and his wife, Dorothy had 10 children and was recognized by his neighbors as a very honorable and pious man and was chosen for public service. At 50 years of age, an interior voice said to him, "Leave everything you love, and God will take care of you." He had to undergo a distressing combat, but decided finally to leave everything — wife, children, house, lands — to serve God. After 25 years of marriage and public service, he kissed his wife and children goodbye, bade farewell to his neighbors and went into the forest to live as a hermit. He left, barefooted, clothed in a long grayish robe of coarse fabric, in his hand a rosary, without money or provisions, casting a final tender and prolonged gaze on his loved ones. His habitual prayer was this: "My Lord and my God, remove from me all that can prevent me from going to You. My Lord and my God, give me all that can draw me to You." One night God penetrated the hermit with a brilliant light, and from that time on he never again experienced hunger, thirst or cold. He settled in a nearby valley called Ranft where he tried to live in a hut of his own making, but the local people insisted upon building him a wooden cabin and a stone chapel. Distinguished persons came to him for counsel in matters of great importance. **He lived for nineteen years only on the Holy Eucharist**; the civil and ecclesiastical authorities, verified this fact as being beyond question.

The auxiliary bishop of Constance consecrated the chapel and even sent a priest to serve as Nicholas' private chaplain so he could attend Mass every day.

He saved Switzerland from civil war in 1480 with his wisdom. At the age of 70, Saint Nicholas fell ill with a very painful sickness which tormented him for eight days and nights without overcoming his patience. He was beatified in 1669 by Pope Clement IX, canonized in 1947, by Pope Pius XII.

St. Malachy

Prophesied the last popes and anti-popes from his time, until the end of the world

Comment: St. Malachy lists several antipopes which means even from his point of view that the last 5 claimants doesn't necessitate them as true popes.

There has been controversy over the last two popes on the list: 111th and 112th. The last "pope" Malachy names Peter Romanus may have been an addition to the list. This "pope" appears not to be listed before the year 1823. The argument goes like this: Rome was getting worried about the accuracy of the list and its end and began promulgating the idea that between "popes" 111 (*Gloria Olivae*) and 112 (*Peter Romanus*) there could be any number of popes leaving it impossible to know precisely how many there would be till the end of the world. Interesting St. Benedict predicted the last pope would be from his order, which Gloria Olivae would be well fit in if Malachy knew this, and never actually had a 112 pope listed. However, perhaps Malachy had another idea about the last listed names if only 111 were on his list.

These are the last 4 St. Malachy listed with a possible connection:

109 *De medietate Lunae* (of the half of the moon)

John Paul I (Albino Luciani), born in Canale d'Agardo, diocese of Belluno, (beautiful moon) and elected on August 26, and last about a month, from half a moon to the next half.

110 *De Labore Solis* (of the eclipse of the sun, or from the labor of the sun)

JP II (Karol Wojtyla) was born on May 18, 1920 during a solar eclipse and was buried on April 8, 2005 during a solar eclipse.

111 *Gloria Olivae* (Glory of the Olive)

Benedict XVI (Joseph Ratzinger) took the name of Benedict because of devotion to the Benedictines, which are known as the Olivetans.

112 In extreme persecution, the seat of the Holy Roman Church will be occupied by Peter the Roman, who will feed the sheep through many tribulations, at the term of which the city of seven hills will be destroyed, and the formidable Judge will judge his people. The End.

Comment: Could the following be what St Malachy had in mind?

Gloria Olivae (Glory of the Olive): a reference to Jesus on Mount of OLIVES, prophesying his Return in GLORY – This is the last "pope" and "pope 112" was truly a later addition and not part of the original prophecy.

Or is the 112th "pope" from the original list actually the 112th "pope" who references the destruction of Rome (city of seven hills)?

This seems to be the most understood version of the list. St Malachy's reference to the destruction of Rome comes right out of the Apocalypse, which describes this city as the "Whore" and will be destroyed because of her harlotry. But how does this fit in with a pope feeding the sheep through many persecutions if Rome is a harlot?

I submit that it could mean the true historic (underground) Church will be in extreme persecution and Peter the Roman is actually the first "Roman" Pope St. Peter considered always to be holding the keys to the kingdom.

In his two Epistles, he speaks to the faithful to remain obedient to the faith, growing in holiness, living a holy Christian marriage, and living in charity, suffering, and faithfulness, while warning against false teachers and prophets.

St. Peter reminds us about the great deluge and Christ's glorious return.

It is from the Epistles of Holy Scripture that St. Peter feeds the sheep through many tribulations. It fits very nicely in the 112th spot whether it is supposed to be there or not.

I guess only time will tell...

Our Lady of Good Fortune (Good Success)

"...the Church will go through a dark night for lack of a Prelate and Father to watch over it..."

Our Lady of Good Fortune appeared to Mother Mary Anne of Jesus Torres, in Quito, Ecuador, on February 2, 1634, with the child Jesus on her left arm and the scepter in her right hand. At her appearance the sanctuary light went out, which Our Lady stated had five meanings. Those having to do with the eclipse of the Church and the lack of a Pope in our century are:

"First meaning: at the end of the 19th century and for a large part of the 20th, various heresies will flourish on this earth which will have become a free republic. The precious light of the Faith will go out in souls because of the almost total moral corruption: in those times there will be great physical and moral calamities, in private and in public. The little number of souls keeping the Faith and practicing the virtues will undergo cruel and unspeakable sufferings...

The third meaning of the lamp's going out is that in those times, the air will be filled with the spirit of impurity which like a deluge of filth will flood the streets, squares and public places. The licentiousness will be such that there will be no more virgin souls in the world.

A fourth meaning is that by having gained control of all the social classes, the sects will tend to penetrate with great skill into the heart of families and destroy even the children. The devil will take glory in feeding perfidiously on the hearts of children. The innocence of childhood will almost disappear. Thus priestly vocations will be lost, it will be a real disaster. Priests will abandon their sacred duties and will depart from the path marked out for them by God. Then the Church will go through a dark night for lack of a Prelate and Father to watch over it with love, gentleness, strength and prudence, and numbers of priests will lose the spirit of God, thus placing their souls in great danger.

Pray constantly, cry out unwearyingly and weep unceasingly with bitter tears in the depths of your heart asking Our Father in Heaven, for love of the Eucharistic Heart of My Most Holy Son, for His Precious Blood, so generously shed for the profound bitterness and sufferings of His Passion and death, that He have pity on His ministers and that He put an end to such fatal times, by sending to His Church the Prelate who will restore the spirit of His priests."

La Salette

"Rome will lose the faith and become the seat of the Antichrist... The Church will be in eclipse... At first, we will not know which is the true pope"
(Words spoken by Our Lady of La Salette to Melanie Calvat in 1846 A.D., a fully approved Church Apparition, except this particular phrase, which was placed on the Index)

(Abbot Combe: "The Secret of Melanie and the Actual Crisis", Rome, 1906, p. 137) comments: "For, in commenting on this part of the secret, Melanie said to the French Abbot Combe, "The Church will be eclipsed. At first, we will not know which is the true pope. Then secondly, the Holy Sacrifice of the Mass will cease to be offered in churches and houses; it will be such that, for a time, there will not be public services any more. But I see that the Holy Sacrifice has not really ceased: it will be offered in barns, in alcoves, in caves, and underground."

"Rome will lose the Faith and become the seat of the Anti-Christ... the Church will be in eclipse. At first, we will not know which is the true pope."

Comment: This coincides with the Apocalypse chapters 17 and 18, which says Rome will become a harlot. This means she was not a harlot at first but will become one. This harlot (modernist Rome) will commit spiritual fornication (idolatry) with the "kings" of the earth (by becoming democratized or conciliarized) as the whole earth follows. She then fornicates with other religions (Assisi Events, synagogues, mosques, etc) becoming drunk on the blood of the Saints (claiming the saints of Jesus as her own children while giving the world false ecumenism).

It reads in (II Thessalonians 2:4) the Anti-Christ will sit in the temple of God. Catholic Rome has the true temple of God, does it not? Now those in the temple teach that one can reject Christ and still worship the same and true God (Vatican 2, *Lumen Gentium*16).

This is the doctrine of anti-Christ.

The great harlot of the Apocalypse is not the true Catholic Church but rather a counterfeit church claiming to be the Catholic Church. She is no bride of Christ, but an apostate religion, which has eclipsed the true Catholic Church, which is now underground (so-to-speak) and has been reduced to a remnant.

As **St Athanasius** once said, *"They may have our churches, but we have the faith."*

Pope Leo XIII's Original Prayer to St. Michael

Pope Leo XIII's composition of the original Prayer to St. Michael the Archangel is one of the most fascinating and prophetic events in modern era.

On September 25, 1888, following his morning Mass, Pope Leo XIII fell into a trance leaving those in attendance thinking that he had just died. After coming to, Leo immediately went into his private chambers and composed the prayer to St. Michael. Afterwards, the Pope described what he had seen: a terrifying Vision of Christ and Satan speaking to each other over the tabernacle. The devil told Jesus, "I could destroy the Church and convert it to himself if he had more time and power over those who will give themselves to his service. Christ asked Satan, "How much time will you need?" Satan said, "75 to 100 years." Our Lord, said, "So be it, you will have the time and power" and then the vision had vanished.

Pope Leo XIII commanded that his original Prayer to St. Michael the Archangel to be recited after all Low Mass as a protection for the Church against the attacks from Satan and his legions.

The Original Prayer

The Raccolta, 1930, Benzinger Bros., pp. 314-315.

O Glorious Archangel St. Michael, Prince of the heavenly host, be our defense in the terrible warfare which we carry on against Principalities and Powers, against the rulers of this world of darkness, spirits of evil. Come to the aid of man, whom God created immortal, made in his own image and likeness, and redeemed at a great price from the tyranny of the devil.

Fight this day the battle of the Lord, together with the holy angels, as already thou hast fought the leader of the proud angels, Lucifer, and his apostate host, who were powerless to resist thee, nor was there place for them any longer in Heaven.

That cruel, that ancient serpent, who is called the devil or Satan, who seduces the whole world, was cast into the abyss with his angels. Behold, this primeval enemy and slayer of men has taken courage. Transformed into an angel of light, he wanders about with all the multitude of wicked spirits, invading the earth in order to blot out the name of God and of his Christ, to seize upon, slay and cast into eternal perdition souls destined for the crown of eternal glory. This wicked dragon pours out, as a most impure flood, the venom of his malice on men of depraved mind and corrupt heart, the spirit of lying, of impiety, of blasphemy, and the pestilent breath of impurity, and of every vice and iniquity.

These most crafty enemies have filled and inebriated with gall and bitterness the Church, the spouse of the immaculate Lamb, and have laid impious hands on her most sacred possessions. In the Holy Place itself, where has been set up the See of the most holy Peter and the Chair of Truth for the light of the world, they have raised the throne of their abominable impiety, with the iniquitous design that when the Pastor has been struck, the sheep may be scattered.

Arise then, O invincible Prince, bring help against the attacks of the lost spirits to the people of God, and give them the victory. They venerate thee as their protector and Patron; in thee holy Church glories as her defense against the malicious power of hell; to thee has God entrusted the souls of men to be established in heavenly beatitude. Oh, pray to the God of peace that He may put Satan under our feet, so far conquered that he may no longer be able to hold men in captivity and harm the Church. Offer our prayers in the sight of the Most High, so that they may quickly conciliate the mercies of the Lord; and beating down the dragon, the ancient serpent, who is the devil and Satan, do thou again make him captive in the abyss, that he may no longer seduce the nations. Amen

Behold the Cross of the Lord; be scattered ye hostile powers.

The Lion of the tribe of Judah has conquered, the root of David.

Let thy mercies be upon us, O Lord.

As we have hoped in thee.

O Lord, hear my prayer.

And let my cry come unto thee.

Let us pray.

O God, the Father of our Lord Jesus Christ, we call upon thy holy name, and as suppliants we implore thy clemency, that by the intercession of Mary, ever Virgin immaculate and our Mother, and of the glorious Archangel St. Michael, thou wouldst deign to help us against Satan and all other unclean spirits, who wander about the world for the injury of the human race and the ruin of souls. Amen.

Comment: Notice the highlighted area. Pope Leo XIII knew how Satan was going to work out his plan. To raise the throne of the Satan's abominable impiety in the Holy Place (Rome) and to strike the shepherd (true Pope) would make the flock scatter.

They also have laid their impious hands on the Church's most sacred possessions.

The Church's most sacred possessions are the deposit of faith (Scripture and Tradition). It was the Tradition of the Church, which was radically altered by the Vatican 2 sect, viz, the seven sacraments, and the Holy Mass.

It has been argued that Pope Leo was referring to his own day when composing this prayer as it coincides with the anti-Catholics trying to destroy the Church.

This may very well be the truth, but it also coincides with today's events.

In 1934, Pope Leo's prayer to St. Michael was changed to a shorter prayer which deleted the specific mention of Satan's plan; the very plan that Our Lady of La Salette, St. Francis of Assisi and St. Nicholas of Flue predicted.

However, John XXIII removed the prayer entirely from the Missal.

He also refused to announce the third secret of Fatima to the world as Our Lady asked it.

Interesting, there was another antipope John XXIII in church history that died during the same time at his council as the second John XXIII died at the Second Vatican Council.

Is this not a sign in itself?

Fatima

Exact words of Sister Lucia (visionary at Fatima) in an interview with Father Augustin Fuentes on December 26, 1957

"Father, the **Blessed Virgin is very sad** because no one heeds her message; neither the good nor the bad. The good continue on with their life of virtue and apostolate, but they do not unite their lives to the message of Fatima. Sinners keep following the road of evil because they do not see the terrible chastisement about to befall them. Believe me, Father, **God is going to punish the world and very soon. The chastisement of heaven is imminent. In less than two years, 1960 will be here and the chastisement of heaven will come and it will be very great.** Tell souls to fear not only the material punishment that will befall us if we **do not** pray and do penance **but most of all the souls who will go to hell."**

Comment: Sister Lucia clearly forewarned a chastisement would occur before 1960 and Our Lady is the one telling her this.

What was it? I submit the death of Pope Pius XII and the uncanonically elected Roncalli to the papacy was it. If it is not then Lucia would be a false seer and prophet, which means Fatima is false.

There is also strong evidence that Sister Lucia was murdered, (1958?) and replaced with an imposter (clear photographs of two different women claiming to be Sister Lucia).

And again...

"Sister Lucy also said to me: Father, we should not wait for an appeal to the world to come from Rome on the part of the Holy Father, to do penance. Nor should we wait for the call to penance to come from our bishops in our diocese, nor from the religious congregations. No! Our Lord has already very often used these means and the world has not paid attention. That is why now, it is necessary for each one of us to begin to reform himself spiritually. Each person must not only save his own soul but also all the souls that God has placed on our path ..." "The devil does all in his power to distract us and to take away from us the love for prayer; we shall be saved together or we shall be damned together."

"Lucia found Jacinta sitting alone, still and very pensive, gazing at nothing. **'What are you thinking of, Jacinta?' 'Of the war that is going to come. So many people are going to die. And almost all of them are going to hell."** (Our Lady of Fatima, p. 94; p. 92 in some versions)

Comment: Jacinta Marto (youngest visionary of Fatima) said almost all those who die in World War II will go to hell. Remember this is not even the Great Apostasy.

How much worse will it be?

Jacinta was found as an incorruptible when they disinterred her body in 1954. We should not take her words lightly.

St. Anselm (Doctor of the Church):

"If thou wouldst be certain of being in the number of the elect, strive to be one of the few, not of the many. And if thou wouldst be quite sure of thy salvation, strive to be among the fewest of the few... Do not follow the great majority of mankind, but follow those who enter upon the narrow way, who renounce the world, who give themselves to prayer, and who never relax their efforts by day or by night, that they may attain everlasting blessedness." (Fr. Martin Von Cochem, *The Four Last Things*, p. 221)

Pope Pius IX

"There will be a great prodigy which will fill the world with awe. But this prodigy will be preceded by the triumph of a revolution during which the Church will go through ordeals that are beyond description."

Pope St. Pius X

In his encyclical letter, Our Apostolic Mandate, on August 25, 1910, Pope St. Pius X already detected "a great movement of apostasy being organized in every country for the establishment of a One World Church which will have neither dogmas, nor hierarchy . . . under the pretext of freedom and human dignity."

Pascendi Dominici Gregis, (On adversaries of the Church), "not from without but from within; hence the danger is present almost in the very veins and heart of the Church."

E Supremi, (On the Restoration of All Things in Christ): 5. When all this is considered there is good reason to fear lest this great perversity may be as it were a foretaste, and perhaps the beginning of those evils which are reserved for the last days; and that there may be already in the world the "Son of Perdition" of whom the Apostle speaks (II. Thess. ii., 3). Such, in truth, is the audacity and the wrath employed everywhere in persecuting religion, in combating the dogmas of the faith, in brazen effort to uproot and destroy all relations between man and the Divinity! While, on the other hand, and this according to the same apostle is the distinguishing mark of Antichrist, man has with infinite temerity put himself in the place of God, raising himself above all that is called God; in such wise that although he cannot utterly extinguish in himself all knowledge of God, he has contemned God's majesty and, as it were, made of the universe a temple wherein he himself is to be adored. "He sitteth in the temple of God, showing himself as if he were God" (II. Thess. Ii., 2).

Pope Pius XII

"We believe that the present hour is a dread phase of the events foretold by Christ. It seems that darkness is about to fall on the world. Humanity is in the grip of a supreme crisis."

"This persistence of Mary [at Fatima] about the dangers which menace the Church is a divine warning against the suicide of altering the Faith in her liturgy...In our [future] churches, Christians will search in vain or the red lamp where god awaits them." (On the message of Our Lady of Fatima)

"I hear around me reformers who want to dismantle the Holy Sanctuary, destroy the universal flame of the Church, to discard all her adornments, and smite her with remorse for her historic past. A day will come when the civilized world will deny its God, when the Church will doubt as Peter doubted. She will be tempted to believe that man has become God. In our churches, Christians will search in vain for the red lamp where God awaits them. Like Mary Magdalene, weeping before the empty tomb they will ask, "Where have they taken Him?" (Cardinal Eugenio Pacelli, later Pope Pius XII, to Count Enrico P. Galeazzi)

"After me the deluge."

Comment: Here we see Pope Pius XII referencing Matt. 24 and I Peter that the end of time will be like that of the great deluge of Noe.

Nursing Nun of Bellay (1810-1830)

This prophecy was written sometime between 1810 and 1830 and was entrusted to Father Fulgence, the Chaplain of the Trappist Monastery of Notre Dame des Gardes, near Angers.

a) "Once again the madmen seem to gain the upper hand! They laugh God to scorn. Now, the churches are closed; the pastors run away; the Holy Sacrifice ceases."

b) "Woe to thee, corrupt city! the wicked try to destroy everything; their books and their doctrine as swamping the world. But the day of justice is come. Here is your King; He comes forward amidst the confusion of those stormy days. Horrible times! The just and the wicked fall; Babylon, is reduced to ashes. Woe to thee, city three times accursed!"

c) "There was also a great battle, the like of which has never been seen before. Blood was flowing like water after a heavy rain. The wicked were trying to slaughter all the servants of the Religion of Jesus Christ. After they had killed a large number, they raised a cry of victory, but suddenly the just received help from above."

d) "A saint raises his arms to Heaven; he allays the wrath of God. He ascends the throne of Peter. At the same time, the Great Monarch ascends the throne of his ancestors. All is quiet now. Altars are set up again; religion comes to life again. What I see now is so wonderful that I am unable to express it."

e) "All these things shall come to pass once the wicked have succeeded in circulating large numbers of bad books." (*Catholic Prophecy*, Yves Dupont, p 51, Tan Books, 1970)

Comment: The new mass is invalid so the Holy Sacrifice ceases, and Rome has completely swamped the world with the dogma of Masonry which is: Everybody is united to God, the bottom line is that it doesn't absolutely matter what you believe because every religion is good enough to get you into heaven.

Blessed Joachim (d. 1202)

"Towards the end of the world, Antichrist will overthrow the pope and usurp his see." (Rev. Culleton, *The Reign of Antichrist*, Tan Books, 1974, p. 130)

Jeanne le Royer (Sister of the Nativity)

"I saw a great power rise up against the Church. It plundered, devastated, and threw into confusion and disorder the vine of the Lord, having it trampled underfoot by the people and holding it up to ridicule by all nations. Having vilified celibacy and oppressed the priesthood, it had the effrontery to confiscate the Church's property, and to arrogate to itself the powers of the Holy Father, whose person and whose laws it held in contempt." (*Catholic Prophecy*, Yves Dupont, Tan Books, 1973)

Venerable Anna-Katrina Emmerick

"I saw also the relationship between the two popes. . . I saw how baleful would be the consequences of this false church. I saw it increase in size; heretics of every kind came into the city of Rome). The local clergy grew lukewarm, and I saw a great darkness..."

"Once more I saw that the Church of Peter was undermined by a plan evolved by the secret sect, while storms were damaging it."

"I saw a strange church being built against every rule. . . No angels were supervising the building operations. In that church, nothing came from high above. . . There was only division and chaos. It is probably a church of human creation, following the latest fashion, as well as the new heterodox church of Rome, which seems of the same kind..."

"I saw again the strange big church that was being built there (in Rome). There was nothing holy in it. I saw this just as I saw a movement led by Ecclesiastics to which contributed angels, saints and other Christians. But there (in the strange big church) all the work was being done mechanically (i.e., according to set rules and formulae). Everything was being done, according to human reason..."

"I saw all sorts of people, things, doctrines, and opinions. There was something proud, presumptuous, and violent about it, and they seemed to be very successful. I did not see a single Angel nor a single saint helping in the work. But far away in the background, I saw the seat of a cruel people armed with spears, and I saw a laughing figure which said: 'Do build it as solid as you can; we will put it to the ground.'"

"Among the strangest things that I saw, were long processions of bishops. Their thoughts and utterances were made known to me through images issuing from their mouths. Their faults towards religion were shown by external deformities. A few had only a body, with a dark cloud of fog instead of a head. Others had only a head, their bodies and hearts were like thick vapors. Some were lame; others were paralytics; others were asleep or staggering."

"Then, I saw that everything that pertained to Protestantism was gradually gaining the upper hand, and the Catholic religion fell into complete decadence. Most priests were lured by the glittering but false knowledge of young school-teachers, and they all contributed to the work of destruction."Matt. 24:39: "And they did not understand until the flood came and swept them all away."

"...The Church is persecuted; the Pope leaves Rome and dies in exile; **an anti-pope is installed in Rome; the Catholic Church is split, leaderless and completely disorganized..."**

"I saw again the new and odd-looking Church which they were trying to build. There was nothing holy about it... People were kneading bread in the crypt below... but it would not rise, nor did they receive the body of Our Lord, but only bread. Those who were in error, through no fault of their own, and who piously and ardently longed for the Body of Jesus were spiritually consoled, but not by their communion. Then, my Guide [Jesus] said: 'THIS IS BABEL.' [The Mass in many languages]." (This prophecy was made circa 1820 by Anna Katarina Emmerick, a stigmatized Augustinian nun and is recorded in The Life of Anne Catherine Emmerich by Rev. Carl E. Schmoeger, C.SS.R.)

Comment: The *Novus Ordo* mass is invalid and this prophecy clearly references the fact.

Six Protestants and the Freemason Annabali Bugnini gave us the *Novus Ordo Missae* by deleting 95% of the prayers, removing the altar and replacing it with a table, and deleting most of the Church's official language. It also changed the very words of Our Lord at the Consecration thus nullifying its validity. As for the Vatican II altar, Pope Pius XII, in Mediator Dei 62, "One would be straying from the straight path were he to wish the altar restored to its primitive table-form."

"In thence days, Faith will fall very low, and it will be preserved in some places only, in a few cottages and in a few families which God has protected from disasters and wars."

"I see many excommunicated ecclesiastics who do not seem to be concerned about it, nor even aware of it. Yet, they are (ipso factor) excommunicated whenever they cooperated to [sic] enterprises, enter into associations, and embrace opinions on which an anathema has been cast. It can be seen thereby that God ratifies the decrees, orders, and interdictions issued by the Head of the Church, and that He keeps them in force even though men show no concern for them, reject them, or laugh them to scorn."

"I saw that many pastors allowed themselves to be taken up with ideas that were dangerous to the Church. They were building a great, strange, and extravagant Church. Everyone was to be admitted in it in order to be united and have equal rights:

Evangelicals, Catholics [SSPX], sects of every description. Such was to be the new Church. . . But God had other designs."

Bernhardt Rembordt (18th century)

"These things will come when they try to set up a new kingdom of Christ from which the true faith will be banished." (*Catholic Prophecy*, Yves Dupont, Tan Books, 1973, pp. 34-35)

St. John Bosco (19th century)

"Your sons ask for the bread of Faith and no one gives it to them . . . Ungrateful Rome, effeminate Rome, arrogant Rome . . . Forgetting that the Sovereign Pontiffs and your true glory are on Golgotha . . . Woe to you; my law is an idle word for you."

Old German Prophecy: "...The doctrine will be perverted, and they will try to overthrow the Catholic Church..." (*Catholic Prophecy*, Yves Dupont, Rockford, IL: Tan Books, 1973, p. 24)

Father E. Sylvester Berry (1921)

Commenting upon the 12th and 13th chapters of the Apocalypse of St. John, foretold that the true pope will be martyred and during the vacancy, the prophet of the Antichrist will set himself up in Rome as anti-pope.

"In the forgoing chapter [12] St. John outlines the history of the Church from the coming of Antichrist until the end of the world [...] In this chapter he shows us the true nature of the conflict. It shall be a war unto death between the Church and the powers of darkness in a final effort to destroy the Church and thus prevent the universal reign of Christ on earth.

"Satan will first attempt to destroy the power of the Papacy and bring about the downfall of the Church through heresies, schisms and persecutions that must surely follow [...] he will raise up Antichrist and his prophet to lead the faithful into error and destroy those who remain steadfast [...] The Church, the faithful spouse of Jesus Christ, is represented as a woman clothed in the glory of divine grace [...]

" [...] In this passage there is an evident allusion to some particular son of the Church whose power and influence shall be such that Satan will seek his destruction at any cost. This person can be none other than the Pope to be elected in those days. The Papacy will be attacked by all the powers of hell. In consequence the Church will suffer great trials and afflictions in securing a successor upon the throne of Peter.

"The words of St. Paul to the Thessalonians may be a reference to the Papacy as the obstacle to the coming of Antichrist: 'You know what withholdeth, that he may be revealed in his time. For the mystery of iniquity already worketh; only that he who now holdeth, do hold until he be taken out of the way. And then that wicked one shall be revealed.'

" [...] St. John [...] sees in heaven a red dragon with seven heads and ten horns [...] The dragon is Satan red with the blood of martyrs, which he will cause to flow. The meaning of the seven heads and ten horns must be sought in the description of the beast that represents Antichrist where they symbolize kings or worldly powers. (II Thessalonians 2:6-7) [...] Satan's attacks against the Church will be organized and carried out by the governments and ruling powers of those days.

"With the beast of Antichrist only the horns have diadems as symbols of royalty or governing power. The heads are branded with names of blasphemy. (Apocalypse, 13:1) Hence they symbolize the sins and errors that will afflict the Church [...] in this final struggle to prevent the universal reign of Christ all forms of sin and error will be marshaled against the Church [...] all errors which have afflicted the Church may be summed up in these seven: Judaism, paganism, Arianism, Mohammedanism, Protestantism, rationalism, and atheism.

"The dragon is seen in heaven which is here a symbol of the Church, the kingdom of heaven on earth. This indicates that the first troubles of those days will be inaugurated within the Church by apostate bishops, priests, and peoples, – the stars dragged down by the tail of the dragon.

" [...] The dragon stands before the woman, ready to devour the child that is brought forth. In other words, the powers of hell seek by all means to destroy the Pope elected in those days.

" [...] It is now the hour for the powers of darkness. The new-born Son of the Church is taken 'to God and to his throne.' Scarcely has the newly elected Pope been enthroned when he is snatched away by martyrdom. The 'mystery of iniquity' gradually developing through the centuries, cannot be fully consummated while the power of the Papacy endures, but now he that 'withholdeth is taken out of the way.' During the interregnum 'that wicked one shall be revealed' in his fury against the Church.

"It is a matter of history that the most disastrous periods for the Church were times when the Papal throne was vacant, or when anti-popes contended with the legitimate head of the Church. Thus also shall it be in those evil days to come.

"The Church deprived of her chief pastor must seek sanctuary in solitude there to be guided by God Himself during those trying days [...] In those days the Church shall [...] find refuge and consolation in faithful souls, especially in the seclusion of the religious life.

" [...] Our Divine Savior has a representative on earth in the person of the Pope upon whom He has conferred full powers to teach and govern. Likewise, Antichrist will have his representative in the false prophet who will be endowed with the plenitude of satanic powers to deceive the nations.

" [...] As indicated by the resemblance to a lamb, the prophet will probably set himself up in Rome as a sort of antipope during the vacancy of the papal throne [...]

" [...] The 'abomination of desolation' has been wrought in many Catholic churches by heretics and apostates who have broken altars, scattered relics of martyrs and desecrated the Blessed Sacrament. At the time of the French Revolution a lewd woman was seated upon the altar of the cathedral in Paris and worshipped as the goddess of reason. Such things but faintly foreshadow the abominations that will desecrate churches in those sorrowful days when Antichrist will seat himself at the altar to be adored as God.

" [...] Antichrist and his prophet will introduce ceremonies to imitate the Sacraments of the Church. In fact there will be a complete organization - a church of Satan set up in opposition to the Church of Christ. Satan will assume the part of God the Father; Antichrist will be honored as Savior, and his prophet will usurp the role of Pope. Their ceremonies will counterfeit the Sacraments [...]" (The Apocalypse of St. John, 1921, The Catholic Church Supply House, Columbus, Ohio, pp. 120-138

Archbishop Fulton J. Sheen (1895-1979):

"He [Satan] will set up a counterchurch which will be the ape of the Church, because he, the Devil, is the ape of God. It will have all the notes and characteristics of the Church, but in reverse and emptied of its divine content. It will be a mystical body of the Antichrist that will in all externals resemble the mystical body of Christ. [...] But the twentieth century will join the counterchurch because it claims to be infallible when its visible head speaks *ex cathedra*." (*Communism and the Conscience of the West*, Indianapolis: Bobbs-Merrill, 1948, pp. 24-25)

Comment: Bishop Sheen was spot on, but unfortunately didn't recognize it when it came. In fact, he helped set the whole thing up. In the picture he is embracing John Paul II in 1979 just before he died.

Communists and Freemasons Plan to Infiltrate the Church

"The fight taking place against Catholicism and Freemasonry is a fight to the very death, ceaseless and merciless." (Bulletin of the Grand Orient of France, 1892, p. 183)

All of the following substance was discussed in a secret meeting of the Jewish Masonic Lodge of B'nai B'rith in Paris, and reported by the London Catholic Gazette of February 1936.

First, a statement concerning B'nai B'rith (Jewish Freemasonry) is needed. Fr. Denis Fahey, in his preface to the "new and revised edition" of Mgr. Dillon's The War of Antichrist with the Church and Christian Civilization, 1885, re-titled as Grand Orient Freemasonry Unmasked as the Secret Power behind Communism, Christian Book Club, Palmdale, CA, states:

FREEMASONRY AND THE JEWISH NATION

"The Jewish connection with modern Freemasonry is an established fact everywhere manifested in its history. The Jewish formulas employed by Freemasonry, the Jewish traditions which run through its ceremonial, point to a Jewish origin, or to the work of Jewish contrivers. . . . Who knows but behind the Atheism and desire of gain which impels them to urge on "Christians" to persecute the Church and destroy it, there lies a hidden hope to reconstruct their Temple, and in the darkest depths of secret society plotting there lurks a deeper society still which looks to a return to the land of Judah and to the rebuilding of the Temple of Jerusalem?"

The discussion...

"Now then, in order to ensure a pope in the required proportions, we must first of all prepare a generation worthy of the kingdom of which we dream . . . Let the clergy move forward under your banner (the Masonic banner) always believing they are advancing under the banner of the apostolic Keys. Cast your net like Simon Bar Jonas; spread it to the bottom of sacristies, seminaries, and convents . . . You will have finished a revolution dressed in the Pope's triple crown and cape, carrying the cross and the flag, a revolution that will need only a small stimulus to set fire to the four corners of the earth." (From April 3, 1844, NUBIUS (Piccolo Tigre), Secret Instructions on the Conquest of the Church, in Emmanuel Barbier, *Les infiltrations masoniques dans l'Eglise,* Paris/Brussels: Desclee de Brouwer, 1901, p. 5)

"Our ultimate end is that of Voltaire and the French Revolution-the final destruction of Catholicism, and even in the Christian idea... The task that we are to undertake...may take years, perhaps a century... We do not intend to win the Popes to our cause,... our principles, propagators of our ideas... Now then, to assure ourselves a Pope of the required dimensions, it is a question first of shaping for this Pope a generation worthy of the reign we are dreaming of..."In a hundred years time . . . bishops and priests will think they are marching behind the banner of the keys of Peter when in fact they will be following our flag . . . The reforms will have to be brought about in the name of obedience." (*The Permanent Instruction of the Alta Vendita*, the Masonic plan to infiltrate the Catholic Church)

The Alta Vendita was the highest lodge of the Carbonari (an Italian secret society). Linked with the Freemasons, the Carbonari was found throughout Europe and operated primarily in Italy and France. The Permanent Instruction was a secret document with the plan to infiltrate the Church all the way to the papacy, change the Faith to the Masonic principles, which is modernism, liberalism, and the religion of man whereby all religions are recognized as legitimate practices pleasing God and all men are united in the one goal of having one secular system of government under this one form of religion.

Popes Pius IX and Leo XIII commanded the Permanent Instruction to be exposed through publication to prevent the plan from taking effect. Popes Pius IX, Leo XIII and St. Pius X all condemned liberalism and modernism as the form found under Masonic principles. Pope St. Pius X was elected in 1903 with Austria vetoing the first election of Cardinal Rampolla, the Mason implant.

"If one takes into consideration the immense development which [the]... secret societies have attained; the length of time they are persevering in their vigor; their furious aggressiveness; the tenacity with which their members cling to the association and to the false principles it professes; the persevering mutual cooperation of so many different types of men in the promotion of evil; one can hardly deny that the Supreme Architect of these associations (seeing that the cause must be proportional to the effect) can be none other than he who in the sacred writings is style the Prince of the World; and that Satan himself even by his physical cooperation, directs and inspires at least the leaders of these bodies physically cooperating with them." (*"Acta Sancta Sedis"*, v. 1, p. 293, 13 July 1865, Pope Pius IX)

Pope Leo warned, "...the Sect's purpose is to reduce to naught the teaching and authority of the Church among the civilian population.... The enmity of the sectarians against the Apostolic See of the Roman Pontiff has increased its intensity... until now the evil doers have reached the aim which had, for a long time that of their evil designs, namely, their proclamation that the moment has come to suppress the Roman Pontiff's sacred power and to completely destroy this Papacy which was divinely instituted." (*Humanum Genus*, 1884, Pope Leo XIII)

"The goal is no longer the destruction of the Church but rather to make use of it by infiltrating it." (*'Ecumenism'* Freemason book, 1908, found in Bishop Graber, St. Athanasius, pp. 64-65)

"A day will come when the pope, inspired by the Holy Spirit will declare that all the excommunications are lifted and all the anathemas are retracted, when all the Christians will be united within the Church, when the Jews and Moslems will be blessed and called back to her . . . she will permit all sects to approach her by degrees and will embrace all mankind in the communion of her love and prayers. Then, Protestants will no longer exist. Against what will they be able to protest? The sovereign pontiff will then be truly king of the religious world, and he will do whatever he wishes with all the nations of the earth." (Notorious Freemason Eliph Levi 1862, found in Dr. Rama Coomaraswamy, *The Destruction of the Christian Tradition*, p. 133)

"Cagliostro was the Agent of the Templars, and therefore wrote to the Free-Masons of London that the time had come to begin the work or re-building the Temple of the Eternal...A lodge inaugurated under the auspices of Rousseau, the fanatic of Geneva, became the center of the revolutionary movement in France... The secret movers of the revolutionary movement in France... The secret movers of the French Revolution had sworn to overturn the Throne and the Altar upon the Tomb of Jacques de Molay. When Louis XVI was executed, half the work was done; and thenceforward the Army of the temple was to direct all its efforts against the Pope." (*Morals and Dogma*, 1871, Albert Pike, pp. 823-824)

In 1878, Masonic Brother and member of the French Parliament, Bethmont boasted to Bishop Pie of Poitiers, "...Violence against the Church leads nowhere; we shall use other means. We shall organize a persecution which shall be both clever and legal; we shall surround the church with a network of laws, decrees and ordinances which will stifle it without shedding one drop of blood." (*Papacy and Freemasonry*, Msgr. Jouin, 1955, pp. 23-24)

"To fight against the Papacy is a social necessity and constitutes the constant duty of Freemasons." (The Report of the Masonic International Congress held in Brussels, in 1904)

'Let us remember that as long as there still remain active enemies of the Catholic Church, we may hope to become Masters of the World...[nevertheless] the future Jewish King will never reign in the world before the Pope in Rome is dethroned as well as all the other reigning Monarchs of the Gentiles upon earth." (Parisian weekly, *Le Revell du Peuple* quote, in The Masonic Plan to Suppress the Papacy as Admitted by the Freemasons Themselves, Exile of the Pope Elect; Part VIII, Gary Giuffre)

"Within the eight city blocks that make up the Vatican State no fewer than four Scottish Rite lodges are functioning. Many of the highest Vatican officials are Masons and in certain countries where the Church is not allowed to operate, it is the lodges that carry on Vatican affairs, clandestinely." (In a 1993 interview with the political weekly *Processo*, Grand Commander of the Supreme Council of Masons of Mexico, Carlos Vazquez Rangel)

Again, Vazquez, "On the same day, in Paris the profane Angelo Roncalli and the profane Giovanni Montini were initiated into the august mysteries of the Brotherhood. Thus it was that much that was achieved at the Council was based on Masonic principles."

"The King of the Jews will be the real Pope of the Universe, the Patriarch of an International Church." (*Protocols of the Learned Elders of Zion*, Sergei Nilus, 1905. Protocol #17)

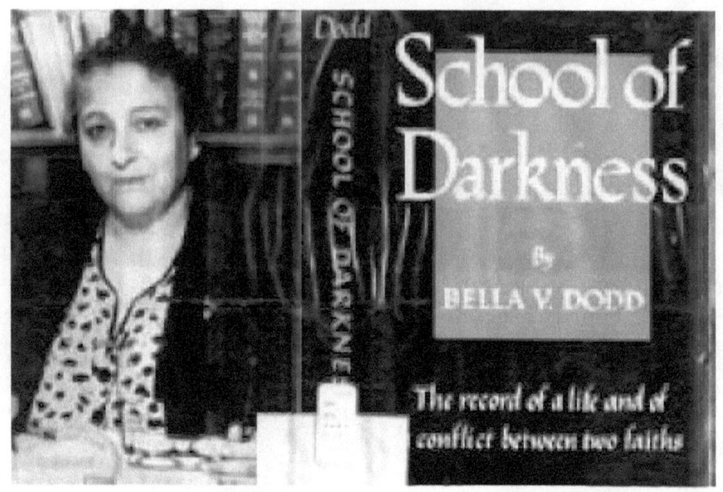

"Dr. Alice von Hildebrand recalled during an interview that "Bella Dodd told my husband and me that when she was an active [Communist] party member, she had dealt with no fewer than four cardinals within the Vatican 'who were working for us'." (Vatican 2 in the Dock, Jan, 2003, this interview took place 20 years before Vatican 2)

Mrs. Bella Dodd was in the Communist Party of America.

She defected and converted to the Catholic Church in 1952 through Bishop Fulton Sheen.

Dodd testified before the House American Activities Committee that she was personally responsible for planting over 1,000 men in Catholic seminaries in order to destroy the Church from within.

She gave lectures in the 1950's telling how in the 1930's "we (Communists) put eleven hundred men into the priesthood in order to destroy the Church from within." She said then that, "Right now they are in the highest places in the Church" with changes that will cause you in the future not to recognize the

Catholic Church as the Faith would be destroyed and apologizing for the past errors of intolerance while not recognizing other religions.

Manning Johnson, (former Communist official) told the same Committee in 1953 that by "concentrating Communist agents in the seminaries" it was intended that "a small Communist minority [would] influence the ideology of future clergymen in the paths conducive to Communist purposes." And he added: "This policy of infiltrating seminaries was successful beyond even our communist expectations."

The Abomination of Desolation

"When therefore you shall see the abomination of desolation, which was spoken of by Daniel the prophet, standing in the holy place: he that readeth let him understand." (The Holy Gospel of Jesus Christ, According to St. Matthew 24:15).

"And when you shall see the abomination of desolation, standing where it ought not (he that readeth let him understand)" (The Holy Gospel of Jesus Christ, According to St. Mark 13:14)

This was the answer Christ gave after being asked by one of his disciples, *"what shall be the sign of thy coming and of the consummation of the world?"* (Matt 24:3)

Later, Christ said, *"But of that day and hour no one knoweth (Matt 24:36), "Watch ye therefore, because ye know not what hour your Lord will come."* (Matt 24:42)

Christ is simply saying that we can't know precisely when He will come again, but that we must be prepared especially during certain events, which will be taking place at that time. In other words, He is hinting to us approximately when it will be.

God gives us other hints as in II Thessalonians 2:3. A Great Apostasy, and the revealing of the man of sin or antichrist will be at the same general time of Christ's Second Coming.

Also, Christ commands us to flee when we see the Abomination of Desolation foretold by Daniel standing in the holy place. (Matt. 24:15, Mark 13:14) Here, Jesus refers to Daniel as speaking about the very last times of history.

The abomination is a false worship service with a false sacrifice and offering. When the true sacrifice and offering ceases due to the false sacrifice, this is the desolation, thus we have the Abomination of Desolation.

The prophecy of Daniel

"And he shall confirm the covenant with many, in one week: and in the half of the week the victim and the sacrifice shall fail: and there shall be in the temple the **abomination of desolation**: and **the desolation shall continue even to the consummation, and to the end**." (Daniel 9:27)

"And arms shall stand on his part, and they shall defile the sanctuary of strength, and **shall take away the continual sacrifice: and they shall place there the abomination unto desolation."** (Daniel 11:31)

"And from the time when the continual sacrifice shall be taken away, and the abomination unto desolation shall be set up, there shall be a thousand two hundred ninety days." (Daniel 12:11)

The prophet Malachi speaks of the continual sacrifice, "For from the rising of the sun even to the going down, my name is great among the Gentiles, and in every place there is sacrifice, and there is offered to my name a clean oblation: for my name is great among the Gentile, saith the Lord of hosts." (Mal. 1:11)

However, this sacrifice will cease at the end of time as foretold in Daniel.

The only sacrifice that Malachi could be speaking about is the Holy Sacrifice of the Mass and the abomination will be its end.

The first time we see the phrase *"Abomination of Desolation"*, is in the books of Maccabees. Under the reign of Antiochus IV Epiphanes in 175 BC, the abomination of desolation takes place in the Holy Temple. To make his abomination of desolation, Antiochus erects a second altar against the first altar in (I Macc. 1:57-62). As part of the new abomination, women began to be involved in the new worship service along with other unlawful acts and the solemn days of the fathers were not observed (II Macc. 6:4).

The second abomination of desolation took place immediately after the death of Our Lord when the Jews who rejected Him kept offering animal sacrifices in the Temple of Jerusalem until approximately 40 to 41 years later, the Gentiles completely destroyed the Temple in 70 AD.

The third abomination of desolation is taking place now as will be demonstrated in relation to the first abomination of history.

The *Novus Ordo Missae* of Paul VI is clearly the abomination God is speaking about. The *Novus Ordo Missae* or New Mass made the true sacrifice (Roman Mass of Popes Sts. Pius V and X) desolate for a time.

The *Novus Ordo* mass also has a second altar against the first, with women serving in the sanctuary as they perform unlawful acts of dancing, speaking, and distributing communion.

The *Novus Ordo* Calendar does not observe the solemn days of the Fathers and leaves out the very verses, which foretells of the great Abomination of Desolation.

Below, in parenthesis, the present situation of the New Mass will be presented as it relates to the first abomination of Antiochus.

I Maccabees Chapter 1:

[20] After subduing Egypt, Antiochus returned in the one hundred and forty-third year. He went up against Israel and came to Jerusalem with a strong force.

(Paul VI went up against the new Israel (Church) with a strong force of modernist prelates.)

[21] He arrogantly entered the sanctuary and took the golden altar, the lampstand for the light, and all its utensils.

(The lampstand indicating the real substantial presence of Our Lord in the Tabernacle has been removed in many churches.)

[22] He took also the table for the bread of the Presence, the cups for drink offerings, the bowls, the golden censers, the curtain, the crowns, and the gold decoration on the front of the temple; he stripped it all off.

(The altars have been removed and replaced with tables.)

[23] He took the silver and the gold, and the costly vessels; he took also the hidden treasures which he found.

(The costly vessels or chalices are now cheap glassware and the hidden treasures or Tabernacles have been taken to back rooms.)

[43] All the Gentiles accepted the command of the king. Many even from Israel gladly adopted his religion; they sacrificed to idols and profaned the sabbath.

(Nearly the whole Catholic world accepted Vatican 2 and the New Mass from Paul VI, and the new idols are money, power, and man's rights.)

[44] And the king sent letters by messengers to Jerusalem and the cities of Judah; he directed them to follow customs strange to the land, **[45]** to forbid burnt offerings and sacrifices and drink offerings in the sanctuary, to profane sabbaths and feasts,

(The Roman Mass was forbidden, and feast days abolished)

[46] to defile the sanctuary and the priests, **[47]** to build altars and sacred precincts and shrines for idols, to sacrifice swine and unclean animals,

(Sanctuaries have been revamped; priests persecuted, and new table altars have been placed while sharing with Protestant services.)

[48] and to leave their sons uncircumcised. They were to make themselves abominable by everything unclean and profane, **[49]** so that they should forget the law and change all the ordinances.

(The Roman Mass was eliminated with all the great feasts and replaced by the new laws of modernists.)

[50] "And whoever does not obey the command of the king shall die."

(Excommunication was exacted on those who openly kept the historic Catholic Faith.)

[51] In such words he wrote to his whole kingdom. And he appointed inspectors over all the people and commanded the cities of Judah to offer sacrifice, city by city. **[52]** Many of the people, every one who forsook the law, joined them, and they did evil in the land; **[53]** they drove Israel into hiding in every place of refuge they had. **[54]** Now on the fifteenth day of Chislev, in the one hundred and forty-fifth year, they erected a desolating sacrilege upon the altar of burnt offering. They also built altars in the surrounding cities of Judah, **[59]** And on the twenty-fifth day of the month they offered sacrifice on the altar which was upon the altar of burnt offering.

(The historic Catholic Church has been driven away and persecuted by the new modernist religion of Rome)

II Maccabees 6:4: "...**And women thrust themselves of their own accord into the holy places**, and brought in things that were not lawful. The altar was also filled with unlawful things, which were forbidden by the laws. And neither were...the solemn days of the fathers observed..."

(Women are all over the sanctuary as altar servers, lectors, dancers, and as acolytes.)

The Indult Mass or the 1962 Missal of John XXIII is also part and parcel with the Abomination of Desolation. First, Christ commands us to flee from the Abomination, not continue some type of true sacrifice alongside of the Abomination so that it no longer makes desolate. So, the Indult Mass begins with disobedience to Christ. The Indult Mass requires that the Abomination be accepted as a true sacrificial offering. The Indult Mass ends with unification with the desolators and anti-Christ's of the last times of history.

There is no justification in assisting at the Indult Mass. It is disobedience in every way: Disobedience to Christ who says to flee, disobedience to the Church, which says not to worship in non-Catholic services, or with heretics, schismatics, and apostates. Disobedience to the Holy Spirit if one is aware or rejects the previous two sentences.

THE NEW MASS OF PAUL VI

In 1969, Paul VI promulgated the second version of the New Mass, which was fabricated by a high-ranking Vatican Official who was a Freemason along with the aid of six Protestants and two Catholics. (*The Eternal War*, Tape 3. *The Keys of the Kingdom* – Fr. Malachi Martin, interviewed by Bernard Janzen, Triumph Communications)

Paul VI publicly thanked them for their assistance in re-editing in a new manner liturgical texts ... so that the *lex orandi* (the law of prayer) conformed better with the *lex credendi* (the law of belief). (Fr. Rama Coomaraswamy, *The Problems with the New Mass*, TAN Books p. 24)

Paul VI rejected the first version of the New Mass presented by the Freemason Annabale Bugnini because it was so evil that Cardinals Ottaviani and Bacci told Paul VI if he didn't reject it, they would declare him a heretic. (*The Eternal War*, Tape 3. *The Keys of the Kingdom* – Fr. Malachi Martin, interviewed by Bernard Janzen, Triumph Communications)

However, the second version is also very evil not only in how it was drawn up but also in the intention of each change.

Evil thoughts are an **abomination** to the Lord: (Book of Proverbs 15:26) and evil thoughts are most certainly on the minds of John XXIII, who knowingly prepared the way of the New Mass with his 1962 missal, and Paul VI, following John's lead, took it to the next level with the new modernist mass.

Since Paul VI approved the Second Vatican Council, he was already quite the heretic.

The *Novus Ordo Missae* had changed from the Roman Mass into what resembled both Luther's Mass and the Anglican Mass.

Jean Guitton, a distinguished French writer as well as the great friend and confidant of Pope Paul VI, described Paul's "intention with regard to the liturgy... (which) was to reform the Catholic liturgy in such a way that it should almost coincide with the Protestant liturgy...beyond the Council of Trent, (and) closer to the Protestant Lord's Supper...(making) less room for all that some would call 'magic,' (namely) ...transubstantial consecration, and for all what is of the Catholic Faith; ...there was with Paul VI an ecumenical intention to remove...what was too Catholic, in the traditional sense, in the Mass, and, I repeat, to get the Catholic Mass closer to the Calvinist mass." (Broadcast December 19, 1993 by Radio-Courtoisie, Paris)

What makes the New Mass an abomination and the 8 lies used by modernists to justify it

According to the infallible decree of Pope Eugene IV, at the Council of Florence in Session 8, on Nov. 22, 1439, "*Exultate Deo*," several things must be present for a Mass to be valid.

"All these sacraments are made up of three elements: namely, things as the matter, words as the form, and the person of the minister who confers the sacrament with the intention of doing what the Church does. If any of these is lacking, the sacrament is not effected." (*Decrees of the Ecumenical Councils*, Georgetown Univ. Press, Vol. 1, p. 542; *Denzinger*, *The Sources of Catholic Dogma*, no. 695)

The focus of this writing is on the form.

The words used at the Consecration over the Chalice at the New Mass in English are: "This is the cup of my Blood...which will be shed for you and for all so that sins may be forgiven."

The words Christ used as well as the entire history of the Church were, "For this is the Chalice of My Blood...Which shall be shed for you and for many unto the remission of sins."

Notice: Christ and the Church did not say, "for all," but instead, "for many."

For this reason, the incorrect form of the Consecration of the New Mass is invalid, therefore, a false worship ceremony is taking place where it should not, and thus you have an abomination.

For every mocker is an abomination to the Lord. (Book of Proverbs 3:32)

The New Mass mocks the Roman Mass as the priests mock our Lord's words.

Lying lips are an abomination to the Lord. (Book of Proverbs 12:22)

The priests are lying when they state at the Consecration that Our Lord says "for all."

The way of the wicked is an abomination to the Lord. (Book of Proverbs 15:9)

Falsifying Our Lord's words at the most solemn moment in time, is the most wicked of ways.

LIE NUMBER 1: The argument used to justify this changed is "all" and "many" can be used interchangeably as sometimes happens in Scripture. The argument, then, was that "all" best shows the meaning of what "many" really means. The Offertory says, "We offer unto Thee, O Lord, the chalice of salvation, humbly begging of Thy mercy that it may arise before Thy divine majesty with a pleasing fragrance, for our salvation and that of all the world. Amen." Therefore, the Offertory shows the Form really means for all.

The words are juxtapose in Scripture at times without changing the meaning however, the Catechism of the Council of Trent promulgated by Pope St. Pius V under St. Charles Borromeo clearly refutes the rest of this lie. It states:

On the Form of the Eucharist:

"The additional words for you and for many, are taken, some from Matthew, some from Luke, but were joined together by the Catholic Church under the guidance of the Spirit of God. They serve to declare the fruit and advantage of His Passion. For if we look to its value, we must confess that the Redeemer shed His Blood for the salvation of all; **but** if we look to the fruit which mankind has received from it, we shall easily find that it pertains **not unto all, but to many of the human race**. When therefore (our

Lord) said: For you, He meant either those who were present, or those chosen from among the Jewish people, such as were, with the exception of Judas, the disciples with whom He was speaking. When He added, And for many, He wished to be understood to mean the remainder of the elect from among the Jews and Gentiles. **With reason, therefore, were the words 'for all' not used**, as in this place the fruits of the Passion are alone spoken of, and to the elect only did His Passion bring the fruit of salvation." (*The Catechism of the Council of Trent*, TAN Books, 1982, p. 227)

Even though "many" and "all" are sometimes used interchangeably in Scripture, we are informed in the official Catechism of the Council of Trent, the Church says specifically "for all" renders a different meaning than "many."

Pope Benedict XIV (1740-1758) discussed this issue and stated that this teaching "explains correctly" Christ's use of "for many," as opposed to "for all" (*De Sacrosanctae Missae Sacrificio*).

Catholics are not at liberty to say the Catechism is in error as some would like to have it. The Catechism is actually addressing the error of previous heretics who wanted the words changed then.

The simple fact is the word "many" can always be used in place of the word "all" unless all of something is a few, but the word all cannot always be used in place of the word many.

If the word many is referring not to all then the word all cannot replace it unless one is using it as hyperbole.

We know Christ would not use hyperbole in the most sacred moment in history. He used many to refer to only the faithful and not to all of humanity as the Catechism explains.

The great 18th century theologian Fr. Martinus von Cochem O.S.F wrote in his book *"The Holy Sacrifice of the Mass Explained"* p. 111:

"Consequently, the Precious Blood of Christ is in real fact shed in the Mass "for you and for many"; that is, for you who are attending and attentive, and for the many who are absent; for those who assisting if they could do so and who therefore desire a memento in it. These are the "many" for the remission of whose sins Christ's Blood is shed in the Mass."

As for the Offertory, it is not Christ but the faithful who is offering the Chalice for all of humanity. The note in some Roman Missals on this part of the Offertory says, "We pray 'for our salvation,' and yes, 'and that of all the world.'" Of course, the faithful would pray and ask for all of the world to come to the truth and receive Communion before they die, but it does not follow that Christ would actually give the Chalice of His Blood to all of the world.

To try to say the Offertory proves the form should also mean **for all** is ludicrous.

LIE NUMBER 2: The essential part of the form is: "This is my Body, and This is my Blood." Therefore, the words "all" and "many" do not matter because they are not essential.

This argument is saying that once the priest says, "For this is the Chalice of My Blood" the wine is changed into the Blood of Christ regardless to what the priest says later in the form.

This lie has a twofold problem.

First, the Council of Florence has pronounced as de fide the whole form is what actuates the change in substance and not just parts of the form.

Pope St. Pius V said in *"De Defectibus"* Chapter 5, Part 1:

"The words of Consecration, which are the **FORM** of this Sacrament, are these: **FOR THIS IS MY BODY. And: FOR THIS**

IS THE CHALICE OF MY BLOOD, OF THE NEW AND ETERNAL TESTAMENT: THE MYSTERY OF FAITH, WHICH SHALL BE SHED FOR YOU AND FOR MANY UNTO THE REMISSION OF SINS. Now if one were to remove, or change anything in the **FORM** of the consecration of the Body and Blood, and in that very **change of words the [NEW] wording would fail to mean the same thing, he would NOT consecrate the sacrament."**

Notice: St. Pius V did not say that one could not remove, or change anything in the form but one could not remove, or change anything, which would give it a different meaning. This is a very crucial distinction, because some forms have variants, which have omissions and changes throughout history.

Pope St. Pius V was reiterating what Pope Eugene IV at the Council of Florence stated in Session 11, Feb 1442:

"However, since no explanation was given in the aforesaid decree of the Armenians in respect to the **form of words** which the holy Roman Church, relying on the teaching and authority of the apostles Peter and Paul, has always been wont to use in the consecration of the Lord's Body and Blood, we concluded that it should be inserted in this present text. It uses this form of words in the consecration of the Lord's Body: FOR THIS IS MY BODY. And of His blood: **FOR THIS IS THE CHALICE OF MY BLOOD, OF THE NEW AND ETERNAL TESTAMENT: THE MYSTERY OF FAITH, WHICH SHALL BE SHED FOR YOU AND FOR MANY UNTO THE REMISSION OF SINS."** (*Decrees of the Ecumenical Councils*, Vol. 1, p. 581).

The Catechism promulgated by Pope St. Pius V says that "all" does not mean the same thing as "many". This pope also stated, "in that very change of words the new wording would fail to mean the same thing, he would not consecrate the sacrament."

St. Alphonsus De Liguori had this to say on the form:

"The words pro vobis et pro multis (for you and for many) are used to distinguish the virtue of the Blood of Christ from its fruits: for the Blood of Our Savior is of sufficient value to save all men **but its fruits are applied only to a certain number and not to all**, and this is their own fault... This is the explanation of St. Thomas, as quoted by [Pope] Benedict XIV." (St. Alphonsus De Liguori, *Treatise on The Holy Eucharist*, Redemptorist Fathers, 1934, p. 44)

The consecration takes place after the whole form is recited and not just parts of it.

To demonstrate this point: Let's suppose over the chalice the priest said only, "For this is the Chalice of My Blood...but only as a symbol and not actually."

Would you really argue the Blood of Christ was actually made present after this particular form?

Of course not, because the form had words which changed the overall meaning and because the added words demonstrated the wrong intention of the priest.

This proves the wine does not change immediately after those "essential" words: "For this is the Chalice of My Blood" precisely because the de fide position is the **WHOLE FORM** is what actuates the change in substance and not just parts of it.

Interesting enough, the documents *Quo Primum* and *De Defectibus* were found in the front of all Altar Missals and placed in the *Missale Romanum* in 1572. In 1969, ICEL (Committee on English in the Liturgy) deleted them in the new versions.

Quo Primum also written by St. Pope Pius V on July 14, 1570 stated:

"It shall be unlawful henceforth and forever throughout the Christian world to sing or to read Masses according to any formula other than this Missal published by us...This present Constitution can never be revoked or modified, but shall forever remain valid and have the force of Law . . . And if, nevertheless, anyone would ever dare attempt any action contrary to this Order of ours, handed down for all times, let him know that he has incurred the wrath of Almighty God, and the Blessed Apostles Peter and Paul."

Why would these important documents be omitted unless there was a sinister agenda to do away with the Tradition of the Church?

The second problem to lie number 2 is the signifying effect of the sacrament would be missing altogether in its wording.

Pope Leo XIII in his 1896 document *Apostolicae Curae* concerning the invalidity of the Anglican Orders states:

"All know that the Sacraments of the New Law, as sensible and efficient signs of invisible grace, must both signify the grace which they effect and effect the grace which they signify.... **That form cannot be considered apt or sufficient for a Sacrament which omits that which it must essentially signify**."

Even though Pope Leo XIII was speaking about the sacrament of Holy Orders, the principle applies to all sacraments. This would apply especially to the Eucharist for this is the greatest and source of all the sacraments.

St. Thomas Aquinas said in his *Summa Theologica*, Pt. III, Q. 78, A. 3:

"I answer that, there is a twofold opinion regarding this form. Some have maintained that the words '**This is the chalice of My blood belong to the substance of the form, but not those words which follow. Now this seems incorrect**, because the words which follow them are determinations of the predicate, that is, of Christ's blood: consequently they belong to the integrity of its (i.e., the form) recitation."

St. Thomas believed all the words must be in the form and he may have been quite correct here. However, the great saint made a good point. All the words in the form must be correct determinations of the predicate.

It is necessary for the words "for many unto the remission of sins" to be correct and not to be omitted because they form part of the **FORM**.

If the words are not the same as Christ's words and the new words mean something different, two parts necessary for a valid Mass are missing: The **Form**, because the words are different having with it a different meaning and the **Intention of the Church** because something else was intended as the very words indicate.

To top it all off, Pope Leo XIII declared the Holy Orders of the Anglican Church invalid due to a defective form. The New Rite of Ordination in the Modernist so-called Catholic Church mirrors that of the Anglican Church and has the very same deficiencies. This means the New Rite of Ordination in the Modernist Church is invalid.

An invalid priesthood would necessarily invalidate the Eucharist. Thus, we now have three necessary parts missing to make a valid Mass. If the ancient Roman Mass were done perfectly, without a valid priest there would be no valid mass.

LIE NUMBER 3: The pope has tolerated the usage and has never disapproved it. He even said the words "for all" himself when he was in America. If the pope did it, so can I. I'm just being obedient to my bishops since the pope followed along.

Supposing the claimants to the papacy were true popes, we know popes sin like everybody else. Perhaps, the pope used the word "all" at Mass and has never disapproved the usage for the same reason Peter would eat only with the Jews in the company of Gentiles as we read in Galatians. In other words, in pleasing men, Peter sinned against God.

The main problem to this argument, however, it is impossible for the pope to have ever approved of the incorrect word to begin with precisely because it would have been a harmful and evil practice. Pope Pius VI solemnly declared in *Auctorem Fidei* that the church could never do such a thing.

The pope is limited in his authority. He cannot officially change the words of Christ anymore than he could change the matter, which Christ used. In other words, the pope could not change bread and wine to pretzels and beer as the heretic Thomas Munzer did in the 16th century. If he did try to do something like this then we are bound to withstand him to the face as Paul did to Peter. You are duty bound to disobey the orders of your superiors if they command you to do something you know to be wrong.

Besides, if a true pope ever did try to do such a thing, he would ipso facto cease to be pope, since it is impossible for a true pope to command a universal discipline that would be wrong.

Because we have claimants to the papacy who hold to extreme blasphemies and heresies, there is no way one could say these men are true popes. To know and understand this and still acknowledge them as legitimate popes is an affront against Almighty God.

What we have is a counterfeit Catholic Church with antipopes eclipsing the true Catholic Church and the new mass is just one of the proofs of this fact.

LIE NUMBER 4: Three Eastern Rites use the words "for all" in the consecration and have done so for years. The first example is the ANAPHORA OF ST. JOHN THE APOSTLE AND EVANGELIST.

"This is the chalice of my Blood of the New Testament: Take, drink ye of it: this is shed forth for the life of the world, for the expiation of transgressions, the remission of sins to ALL that believe in him forever and ever."

The second example is the ANAPHORA OF ST. MARK THE EVANGELIST. "This is the chalice my Blood of the New Testament: Take, drink ye all of it, for the remission of sins of you and of ALL the true faithful, and for eternal life."

The third example is one of twenty-two Anaphoras once used in the Maronite Rite said "shed for you and for all" just as the New Mass says today. For over 300 years this Maronite Anaphora was used until it was changed to "for many."

Therefore, since it was once used in the East without condemnation from Rome, it must be permissible.

According to Dr. Rama Coomaraswamy, never did any of the Eastern Rites or Oriental Rites amounting to some 76 different rites in various languages going back to apostolic times ever use the word "all" in the Form of Consecration. (*The Problems with the New Mass*)

However, for the sake of the argument, let's assume this lie is true.

In the first two examples, notice the words used in the anaphoras were "all that believe" and "all the true faithful." Though this is not exactly the word Christ used, they do mean the same thing as the word "many" as it is understood from Trent's Catechism.

The words "for all" were not used by themselves but were used with qualifying words to explain that the words "for all" did not mean for all mankind but only Catholics.

When using words indicating "many" and not to all mankind, the correct meaning and intention stays intact, even though the words themselves are not a perfect translation. If one were to use "for all" without any additional or qualifying words, naturally one would think for all mankind.

As for the third example, because something was believed, practiced, or understood by one part of the Church would not ipso facto be correct. This is how the Protestant argues. He looks for something in history and assumes it makes it okay to hold to it today.

Saints believed incorrectly about many doctrines until they were defined, such as the Immaculate Conception, which was denied by Sts. Thomas Aquinas and John Chrysostom.

There are many more examples but this one should suffice. The same goes with practices and disciplines.

Again, assuming this lie is true, one would have to ask several questions:

Why would one out of 22 anaphoras, which used the original language used by Christ, have a different word than what Christ actually used?

Why would it be considered a valid anaphora if the wrong word was used?

Why after 300 years did the anaphora get changed back to "many" if "all" was acceptable?

Could it be the word were incorrect, it was finally realized to be the wrong word after so many years, and then it was changed precisely because it invalidated the consecration and they knew it?

There are too many questions to establish de fide practice.

However, we do have de fide stance at the Council of Florence, which establishes the dogma and the practice for all rites, not just Rome.

It ultimately does not matter what was used in history before the Council of Florence, for if it was done differently, then in light of the definition we can know for sure that it would have been invalid.

LIE NUMBER 5: Rome approved of the words in a 1970 query known as Notitiae 6. It states:

"In certain vernacular versions of the text for consecrating the wine, the words *pro multis* are translated thus: English, *for all;* Spanish, *por todos,* Italian, *per tuti*

Query:

a. Is there a sufficient reason for introducing this variant and if so, what is it?
b. Is the pertinent traditional teaching in the Catechism of the Council of Trent to be considered superseded?
c. Are all other versions of the biblical passage in question to be regarded as less accurate?
d. Did something inaccurate and needing correction or emendation in fact slip in when the approval was given for such a version?

Reply:

a. According to exegetes [experts] the Aramaic word translated in Latin by *pro multis* has its meaning "for all;" the many for whom Christ died is without limit; it is equivalent to saying Christ has died for all. The words of Saint Augustine are apposite [being of striking appropriateness and pertinence]: "See what he gave and you will discover what he bought. The price is Christ's. What is it worth but the whole world? What, but all peoples? Those who say either that the price is so small that it has purchased only

Africans are ungrateful for the price they cost; those who say that they are so important that has been given for them alone are proud" [Enarr. in Ps. 95, 5].

b. The teaching of the Catechism (Trent's Catechism) is in no way superseded: the distinction that Christ's blood is sufficient for all but efficacious for many remains valid.

c. In the approval of this vernacular variant in the liturgical text nothing inaccurate has slipped in that requires correction or emendation."

It was the Freemason Annabale Bugnini who was then the Secretary of Divine Worship. It was he who concocted the New Mass. This is the same man whom in his first version of the New Mass left out the words of Consecration altogether and was told by Paul VI to change it.

The secretary is not Rome. The secretary is not infallible and neither is a false claimant to the papacy as was Paul VI. As a matter of fact, he was also a Freemason.

Fr. Malachi Martin said the freemason Bugnini was a very wicked individual, an agent of Lucifer. His intention for the New Mass "was to make any Protestant, any Jew, or any partaker feel right at home." (*The Kingdom of Darkness*, Tape 1, Fr. Malachi Martin, interviewed by Bernard Janzen, Triumph Communications)This being said, the following responses will expose the lies and nonsense of the three answers Bugnini gives in the 1970 query.

a. Contrary to the reply, the Aramaic word does not have as its meaning "for all." Never in history or in Scripture do we see this in the Consecration. According to Fr. Malachi Martin, doctor and the premier expert in ancient Semitic Languages, states that there are two Aramaic words for "all" and two for "many." (*The Eternal War*, Tape 3. *The Keys of the Kingdom* – Fr. Malachi

Martin, interviewed by Bernard Janzen, Triumph Communications)

The words Christ used are not the ones that apply to "all" which of course, corresponds and confirms Trent's Catechism.

If the meaning were the same then the Catechism of Trent is in error for it says just the opposite.

Also, St. Augustine never said that the Consecration of the Chalice is for all, which is the point of the matter. The Secretary is taking St. Augustine out of context and then used to justify the lie.

b. We already know that the Catechism of Trent is right and valid. The secretary doesn't want to say the Catechism is wrong but he wants his way also. However, if the change of "many" can be changed to "all" then the Catechism is incorrect in its statement. It's that simple. You can't have it both ways as the secretary is trying to do.

c. This is an amazing statement by the secretary. The Catechism already answered this question hundreds of years ago and now the secretary is contradicting it. If nothing inaccurate slipped in then the Catechism and St. Alphonsus are incorrect because they are saying the word "all" is inaccurate because the chalice is for the fruit of Christ's passion, and not for all mankind. The secretary implies in his first answer that it is for all mankind which contrary to the Catechism. Please reread the Catechism and St. Alphonsus and see for yourself how the secretary contradicts them. The problem is the secretary wants to have it both ways. Annabale Bugnini's statement flies right in the face of the historical understanding.

LIE NUMBER 6: You can't have only half of the sacrament. The host cannot change without the chalice, therefore, if the host changes, the wine in the chalice must also change.

First of the all, the Host alone is not just half of the sacrament. The whole Christ is present in the consecrated Host: Body, Blood, Soul, and Divinity. This is basic catechetics 101.

The 1917 Code, Canon 817 states: "It is unlawful even in the case of necessity, to consecrate one species without the other, or to consecrate both outside the Mass."

Though it is unlawful, it would not necessarily invalidate the Host. The law is not saying anything about whether one species can be consecrated without the other, but only that it should not be done.

Maximillian Kolbe canonized by John Paul II reportedly broke this law while at Auschwitz.

At every Holy Mass, presuming all the elements are present, the host will change before the chalice since Catholics adore the Host before the second part of the Consecration takes place.

If a valid priest honestly forgets to consecrate the wine in the chalice, the Host would still remain valid with Christ fully present, if it did not, then Christ would be present one moment and cease being present a moment later. The only other possibility would be that Christ would have never been present in the host thus rendering adoration to a piece of ordinary bread by the faithful a moment earlier.

Though the Church has never defined what would happen in either scenario, the argument does not follow that the chalice must be valid. It could only support the possibility Christ is not present in the host as well.

Without the correct intention in the second part of the Consecration, the host would also not transubstantiate precisely because there was never the correct intention in the beginning.

LIE NUMBER 7: Based on the Scriptural usage, the replacement of "many" with "all" does not represent a material change in the consecration formula, for both "many" and "all" can be either inclusive or exclusive. Whether the inclusive or exclusive meaning is intended in Matthew 26:28 and Mark 14:24 is neither specified by Scripture nor taught in any papal or conciliar dogma. Yet we must add that even in its most inclusive sense, the Scriptural usage of "all" does not mean that every person in the world *will be* saved, but only that every person has the *opportunity* to be saved.

This argument was partly covered in LIE NUMBERS 1, 2, and 3.

Regardless of the wording whether "many" or "all" if the intention of either word is inclusive, then the wrong intention would be present because it is not referring to who or who is not going to be saved.

The form is not merely referring to every person who has an opportunity to be saved because all of mankind has the opportunity to be saved.

The Chalice is offered only to those who believe. The faithful are the fruits of Christ's redemption.

The assumption is not made whether the faithful will remain faithful to the end, just as the fruits may not remain good until harvest.

This is the key. It doesn't matter whether the ones receiving the Cup will be saved or not because the potentiality of salvation of the soul is based on the endurance of the individual.

This is why the Eucharist is given to the believers. The Eucharist is our daily bread to help keep us spiritually alive and healthy and to give us strength.

Thus, the statement that said, "...**for both "many" and "all" can be either inclusive or exclusive... Whether the inclusive or exclusive meaning is intended in Matthew 26:28 and Mark 14:24 is neither specified by Scripture,**" is denied in the *Catechism of the Council of Trent* and by St. Alphonsus and Scripture itself.

It would be the height of arrogance, not to mention outright heretical, to argue against the Catechism of Trent and St. Alphonsus and say anyone whosoever can receive from the Chalice and that it could be inclusive.

For it is and has always has been only for those who believe, viz, Catholics **making this understanding a dogma** precisely because it is in Scripture itself, and confirmed by the consistent and unambiguous writings of Pope St. Pius V, St. Charles Borremeo, and St. Alphonsus De Liguori.

"For any one who eats and drinks without discerning the body eats and drinks judgment upon himself." (First Letter to the Corinthians 11:29)

This is dogma!

LIE NUMBER 8: In *De Defectibus*, Pope St. Pius V tells us exactly what the "intention" required to consecrate the sacrament must be. And that intention has absolutely *nothing* to do with whether the priest intends to share the fruits of the Lord's blood with "many" or "all" men. In paragraph 23 of the document, Pope Pius V states:

"The intention of *consecrating* is required"

The intention of consecration is required, but we are dealing with the requirement of consecrating.

The intention of consecration lies in the form, which is why it is in the form. Pope St. Pius V said that if you change the form to mean something different such as consecrating it for all mankind, then you would have the wrong intention. It wouldn't be in the form if the intention were not going to be a part of it.

The intention is consecrating, but that doesn't mean merely changing the substance without the purpose of changing it. This is why all the words matter as St. Thomas and St. Alphonsus said.

The Council of Florence has given us the de fide position; the whole form is what changes the substance.

Again, the consecration requires the intent to change the wine and its purpose if that purpose is part of the form.

All of this could simply be avoided if one word were changed. The hierarchy knows this, but they won't change that one word back to the one Christ actually used precisely because the New Mass as a whole is profoundly non-Catholic, non-historical, and non-biblical and that is the way it was meant to be according to those who drew it up.

Amazingly, the Liturgy of the Word in the New Mass will quote Christ saying "for many" and the priest's duty is to explain the Liturgy of the Word in his homily. A few minutes later, the priest uses the words "for all" during the Consecration right after everyone just heard Christ saying it is not for all but for the many, and nobody is the wiser. The modernist church keeps up the mockery and sacrilege.

Don't be surprised if the modernist Counterfeit Church changes the words back after all the real priests are gone due to the break in Apostolic Succession. Remember, only valid priests can say valid masses.

If any doubt lingers whatsoever over the validity of any mass due to faulty words of consecration or doubtful priests, then you are obligated **NOT** to attend it.

Pope Innocent XI, in a decree of the Holy Office, March 4, 1679, condemned the idea that a person could follow a probable opinion regarding the value of a sacrament and abandon the safer course. He not only condemned this once but twice.

It should be noted, the **Council of Trent in the 7th Session, Canon 13 said:** "If anyone says that the received and approved rites of the Catholic Church, customarily used in the solemn administration of the Sacrament, can be despise or can be freely omitted by the ministers without sin, or can be changed into other new rites by any pastor in the Church whomsoever, let him be anathema"

The key phrases are "other new rites...by any pastor...whomsoever."

Was this statement of Trent binding on future popes? Many say no, yet, today we still have two distinct rites: the Ancient (Roman) Rite and the New Rite.

How can this be possible? The answer is it is not possible.

Even if Paul VI were the true pope at that time, the new rite of mass would have caused his own automatic anathema.

Again, in the Ancient or Roman Rite, there is an Altar, and in its Rubrics, there is an offering of Christ's Body and Blood.

In the New Rite, there is a table and in its Rubrics, there is an offering of bread and wine.

The abomination of desolation found in the two books of Maccabees had two altars. One was placed over the other just as in today's so-called Catholic Church. This is quite a coincidence. The Old Testament abomination also had women serving in the sanctuary. (II Maccabees 6:4)

Again, Jesus spoke of a future abomination of desolation in Matthew 24:15, *"So when you see the desolating sacrilege spoken of by the prophet Daniel, standing in the holy place (let the reader understand)..."*

This is the last Gospel reading of the liturgical year on the Roman calendar, yet this verse is not found in all of the Gospel readings throughout the entire year in the new liturgical (New Mass) calendar. Why?

Because Christ was referring to the New Mass and Masonic Rome knows it.

The New Mass should be avoided with all our power for it does not fit in the Catholic belief system of worship. Even when the New Mass is valid and done properly, it should still be avoided just as every valid schismatic mass should be avoided. This would include the indult mass of the 1962 Missal. Even some Black Masses are valid and they of course should be avoided.

The *Novus Ordo* (New Mass) is truly a Black (Satanic) Mass because Freemasons and Protestants concocted it.

In Matthew 5:48, Christ said, *"You, therefore, must be perfect, as your heavenly Father is perfect."* In Matthew 22:39, Christ said, *"You shall love the Lord your God with all your heart, and with all your soul, and with all your mind. This is the great and first commandment."*

He that turneth away his ears from hearing the law, his prayer shall be an abomination. (Book of Proverbs 28:9)

The Holy Sacrifice of the Mass is the greatest thing in Heaven and on earth!

How could anyone knowingly participate and even defend a Protestant, New Age, and Masonic Mass in the name of Christ and then call himself or herself Catholic?

Perhaps, as only one drunk on that wine of abomination of which St. John saw in the Apocalypse.

The Lord hateth all abomination of error, and they that fear him shall not love it. (Ecclesiasticus 15:13)

Return to the Lord, and turn away from thy injustice, and greatly hate abomination. (Ecclesiasticus 17:23)

In 2011, Rome admitted that "for all" was a faulty translation and changed the words back to "for many." However, very few priests are most assuredly valid. Therefore, the *Novus Ordo* mass continues to be an abomination since there's no valid Eucharist.

The New Rite of Holy Orders for Priests and Bishops

According to the infallible decree of Pope Eugene IV, at the Council of Florence in Session 8, on Nov. 22, 1439, *Exultate Deo, "All these sacraments are made up of three elements: namely, things as the matter, words as the form, and the person of the minister who confers the sacrament with the intention of doing what the Church does. If any of these is lacking, the sacrament is not effected."* (*Decrees of the Ecumenical Councils*, Georgetown Univ. Press, Vol. 1, p. 542; *Denzinger*, The Sources of Catholic Dogma, 695)

Popes, such as Pope St. Pius X, have taught that *"It is well known that to the church there belongs no right whatsoever to innovate anything on the substance of the sacraments. (Ex quo nono)."*

Session 21, Chapter 2 of The Council of Trent taught, *"It* [Council of Trent] *declares further that this power has always been in the Church, that in the administration of the sacraments, without violating their substance, she may determine or change whatever she may judge to be more expedient for the benefit of those who receive them."*

Pope St. Pius V, in *De Defectibus,* implies that the substance is the meaning.

During the Protestant Revolt, the Anglican Church altered the rite of Holy Orders. On June 20, 1555, Pope Paul IV issued the Bull *Praeclara carissimi*, which stated *"that anyone not properly and correctly ordained was to be reordained."* On Oct. 30, 1555, Pope Paul IV issued the papal brief, *Regimini universalis,* against the bishops consecrated in the Anglican rite that *"anyone ordained to the rank of bishops or archbishops by rites other than those used by the Church are not properly and correctly ordained."* The proper and correct way for ordination and consecration comes from the *"customary form of the Church."* (*Bishops and Reform in the English Church*, 1520-1559, by Kenneth Carleton, and *The Destruction of the Christian Tradition*, by Rama P. Coomaraswamy, pp. 321-322, *Apostolicae Curae*, Promulgated September 18, 1896 by Pope Leo XIII)

In 1896, Pope Leo XIII specified in *Apostolicae Curae* the cause for the invalidity of the Anglican Orders: *"From them has been deliberately removed whatever sets forth the dignity and office of the priesthood in the Catholic rite. That form cannot be considered apt or sufficient for a Sacrament which omits that which it must essentially signify. 28. The same holds true of episcopal consecration. For to the formula, "Receive the Holy Ghost", not only were the words "for the office and work of a bishop", etc. added at a later period, but even these, as we shall presently state, must be understood in a sense different to that which they bear in the Catholic rite. Nor is anything gained by quoting the prayer of the preface, "Almighty God", since it, in like manner, has been stripped of the words which denote the summum sacerdotium [high priesthood].... So it comes to pass that, as the Sacrament of Order and the true sacerdotium of Christ were utterly eliminated from the Anglican rite, and hence the sacerdotium is in no wise conferred truly and validly in the episcopal consecration of the same rite, for the like reason, therefore, the episcopate can in no wise be truly and validly conferred by it, and this the more so because among the first duties of the episcopate is that of ordaining ministers for the Holy Eucharist and sacrifice.... Being fully cognizant of the necessary connection between faith and worship, between "the law of believing and the law of praying", under a pretext of returning to the primitive form, they corrupted the Liturgical Order in many ways to suit the errors of the reformers. For this reason, in the whole Ordinal not only is there no clear mention of the sacrifice, of consecration, of the priesthood (sacerdotium), and of the power of consecrating and offering sacrifice but, as we have just stated, every trace of these things which had been in such prayers of the Catholic rite as they had not entirely rejected, was deliberately removed and struck out."*

Other parts of the ceremonial rite, known as the *signification ex adjunctis*, clarify the meaning of the form. Pope Leo XIII was referring to the *signification ex adjunctis* of the Anglican rite, which omits all the references of the meaning of the priesthood therefore, being the essential cause of the demise and invalidation of the rite. In other words, the form can take on a different meaning with *signification ex adjunctis,* which it clearly does in the Anglican rite. As Pope Leo XIII taught in *Apostolicae Curae, "Sacraments of the New Law, as sensible and efficient signs of invisible grace, must both signify the grace which they effect and effect the grace which they signify."* The *signification ex adjunctis* found in the Anglican rite demonstrated that their sacramental form didn't *"signify the grace which they effect."*

The reason for pointing out this solemn and infallible condemnation of the Anglican rite of Orders by Pope Leo XIII is due to the fact that, when it made its big splash in the Catholic world, Paul VI's new 1968 rite came bearing precisely the same deficiencies as the condemned Anglican rite.

The form for the Sacrament of Holy Orders was infallibly taught by Pope Pius XII in *Sacramentum Ordinis*, Nov. 30, 1947: *"But regarding the matter and form in the conferring of every order, by Our same supreme apostolic authority We decree and establish the following: ... the form consists of the words of the preface of which the following are essential and so required for validity:*

Grant, we beseech You, Almighty Father, to these Your servants, the dignity of the Priesthood renew the spirit of holiness within them, so that they may hold from You, O God, the office of the second rank in Your service and by the example of their behavior afford a pattern of holy living."

In the new 1968 rite, the essential phrase *"so that"* is missing, which affects the substance. Without *"so that"* what was implied isn't necessarily the same. Pope Pius XII taught the necessity of this phrase *"so that"* in order for the validity of the sacrament and to remove all doubt about it.

However, the 1968 rite does more than merely leave out a simple phrase in the form. It eliminated all references to the *summum sacerdotium* [high priesthood] in the *signification ex adjunctis,* as did the Anglican rite. Wouldn't you know, the Anglican Church has no problem with Paul VI's new rite, unlike the traditional Catholic rite. As you'll find in the Anglican rite, words like: sacrifice, priesthood, and mass are present, but they are ambiguously phrased. For example, *"offering sacrifice to God"* is not the same as *"offering THE sacrifice to God."* Everyone offers sacrifice to God, and the faithful can only offer *THE* sacrifice through the priest, but without the high priesthood, *THE* sacrifice to God is impossible. Therefore, there are two types of priesthood: the priesthood of all believers, and the ministerial [high] priesthood. The distinction must be made in favor of the high priesthood, with the understanding that this priesthood represents Christ and not the faithful.

Paul VI's novel 1968 rite eliminated and abolished the following:

"Receive the power to offer the Sacrifice to God and to celebrate Masses for the living and the dead."

"Theirs be the task to change with blessing undefiled, for the service of thy people, bread and wine into the Body and Blood of Thy Son."

"Receive the Holy Ghost, whose sins you shall forgive, they are forgiven them, and whose sins you shall retain, they are retained."(John 20:22)

"Be pleased, Lord, to consecrate and sanctify these hands by this anointing, and our blessing. That whatsoever they bless may be blessed, and whatsoever they consecrate may be consecrated and sanctified in the name of Our Lord Jesus Christ."

"For it is a priest's duty to offer sacrifice, to bless, to lead, to preach and to baptize."

"The new priests then promise obedience to their bishop who 'charges' them to bear in mind that offering Holy Mass is not free from risk and that they should learn everything necessary from diligent priests before undertaking so fearful a responsibility."

"That Thou wouldst recall all who have wandered from the unity of the Church, and lead all believers to the light of the Gospel."

"The blessing of God Almighty, the Father, the Son, and the Holy Ghost, come down upon you, and make you blessed in the priestly Order, enabling you to offer propitiatory sacrifices for the sins of the people to Almighty God."

The hatchet job to the rite for bishops is more drastic. It's also more important than the rite for priests since bishops make priests. If any doubt is found in the episcopacy, then those priests whom they ordain automatically become doubtful. Invalidity must be presumed when there is reasonable doubt. (Pope Innocent XI, in a decree of the Holy Office, March 4, 1679)

In Sacramentum Ordinis, Pope Pius XII declared: *"But regarding the matter and form in the conferring of every order, by Our same supreme apostolic authority We decree and establish the following:... in the Episcopal ordination or consecration... the form consists of the words of the 'Preface,' of which the following are essential and so required for validity: Complete in Your Priest the fullness of Your ministry, and sanctify him, adorned (as he is) with the ornament of all glorification, with the dew of heavenly anointing.*

Pope Pius XII's intention was to settle the matter once and for all to clear up the mess and remove all doubt for priests and bishops. But within 21 years, Paul VI completely changed it all again, especially the rite for bishops. The new rite: *"So now pour forth upon this chosen one that power which is from You, the governing Spirit whom You gave to your beloved Son, Jesus Christ, the Spirit given by Him to the holy Apostles, who found the Church in every place to be your temple for the unceasing glory and praise of your name."*

Do the two forms mean the same thing? What do we find in the *signification ex adjunctis* but more eliminations and abolishment. For instance, the bishop elect was once asked to confirm his belief in each article of the Apostles' Creed, and if he would, *"anathematize every heresy that shall arise against the Holy Catholic Church."* However, Paul VI's new ecumenical rite did away with these all important aspects of the rite. Other words and prayers were eliminated in the new rite, such as:

"A bishop judges, interprets, consecrates, ordains, offers, baptizes and confirms."

And

"Give him, O Lord, the keys of the Kingdom of Heaven... Whatsoever he shall bind upon earth, let it be bound likewise in Heaven, and whatsoever he shall loose upon earth, let it likewise be loosed in Heaven. Whose sins he shall retain, let them be retained, and do Thou remit the sins of whomsoever he shall remit... Grant him, O Lord, an Episcopal chair."

The Anglicans have no problem with new rite because all things absolutely Catholic have been removed. According to sacramental requirements taught as the customary form of the Church by Popes Leo XIII and Pius XII, the new 1968 rite of Holy Orders by Paul VI is lacking that which is required for validity, at least, it appears so. Therefore, serious and reasonable doubt about the validity of the new rite is present and an honest Catholic cannot in good faith accept it. The real kicker is that a true pope can't do what Paul VI has done, namely, create reasonable doubt about the sacraments. The new rite by Paul VI is the bad fruit Christ instructs his followers to recognize in order that we know and *"beware of false prophets who come to you in sheep's clothing but inwardly are ravenous wolves."* (Matt. 7:15)

Introduction to the Antipopes

Every time evidence is presented that a Vatican 2 pope was involved with Masonry, their defenders discount it as hearsay. Every time those popes can be shown teaching a heresy or practicing some abomination, their defenders will either say that they are being taken out of context or call their heretical teachings and practices good and orthodox, because in their minds, their popes are just too wonderful. Just as Protestants who defend the heresy of justification by "Faith Alone" with "man is justified by faith alone but not by a faith that is alone" despite the fact St. James in his Epistle states that justification is NOT BY FAITH ALONE, Vatican 2 defenders likewise defend the heresies and apostasies of their popes.

Two arguments specifically will be given against John Paul II and Benedict XVI on how their particular heresy among many is unjustifiable and indefensible. When the conciliar popes are shown in acts of apostasy, their defenders dismiss it altogether with "we don't know what the intent was." Some will even deny that the acts of apostasy are acts of apostasy. An anecdote will be given in one particular John Paul II case to demonstrate how ridiculous some apologetics used by Vatican 2 defenders can be.

While it is true that a pope cannot teach a heresy formally, an antipope most certainly can. Defenders of the conciliar popes will not consider that their popes might really be antipopes.

True popes can be evil scoundrels as many have been, however, they must be Catholic and members of the Church. Masons, heretics, and apostates are non-Catholics and therefore cannot be true popes. Only the highlights of the conciliar antipopes will be given, but many more examples could be supplied.

Catholics (sedevacantists) confess that Rome was usurped with a new religion altogether. It has new laws, practices, doctrines, worship services, worship manuals, and even a new calendar.

Under the guise of modernism, the counterfeit Catholic Church (Vatican 2 Church) is no doubt Satan's grand masterpiece. The Devil could not have better orchestrated his ape church as he usurped the Catholic Church mocking her every sacrament. For every heresy and blasphemy that is spewed out of the Vatican 2 documents and her popes, their defenders actually justify in the name of Our Lord as great teachings given by the Holy Ghost. This is an astounding feat even for the devil. However, we know that all of Satan's power was given him by God for God's greater glory.

The only pope saint since Pope St. Pius V is Pope St. Pius X. His greatest works are against modernism known as the *Syllabus* Condemning the Errors of the Modernists (*Lamentabili Sane*) and On the Doctrine of the Modernists (*Pascendi Dominici Gregis*) with an Oath Against Modernism.

All of these great works by Pope St. Pius X were rejected and eliminated by Paul VI. Not once are these documents mentioned in the new 1992 Catechism of the Catholic Church produced by Ratzinger and John Paul II. To condemn modernism would be the condemnation of the Vatican 2 Church. Ratzinger taught that dogmatic formulas must constantly change. This is the very definition of modernism. No wonder, he said that those past papal teachings against modernism are obsolete.

Pope St. Pius X infallibly declared in *"Pascendi 39"* that Modernism *"should be defined as the synthesis of all heresies."* Since this is so, then modernists should be defined as the synthesis of all heretics. Heretics cannot be true popes as taught unanimously by the Church Fathers. Therefore, 5 claimants to the papacy are actually antipopes since they all are modernists. This means that either the Gates of Hell have prevailed against the Church or the position offered as sedevacantism is true. There is no middle ground. May Our Lord have mercy on us all!

The Papal Oath

Council of Florence, Session 23, March 26, 1436:

[On the profession of the supreme pontiff]

The holy synod decrees that the person elected as pope is obliged to express his consent to the election in the manner stated below. It is fitting that this consent should be made to the cardinals, if the person elected is present in the curia, or to one of the cardinals or someone mandated by them if he is not present there, in the presence of a notary and at least ten persons. After he has been informed of the election, he is bound to act within a day of the demand. If he does not do so, his election is annulled and the cardinals must proceed in the Lord's name to another election. But if he expresses his consent, as stated above, the cardinals shall straightaway make due obeisance to him as supreme pontiff. Once the obeisance has been made by the cardinals, nobody has any right to challenge his pontificate.

[Form of consent]

In the name of the holy and undivided Trinity, Father, Son, and holy Spirit. I, N., elected pope, with both heart and mouth confess and profess to almighty God whose church I undertake with his assistance to govern, and to blessed Peter, prince of the apostles, that as long as I am in this fragile life I will firmly believe and hold the catholic faith, according to the tradition of the apostles, of general councils and of other holy fathers, especially of the eight holy universal councils - namely the first at Nicaea, the second at Constantinople, the third which was the first at Ephesus, the fourth at Chalcedon, the fifth and sixth at Constantinople, the seventh at Nicaea and the eighth at Constantinople – as well as of the general councils at the Lateran, Lyons, Vienne, Constance and Basel, and to preserve intact this faith unchanged to the last dot, (see Matt 5, 18) and to defend and preach it to the point of death and the shedding of my blood, and likewise to follow and observe in every way the rite handed down of the ecclesiastical sacraments of the church. I promise also to labour faithfully for the defense of the catholic faith, the extirpation of heresies and errors, the reform of morals and the peace of the Christian people. I swear also to continue with the holding of general councils and the confirmation of elections in accordance with the decrees of the holy council of Basel. I have signed this profession with my own hand; I offer it on the altar with a sincere mind to you almighty God, to whom on the day of tremendous judgment *I shall have to give an account of* this and *all my deeds* (Athanasian Creed; see Heb 13, 17.); and I will repeat it at the first public consistory.

So that this salutary institution may not fade from the supreme pontiff's memory with the passage of time, every year on the anniversary of his election or of his coronation, the first cardinal present shall, during mass, publicly and in a loud voice address the supreme pontiff thus: Most holy father, may your holiness heed and carefully ponder the promise which you made to God on the day of your election. He shall then read out the promise and shall continue as follows: May your holiness, therefore, for the honour of God, for the salvation of your soul and for the good of the universal church, strive to observe to your utmost all these things in good faith and without guile or fraud. Recall whose place it is that you hold on earth, namely of him who *laid down his life for his sheep* (John 10, 11, 15), who thrice asked the blessed Peter if he loved him, before he entrusted his sheep to him (John 21:15-17), and who, as the just judge *whom nothing secret escapes* (Prayer before Mass; Job 42, 2.), will exact from you an account of everything to the very last farthing (Matt 5, 26). Remember what blessed Peter and his successors as pontiffs did; they thought only of the honour of God, the spread of the faith, the public good of the church and the salvation and benefit of the faithful; finally, imitating their master and Lord, they did not hesitate to lay down their lives for the sheep entrusted to them.

John XXIII Highlights

Angelo Giuseppe Roncalli was the beginning of the end for the Church of Rome.

He had a very suspicious election and it was proclaimed on a full moon.

Roncalli in 1958 took the name of John XXIII, the same name as the Anti-Pope Baldasar Cossa, who usurped the papal office during the exile of the true pope, and for a time carried out his usurpation in Rome itself. The policy in the Roman Church is to never take the name of an anti- pope.

After his death, the Vatican sent for Gennar Goglia, who with his colleagues embalmed John XXIII. Goglia injected ten liters of embalming fluid into John XXIII's wrist and stomach to neutralize any putrefaction. This explains his incorruptible body not to mention he was found face down in his casket.

A laundry list of words, deeds, and associations will easily demonstrate that John XXIII was not a Catholic and therefore not a true pope.

Keep in mind that John Paul II beatified the man you're about to read about.

He was a modernist. Modernism is the synthesis of all heresies (Pope Pius X), which would make him a modernist, the synthesis of all heretics.

His associations alone with such notorious enemies of the Catholic Church should disqualify him as a true pope.

Associations with Communists, Marxists, and terrorists would disqualify a man from the FBI and CIA of the USA. John XXIII's friends and comrades were these very men, and yet there is no problem that he could be pope at the same time?

He was a mason. Masons are automatically excommunicated.

He was a liar. He took the papal oath with no intention to comply.

Since much has been written about John XXIII, only a very brief description will be given as to why he is not recognized as a true pope.

Some highlights of his modernist associations and statements:

-Was influenced by the excommunicated modernist Loisy and by modernist writer Duschene. (*The Destruction of the Christian Tradition*, updated and revised, 2006, Rama P. Coomaraswamy p. 134)

-Was involved in the youth organization "Opera Dei Congress" that was dissolved by Pope St. Pius X for modernism. (*The Destruction of the Christian Tradition*, updated and revised, 2006, Rama P. Coomaraswamy p. 134)

-Was associated with notorious modernists such as Bishop Radini Tedeschi, Bishop Carlo Ferrara of Milan, Bishop Bonomello of Cremona, and Lamberdo Beauduin. (*The Destruction of the Christian Tradition*, updated and revised, 2006, Rama P. Coomaraswamy p. 134 cited Giancarlo Zizola's, The Utopia of Pope John XXIII (Orbis: N.Y., 1978)

-His closest seminary friends including roommate (later Bishop of Bergamo) who assisted at his ordination were excommunicated for modernism. (*The Destruction of the Christian Tradition*, updated and revised, 2006, Rama P. Coomaraswamy p. 134 cited E. Poulat (*Integrisme et Catholicisme integral*)

-Was a Professor of Patristics at the Lateran University, and removed several months "on suspicion of modernism" and for teaching the theories of Rudolf Steiner, an illuminati member and originator of "The Science of the Spirit known as Anthroposophy." A file dated to 1925, the Holy Office had maintained a dossier on Angelo Roncalli which read "suspected of Modernism."

-Roncalli continued a close association with the defrocked priest, Ernesto Buonaiuti, who was excommunicated for heresy in 1926. (Lawrence Elliott, *I Will Be Called John*, 1973, pp. 90-92)

-When Roncalli was Nuncio to France, he was appointed Observer for the Holy See to the United Nations cultural agency, UNESCO. In July 1951, he gave a speech "lavishly praising UNESCO..." Roncalli called UNESCO "this great international organization..." (Alden Hatch, *A Man Named John*, p. 117 -118)

-During his Nunciature in Paris, "Cardinal Roncalli attended in civilian clothes the Great Lodge where he found again the Jesuit Riquet. His adviser was Maurice Bredet, author of 'Mystic and Magic,' who boasted that he had prophesied the Tiara to Cardinal Roncalli." (*The Hidden, But Victorious Way Of The Free-Masonry*, Rev. Fr. Henri Mouraux)

-As "pope" he broke most all papal traditions.

- "When necessary he simply contradicted previous Popes. He rejected *in toto* Gregory XVI's *Mirari Vos* and *Singulari Nos,* and the *Quanta Cura* of Pius IX, to which was attached, as appendix, The *Syllabus of Errors.* John was ruthless in dismissing the views of his predecessors." When asked about following in the footsteps of so great a man as Pius XII, John XXIII responded, "I try to imagine what my predecessor would have done, and then I do just the opposite."('*Pope John XXIII*' Catholic Writer Paul Johnson)

-Again Johnson, "If we take *Mater et Magistra* and *Pacem in Terris* together, they effectively demolish most of the internationalist, social, economic, and political teachings of the Popes for the previous hundred years with the one exception of Leo XIII's *Rerum Novarum."*

-Was greatly influenced by super modernist heretic Teilhard de Chardin.

-Greatly admired super modernist Maritain. (Giancarlo Zizola's, *The Utopia of Pope John XXIII,* Orbis: N.Y., 1978)

-Calls on a Council and invites everybody, Protestants, Eastern Orthodox and Communists. He thought up the event 2 days from his election.

-Revolutionized the mass in 1962 and eliminated many traditional prayers.

-He removed the St. Michael Prayer of Pope Leo from the low masses.

-He refused to read the 3rd Secret of Fatima and called the Fatima seers "Prophets of Doom." (Malachi Martin)

·Removed the Patron Saint of St. John Vianney off the Calendar, St. Philomena. (Pope Gregory XVI had given her the titles of: "Great Wonder Worker of the 19th century" and "Patroness of the Living Rosary, and then canonized her in 1837.) He, also, removed other great saints.

· "...the Christian doctrine of original sin as the cause of human susceptibility to evil, and of the existence of a personal principle of moral evil that Christians always called the Devil or Satan. Both these fundamental doctrines Roncalli had sworn to uphold, and any of his predecessors would have condemned him for not doing so." (Malachi Martin, *The Decline and Fall of the Catholic Church*, (Putnam: N.Y. 1981), p 274)

Fr. Malachi wrote of John as a man with good intentions but very ignorant of those collaborators of evil around him.

Fr. Malachi Martin later changed his views and became a sedevacantist just before he died.

·Vatican insiders were aware that Roncalli was a homosexual.

·One of his first acts was to make Giovanni Baptiste Montini (the future Paul VI) a cardinal, something Pope Pius XII refused to do after it was found Montini had been secretly communicating with Stalin during World War II. Making Montini a cardinal positioned him to become "Pope" Paul VI, which was apparently the game-plan all along, as suggested by *LIFE* magazine's promotion of Montini for Pope in 1956 when he was still only a bishop.

Reproduced here is a de-classified secret World War II document establishing Montini's contacts and cooperation with the Communist-enemy during World War II.

From the Italian magazine *Il Borghese* (March 3, 1974) comes disclosure of how Montini behaved behind Pius XII's back. Evidence has come to light that Montini had been making secret contact with Communist leader Togliatti and others, treacherously compromising the Holy See

Montini (Paul VI) was made a "cardinal" by John

Some highlights involving associations with enemies of the Church:

Roncalli receiving the red hat from a notorious Freemason

-When elevated to the College of Cardinals, Roncalli insisted upon receiving the red hat from the notoriously anti-clerical Vincent Auriol, President of the Masonic "Fourth Republic" of France, kneeling before him to have the red hat placed upon his head. John XXIII said of Vincent Auriol that he was "an honest socialist." (Alden Hatch, *A Man Named John*, p. 121)

-John XXIII was also known as a "good friend and confidant" of Edouard Herriot, Secretary of the Anti-Catholic Radical Socialists (of France). "Perhaps Roncalli's greatest friend was the grand old socialist and anti-clerical, Edouard Herriot." (Rev. Francis Murphy, *John XXIII Comes To The Vatican*, 1959, p. 139. Alden Hatch, *A Man Named John*, p. 114)

-One of John XXIII's good friends was the Communist and Lenin Peace Prize winner Giacomo Manzu. (Curtis Bill Pepper, *An Artist and the Pope*, London, England: Grosset & Dunlap, Inc. Front cover & inside slip cover of book; also look at p. 5)

-John XXIII said: "I see no reason why a Christian could not vote for a Marxist if he finds the latter to be more fit to follow such a political line and historical destiny." (Fr. Joaquin Saenz Y Arriaga, *The New Montinian Church*, Brea, Ca., p. 570)

- At social functions in Paris Roncalli was frequently seen fraternizing with the Soviet Ambassador, M. Bogomolov, even though the Soviet Union had resumed its pre-war policy of brutal extermination of Catholics in Russia. Also a good friend of Edouard Herriot, Secretary of the anti-Catholic Radical Socialists (of France) (*John XXIII Comes To The Vatican*, by Rev. Francis X. Murphy, C.SS.R., 1959, p. 139)

Some highlights involving Freemasonry:

Cardinal Angelo Roncalli was a documented Freemason seated next to Edouard Herriot, Secretary of the Radical Socialists whom Roncalli hosted, along with other officials of the Masonic "Fourth Republic" of France, in 1953

-Was Papal Nuncio in Paris and would visit the Grand Lodge of that city in civilian clothes every Thursday evening as testified by several members of the French police appointed to guard him. (This information can be substantiated by Commandant Rouchette, the retired French police at B.P. 151, 18105 Cognac Cedex. France. Also noted in Mary Ball Martinez, The Undermining of the Catholic Church, Hillmac, Mexico, 1999, p. 117)

-Yves Marsaudon, 33rd degree Scottish Rite Freemason: "The sense of universalism that is rampant in Rome these days is very close to our purpose for existence... with all our hearts we support the revolution of John XXIII." (Yves Marsaudon in his book *Ecumenism Viewed by a Traditional Freemason*, Paris: Ed.

Vitiano; quoted by Dr. Rama Coomaraswamy, *The Destruction of the Christian Tradition*, p. 144)

Freemason Baron Yves Marsaudon

-Yves Marsaudon, the aforementioned French Freemason and author, also claims that Roncalli [John XXIII] became a thirty-third degree Mason while a nuncio at France.

-The Grand Master of the Grand Orient of Italy of Italian Freemasonry told *30 Days Magazine*: "As for that, it seems that John XXIII was initiated (into a Masonic Lodge) in Paris and participated in the work of the Istanbul Workshops." (Giovanni Cubeddu, *30 Days,* Issue No. 2-1994 p. 25)

-From 30 Days magazine, Nov. 2, 1994 edition entitled "A John XXIII Update": "Our readers will remember that in our June 1994 newsletter (Nuclear Horizons) we published a sensational statement by the Grand Master of the Italian Grand Orient Order of Freemasons to the effect that 'Pope' John XXIII had been initiated into the Freemasons when he was Nuncio in Paris in the late forties. We pointed out, that if this statement were true, Angelo Roncalli (John XXIII) could not possibly have been validly elected to the Supreme Pontificate. He would have been intrinsically ineligible by reason of his automatic excommunication under Canon Law (No. 2335). Not being a Catholic, it was not possible for him to be head of the Catholic Church."

-When Angelo Roncalli was the nuncio to France, he appointed a thirty-third degree Freemason and close friend, the Baron Yves Marsaudon, as head of the French branch of the Knights of Malta, a Catholic lay order, causing a major scandal for the Pius XII papacy. (Paul I. Murphy and R. Rene Arlington, *La Popessa*, 1983, pp. 332-333)

- "If there are still some remnants of thought, reminiscent of the Inquisition, they will be drowned in a rising flood of ecumenism and liberalism. One of the most tangible consequences will be the lowering of spiritual barriers that divide the world. With all our hearts we wish for the success of John XXIII's Revolution." (*L'oecumenisme vu par un Franc Macon de Tradition*, Yves Marsaudon, 1964, Paris, p. 26)

-The dedication and preface for Marsaudon's book was written by Charles Riandley, Sovereign Grand Commander of the Supreme Council of France (Scottish Rite). Riandley wrote: "To the memory of Angelo Roncalli,... Pope under the Name of John XXIII, Who Has Deigned to Give Us His Benediction, His Understanding and His Protection,... [and] To His August Continuer, His Holiness Pope Paul VI." Riandley confidently predicted how the policies of Roncalli and Montini would advance the Masonic agenda: "We are convinced of the narrowness of the spiritual, cultural, scientific, social and economic structures which up to our own time, have hindered the actions and the thoughts of man... But these structures have already been shattered in part. Some pontifical decisions have contributed to this. We feel sure that they will be all destroyed eventually... True, not everything is to be rejected; but what cannot be saved will not be saved unless it is renovated." (*L'oecumenisme vu par un Franc Macon de Tradition*, Yves Marsaudon, 1964, Paris, pp. 15, 16)

-John XXIII wrote a Masonic type of encyclical Pacem et Terris and was praised by General Secretary of the British Communist Party, John Gollan, before television cameras on April 21, 1963, said the "encyclical (*Pacem in Terris*) [of John XXIII] had surprised and gladdened" him and, therefore, he had externalized his "most sincere satisfaction at the recent 28th Party Congress." (Fr. Joaquin Saenz Y Arriaga, *The New Montinian Church,* Brea, CA., p. 170)

-John XXIII, *Pacem in terris* #14, April 11, 1963: "Also among man's rights is that of being able to worship God in accordance with the right dictates of his own conscience, and to profess his religion both in private and in public."

-When the theologian of the Holy Office, Fr. Ciappi, told John XXIII that his encyclical *Pacem in Terris* contradicted the teaching of Popes Gregory XVI and Pius IX on religious liberty, John XXIII responded: "I won't be offended by a few spots if most of it shines." (*Catholic Restoration*, March-April 1992, Madison Heights, MI, p. 29)

-The *Masonic Bulletin*, the official organ of the Supreme Council of the 33rd Degree of the Ancient and Accepted Scottish

Rite of Masons, for the Masonic District of the United States of Mexico, located at 56 Lucerna St., Mexico, D.F. (Year 18, No. 220, May 1963):

"THE LIGHT OF THE
GREAT ARCHITECT OF THE UNIVERSE
ENLIGHTENS THE VATICAN

"Generally speaking, the encyclical *Pacem in Terris,* addressed to all men of goodwill, has inspired comfort and hope. Both in democratic and Communist countries it has been universally praised. Only the Catholic dictatorships have frowned upon it and distorted its spirit. "To us many concepts and doctrines it contains are familiar. We have heard them from illustrious rationalist, liberal, and socialist brothers. After having carefully weighed the meaning of each word, we might say that, the proverbial and typical Vatican literary rubbish notwithstanding, the encyclical *Pacem in Terris* is a vigorous statement of Masonic doctrine... we do not hesitate to recommend its thoughtful reading." (Fr. Joaquin Saenz Y Arriaga, *The New Montinian Church*, pp. 147-148)

- "The direction of our action: Continuation of the Work of John XXIII and all those who have followed him on the way to Templar Universalism." (*Resurgence du Temple,* published and edited by the Knights Templar (Freemasons), 1975 A.D.O. Datus, "*Ab Initio,*" p. 60)

-From the June 4, 1963, edition of *The Reporter (El Informador):*

"The Great Western Mexican Lodge of Free and Accepted Masons, on the occasion of the death of John XXIII, makes known its sorrow for the disappearance of this great man who revolutionized the ideas, thoughts, and forms of the Roman Catholic liturgy. His encyclicals *Mater et Magistra* and *Pacem in Terris* have revolutionized the concepts favoring human rights and liberty. Mankind has lost a great man, and we Masons acknowledge his high principles, his humanitarianism, and his being a great liberal. Guadalajara, Jal., Mexico, June 3, 1963 *Dr. Jose Guadalupe Zuno Hernandez"* (Fr. Joaquin Saenz Y Arriaga, *The New Montinian Church,* p. 147)

-Charles Riandey, a sovereign Grand Master of secret societies, in his preface to a book by Yves Marsaudon (State Minister of the Supreme Council of French secret societies), stated: "To the memory of Angelo Roncalli, priest, Archbishop of Messamaris, Apostolic Nuncio in Paris, Cardinal of the Roman Church, Patriarch of Venice, Pope under the name of John XXIII, who has deigned to give us his benediction, his understanding, and his protection." (Piers Compton, *The Broken Cross,* Cranbrook, Western Australia: Veritas Pub. Co. Ptd Ltd, 1984, p. 50)

- "I know Cardinal Roncalli very well. He was a Deist and a Rationalist whose strength did not lie in the ability to believe in miracles and to venerate the sacred." (*Journal de Geneve,* by Freemason Carl Jacob Burckhardt, A.D.O Datus, *"AB INITIO,"* p. 60)

-John XXIII made a notorious Freemason, Umberto Ortolani, a "Gentleman of His Holiness."

-Cardinal Heenan, who was present at the 1958 conclave which gave us John XXIII, once mentioned: "There was no great mystery about Pope John's election. He was chosen because he was a very old man. His chief duty was to make Msgr. Montini (later Paul VI), the Archbishop of Milan, a cardinal so that he could be elected in the next conclave. That was the policy and it was carried out precisely." (Cardinal Heenan's biography, *Crown of Thorns*)

After 1958 conclave, he summoned the conclavists back for an unusual overnight post-election session: "John XXIII asked the cardinals to remain in the conclave another night instead of leaving immediately as was customary...to caution them again against revealing the secrets of his election to outsiders..." (Alden Hatch, A Man Named John, Hawthorn Books, 1963, p. 163)

"After greeting and blessing the cheering throng in St. Peter's Square . . . John XXIII ordered the Cardinals not to disperse. He wished to meet with them in secret. This was a burden on several of the Cardinals who were in their nineties and in failing health, but in deference to the new Pope they all stayed. It must have been a very sensitive meeting, for when Secretary of State Tardini tried to enter, mistakenly believing the conclave was over, he was promptly excommunicated by France's Cardinal Tisserant." (Mark Fellows, *Fatima in Twilight*, p. 154)

In October 1958, the greatest conspiracy ever is made manifest.

The Freemasonic plan is finally realized when one of their own is recognized as the visible head of the Catholic Church.

CONSPIRACY WITHIN A CONSPIRACY

A series of misinformation and disinformation has led to the false and unsubstantiated theory that Cardinal Siri was elected at the 1958 conclave and forced to resign.

Such stories when investigated can hurt the position of sedevacantism as a position bent on believing anything that supports it. There were no real FBI documents to support it. It was all a lie. Cardinal Siri was good friends with all the antipopes especially John Paul II.

However, sedevacantism doesn't need the fable of Cardinal Siri, since the theory was used as a defense for the false understanding of Vatican I and perpetual successors. Roncalli's own life is testimony enough to demonstrate the truth of sedevacantism.

Lastly, even if Cardinal Siri was elected and forced to resign, all that happened in secret and we the faithful couldn't know for sure if Siri was indeed the true pope during his lifetime. We can't have secret popes. A secret pope amounts to a doubtful pope which would negate the Siri thesis even if it were all true.

Therefore, it's impossible for Siri to be a true successor to Peter.

Is the following a coincidence?

The first John XXIII lasted five years, 1410 – 1415.
The Second John XXIII lasted five years, 1958 - 1963.

The first John XXIII called the Council of Constance.
The Second John XXIII called the Second Vatican Council.

The first John XXIII opened his Council in the 4th year of his reign, 1414.
The second John XXIII opened his Council in the 4th year of his reign, 1962.

The first John XXIII died in 1415, just before the 3rd Session of his Constance.
The second John XXIII died in 1963, just before the 3rd Session of Vatican II.

Paul VI Highlights

Giovanni Battista Montini sealed the fate for the Church in Rome. He took the name of Paul VI. As his predecessor, he had a very suspicious election.

A laundry list of words, deeds, and associations will easily demonstrate that Paul VI was also not a Catholic and therefore not a true pope.

He, like his predecessor John XXIII, was a modernist. Modernism is the synthesis of all heresies (Pope Pius X), which would make him a modernist, the synthesis of all heretics.

He was a mason. Masons are automatically excommunicated.

He was a liar. He took the papal oath with no intention to comply.

Only a very brief description will be given as to why he is not recognized as a true pope. All of the following can be found in the books at the end of the highlights for further reading and researching.

Highlights on his background and with Freemasonry:

·His mother was a convert from Judaism. Her funeral monument has Masonic symbols engraved all over it. There are so blatant, that a wall was built in front of it to hide them. The Montini family is listed in the *Golden Book of Noble Italian Heritage* (1962-1964, p. 994): "A branch of the... noble family from Brescia... wherefrom their noble blazon comes and which avows as its sure trunk and founder, a Bartholomew (Bartolino) de Benedictis, said Montini was of Hebrew origin." (Fr. Joaquin Saenz Y Arriaga, *The New Montinian Church*, p. 391)

Jesuit Father Joaquin Saenz Y Arriaga was a doctor of Theology, Church History, and Canon Law. He was one of the first sedevacantists recognizing it in the mid to late 1960's, perhaps earlier.

Father Joaquin Sáenz Y Arriaga S.J.

-There is no record of Baptism for Giovanni Montini (Paul VI).

- Was known in his seminary days as a notorious homosexual.

-In 1944, he worked with the Soviets through a childhood friend Togliatti, who was head of the communist Party in Italy. The Archbishop Primate of the Protestant Church in Sweden, who was state official, informed Pope Pius XII of the situation. It came as shock to Pius XII who exiled Montini to Milan without the traditional red hat. He was so angry that he refused the cardinal's beretta from Pius XII. Investigations into Montini's Soviet affair resulted in finding that his private secretary, the Jesuit Tondi, was a KGB agent who was once the Professor of Atheism at the University of Maxism-Leninism. Tondi gave the Soviets the names of all the clergy sent to Russia who were immediately caught and executed. Tondi was imprisoned and later married his mistress, the militant communist Carmen Zanti in a civil service. After Montini's election to the papacy, Tondi returned to Rome to work in the Vatican's Civil Service as a cover for his KGB activities. Paul VI was greeted on the balcony after his "election" with cries of "*il Papa Montinovsky.*"

-Paul VI was a communist sympathizer. The Pact of Metz held in 1962, guaranteed that the Vatican would not condemn communism at the Second Vatican Council. However, earlier, in 1942, talks already were in the works with communist Moscow. "It was in that year, that Vatican Monsignor Giovanni Battista Montini, who himself later succeeded to the Papacy as Paul VI, talked directly with Joseph Stalin's representative. Those talks were aimed at dimming Pius XII's constant fulminations against the Soviet dictator and Marxism. Stato himself had been privy to those talks. He had also been privy to the conversations between Montini and the Italian Communist Party leader, Palmiro Togliatti, in 1944... "*Stato* offered to supply reports from the *Allied Office of Strategic Services* about the matter, beginning, as he recalled, with OSS Report JR-1022 of August 28, 1944." (Malachi Martin, *The Jesuits - The Society of Jesus and the Betrayal of the Roman Catholic Church*, New York: Simon & Schuster, 1987; pp. 91-92)

-Mark Winckler, interpreter working at the Vatican, tells of a meeting he had with Cardinal Pignedoli (then Msgr.) Pignedoli told him in 1944 that the failed Freemasonic plan to have Cardinal Rampolla elected pope in 1903 would be corrected when they elect Montini. (*The Destruction of the Christian Tradition*, updated and revised, 2006, Rama P. Coomaraswamy p. 145)

-Montini stated, "Our times, can they also not have an Epiphany which corresponds to its spirit, to its capacities? The marvelous scientific evolution of our days, can it not become this star, this sign that thrusts modern humanity towards a new quest for God, towards a new discovery of Christ?" (Milan, 1956, *Le Pape de l'Epiphanie*)

-Montini stated, "Modern man, will he not gradually come to the point where he will discover, as a result of scientific progress, the laws and hidden realities behind the mute face of matter and give ear to the marvelous voice of the spirit that vibrates in it? Will this not be the religion of our day? Einstein himself glimpsed this vision of a universal religion produced spontaneously [i.e., without revelation]. Is this not perhaps today my own religion?" (Conference in Turin, Mar. 27, 1960)

-Montini stated, "We...Catholics...must...first of all, love the world...our times...our civilization...our technical achievements...and above all...love the world." (Bodart's *La biologie et l'avenir de l'homme*)

This statement is one of the foundations for historic Masonry. Historic Catholicism teaches us to despise the world with her achievements and above all to love God.

- "At his coronation as Pope Paul VI, several American newspapers accused him of being a member of the Lodge B'nai B'rith - a photograph served as proof." (*The Hidden, But Victorious Way Of The Free-Masonry,* Rev. Fr. Henri Mouraux)

-30 Days magazine reported the Chair of Peter for Paul VI was engineered by a large group of Masonic and Modernist cardinals meeting in the home of a leading freemason named Umberto Ortolani just prior to the conclave. (November 3, 1993)

- "The sense of universalism that is rampant in Rome these days is very close to our purpose for existence. Thus we are unable to ignore the Second Vatican Council and its consequences... With all our hearts we support the Revolution of John XXIII... This courageous concept of the Freedom of Thought that lies at the core of our Freemasonic lodges, has spread in a truly magnificent manner right under the Dome of St. Peter's." (*L'oecumenisme vu par un Franc Macon de Tradition*, Yves Marsaudon, 1964, Paris)

·Yves Marsaudon wrote, "Born in our Masonic Lodges, freedom of expression has now spread beautifully over the Dome of St. Peter's... This is the Revolution of Paul VI. It is clear that Paul VI, not content merely to follow the policy of his predecessor, does in fact intend to go much further..." (*Freemasonry and Vatican Two,* Y.L. Dupont, Britons: London, 1968)

·Carlos Vazquez Rangel, Grand Commander of the Supreme Council of the Masons of Mexico, in a 1993 interview with the political weekly Processo stated: "On the same day, in Paris the profane Angelo Roncalli and the profane Giovanni Montini were initiated into the august mysteries of the Brotherhood. Thus it was that much that was achieved at the Council was based on Masonic principles."

·He meditated in a room at the UN filled with Masonic symbols, and received B'nai B'rith members at the Vatican.

·Paul VI promised to pray for the success of Mrs. Hollister and her "Temple of Understanding" (which Cardinal Bagnozzi told him was "an occult enterprise of the Illuminati whose aim is the founding of 'the World Religion of Human Brotherhood').

·The Masonic plans were, of course, to infiltrate the Church until one of their own became pope, knowing full well that obedience will be given to him. Thus, the Masonic doctrines will be held as Catholic Orthodoxy. Paul VI stated, "All men must obey him [the pope] in whatever he orders if they wish to be associated with the new economy of the Gospel." (Allocution, June 29, 1970)

The Masonic goal is to change Catholicism to conform to the world and be cultural and perhaps to lead the way in the New World Order. Historic Catholicism is counter-cultural and the reason for the Old World Order.

So when Montini is elected as Paul VI, he finishes the work that began under John XXIII and undoes the historic faith and replaces it with the new modernist Masonic religion and usurps the Catholic name.

·Paul VI stated, "If the world changes, should not religion also change?" (Dialogues, Reflections on God and Man)

·Paul VI closed the Second Vatican Council, which changed the way the Church understood Herself and the world.

·Following Vatican II, Paul VI changed all seven of the sacraments. Only three remain valid, Baptism and Matrimony and Confession in cases where priests are valid.

·Paul VI appointed the Freemason "Fr" Annibali Bugnini including six Protestants to concoct the '*novus ordo missae*' (the new mass). "He who goes about to take the Holy Sacrifice of the Mass from the Church plots no less a calamity than if he tried to snatch the sun from the universe." (St. John Fischer, English martyr under King Henry VIII)

·Paul VI stated in his *General Audience*, June 27, 1973: "...everything must change, everything must progress. Evolution seems to be the law that brings liberation. There must be a great deal that is true and good in this mentality..." (*L'Osservatore Romano*, July 5, 1973, p. 1)

The new religion of Rome only appears to be Catholic but in reality has been radically altered. New Laws, new practices, new worship ceremony, and new doctrines, which are really heresies as all heresies are new doctrines.

All this change came under the guise of papal authority under papal infallibility, which made the Masonic Plan a success.

Only 50 years earlier did Pope St. Pius X warn of this very event as the Masonic Plan was made public.

Paul VI wearing the Ephod

Wearing the Ephod in Yankee stadium	12 Stones

Colombia in 1968

Montini Wearing the Jewish Ephod in place of his pectorial cross

- "Now then, the breastpiece was a prominent Jewish emblem. It symbolically represented the twelve tribes of carnal Israel at the ritual celebrations. Nothing, then, justifies the wearing of this ritual object by a Pope, its visible head of the new people of God, the children of the New Covenant. Even the fact that no previous Pope during the 2,000-year history of the Church has ever worn this ritualistic object of religious Judaism, seems to demonstrate that there is an absolute incompatibility between the profession of our Catholic Faith and the wearing of the ephod or "breastplate of judgment," thoroughly described in the Exodus as characteristic and exclusive of the Levitical high priest.

Since Paul VI wore it publicly, we have the right, and moreover, a grave obligation of conscience to investigate why...*John Baptist Montini wears the breastpiece because in his heart, rather than a Pope, he is a Levitical high priest.* Consciously or unconsciously, only God knows, he seems to be associated with international Judaism, its mighty leaders, and its destructive tools of Communism and Masonry. On the other hand, in his genealogical line of ancestors we find actual roots of Jewish origin, just as in the cases of other cardinals, monsignors, and theologians who have masterminded this dreadful revolution in God's Church." (Fr. Joaquin Saenz Y Arriaga, S.J. PHD., *The New Montinian Church*, 1971 A.D. pp. 302-303)

Exorcist Fr. Malachi Martin reported that on June 29, 1963, the night before Paul VI's coronation, a black mass was celebrated and Satan was enthroned in the Vatican! (Windswept House)

Fr. Malachi has confirmed several times in interviews that this is a fact from his book, and has believed the Vatican has been possessed by Satan ever since.

-Paul VI, *Address to Dalai Lama*, Sept. 30, 1973: "We are happy to welcome Your Holiness today... You come to us from Asia, the cradle of ancient religions and human traditions which are rightly held in deep veneration." (*L'Osservatore Romano*, Oct. 11, 1973, p. 4)

Rightly held? Does this sound like a Catholic Pope?

-Paul VI stated, "We would also like you to know that the Church recognizes the riches of the Islamic faith – a faith that binds us to the one God." (*L'Osservatore Romano*, Sept. 21, 1972, p. 2)

-Paul VI, *Address*, Sept. 18, 1969: "...Moslems... along with us adore the one and merciful God, who on the last day will judge mankind." (*L'Osservatore Romano*, Oct. 2, 1969, p. 2)

-Paul VI, *Address to Muslim Ambassador*, June 4, 1976: "... Moroccan Moslems ... our brothers in faith in the one God. You will always be made very welcome and you will find esteem and understanding here." (*L'Osservatore Romano*, June 24, 1976, p. 4)

-Paul VI, *Address*, Dec. 2, 1977: "...the Moslems (who) profess to hold the faith of Abraham, and together with us they adore the one, merciful God, mankind's judge on the last day, as the Second Vatican Council solemnly declared." (*L'Osservatore Romano*, Dec. 22, 1977, p. 2)

These statements all stem from the Dogmatic Constitution *Lumen Gentium* of Vatican 2 that heretically declares that Muslims worship the one and same true God as Catholics even though they reject God in Christ.

-Paul VI, *Address,* July 9, 1969: "She [the Church] has also affirmed, during Her long history, at the cost of oppression and persecution, freedom for everyone to profess his own religion. No one, She says, is to be restrained from acting, no one is to be forced to act in a manner contrary to his own beliefs... As we said, the Council demanded a true and public religious freedom..." (*L'Osservatore Romano*, July 17, 1969, p. 1)

-Paul VI, Letter, July 25, 1975: "...the Holy See rejoices to see specifically emphasized the right of religious liberty." (*L'Osservatore Romano*, Aug. 14, 1975, p. 3)

These statements stem from *Dignitatis Humanae* (Declaration of religious freedom) of Vatican 2 that heretically declares that man has the right to be wrong. The Council of Vienne declared by implication that man does not have religious freedom as declared in Vatican 2. See p. 348.

-Paul VI, *Telegram after the election of a new Patriarch of Constantinople*, July, 1972: "At the moment when you assume a heavy charge in the service of the Church of Christ..." (*L'Osservatore Romano*, July 27, 1972, p. 12)

Notice that Paul VI is recognizing a schismatic church as the Church of Christ.

-Paul VI, *Address*, Dec. 14, 1976: "...very dear Brothers, sent by the venerable Church of Constantinople... we carried out the solemn and sacred ecclesial act of lifting the ancient anathemas, an act with which we wished to remove the memory of these events forever from the memory and the heart of the Church..." (*L'Osservatore Romano*, Jan. 1, 1976, p. 6)

-Paul VI, *General Audience*, Nov. 30, 1977: "We greet you joyfully, beloved brothers, who represent here His Holiness Patriarch Pimen and the Russian Orthodox Church... all our esteem and brotherly love to His Holiness Patriarch Pimen, to his clergy and to the whole people of the faithful." (*L'Osservatore Romano*, Dec. 15, 1977, p. 4)

-Paul VI, *Joint Declaration with the* [schismatic/heretic] *Shenouda III*, May 10, 1973: "Paul VI, Bishop of Rome and Pope of the Catholic Church, and Shenouda III, Pope of Alexandria and Patriarch of the See of St. Mark... In the name of this charity, we reject all forms of proselytism... Let it cease, where it may exist..." (*L'Osservatore Romano*, May 24, 1973, p. 6)

-Paul VI, *Address,* April 28, 1977: "...relations between the Catholic Church and the Anglican Communion... these words of hope, 'The Anglican Communion united not absorbed,' are no longer a mere dream." (*L'Osservatore Romano*, May 5, 1977, p. 1)

-Paul VI, *Message*, Sept. 8, 1977: "Stress is legitimately laid nowadays on the necessity of constructing a new world order..." (*L'Osservatore Romano*, Sept. 22, 1977, p. 11)

All these statements stem from the Dogmatic Constitution *Lumen Gentium* of Vatican 2 that heretically implies that the Church of Christ exists outside the Catholic Church, as Paul VI actually states about the Church of Constantinople.

If that were not enough, he invited Anglicans to use Catholic altars in the Vatican for their services (a sacrilegious act), and place his papal ring on the Anglican "archbishop" and invited him to bless the faithful in St. Peter's Square. (*The Destruction of the Christian Tradition*, updated and revised, 2006, Rama P. Coomaraswamy p. 152)

For the sake of ecumenism he did not hesitate to even desecrate the Sacred Body of Our Lord, as for example when he personally authorized giving communion to Barbara Olson, a Presbyterian, at her Nuptial Mass (Sept. 21, 1966) without her abjuring her Presbyterian views or her going to Confession.. Not an isolated act by any means, for he also gave Communion under the same circumstances to the Lutherans (*Forts dans la foi,* No. 47). As the Abbe of Nantes said, "No one in the world, bishop or cardinal, Angel or even the Pope himself, has any right whatever to give the Sacrament of the Living to those who are spiritually dead." (Liber Accusationis) quoted in (*The Destruction of the Christian Tradition*, updated and revised, 2006, Rama P. Coomaraswamy p. 152)

·He joined Cardinal Willebrands in "the common prayer of the World Council of Churches" (Doc. Cath. Jan 17, 1971)

·Paul VI, *Message to United Nations*, May 24, 1978: "...we are aware that the path which must lead to the coming of a new international order... cannot in any case be as short as we would like it to be... Disarmament, a new world order and development are three obligations that are inseparably bound together..." (*L'Osservatore Romano*, June 15, 1978, p. 3)

-Paul VI, *Address*, Aug. 1, 1969: "...do not let yourselves become discouraged by the obstacles and difficulties that constantly arise; do not lose faith in man." (*L'Osservatore Romano*, Aug. 14, 1969, p. 8)

-Paul VI, *Audience*, Jan. 10, 1972: "For the demands of justice, Gentlemen, can only be gathered in the light of truth, that truth which is man..." (*L'Osservatore Romano*, Jan. 20, 1972, p. 7)

Such statements could be multiplied tenfold, but as one can see that Paul VI belonged to the Masonic religion, which is the religion of man, not the Catholic religion, which is the religion of God.

These statements also prove the official interpretation of Vatican 2. We'll see later that John Paul II and Benedict XVI make the same types of statements, which again, prove how Rome understands its own Vatican 2 council.

More atrocious deeds of Paul VI

Paul VI giving away the Papal Tiara

·On November 13, 1964, Paul VI gave away the triple-crowned papal tiara. Paul VI had the tiara auctioned at the New York World's Fair. (Fr. Joaquin Saenz Y Arriaga, *The New Montinian Church*, pp. 394-395)

The Papal Tiara is a sign of a true Pope's authority – the three crowns representing the dogmatic, liturgical and disciplinary authority of a pope. In giving it away, Paul VI was symbolically giving away the authority of the Papacy. "Cardinal" Ottaviani is by the side of Paul VI as he does this atrocious deed.

·Paul VI gave his Shepherd's Crook and Fisherman's Ring to U Thant, head of the UN, who sold them to a Jewish businessman in the Midwest. (*The Voice,* Dec. 9, 1972 and documented in Hubert Monteilhet, *Papa Paul VI – L'Amen·Dada)*

·Paul VI abolished the oath against Modernism, at a time when Modernism was everywhere, and why not, for the new religion of Rome, it's heretical to be against modernism.

·On Nov. 21, 1970, Paul VI also excluded all cardinals over 80 years of age from participating in papal elections. (*L'Osservatore Romano*, Dec. 3, 1970, p. 10)

This fixes the next conclave and keeps the devils in power.

·Paul VI gave all the bishops a new gold ring in place of the traditional ones as a sign of the new church. He asked the bishops not to use their shepherd's crooks.

·Paul VI abolished the rite of Tonsure, all four Minor Orders, and the rank of Subdiaconate. (*The Reign of Mary*, Vol. XXVI, No. 81, p. 17)

· "Paul VI gave back to the Muslims the Standard of Lepanto. The history of the flag was venerable. It was taken from a Turkish admiral during a great naval battle in 1571. While Pope St. Pius V fasted and prayed the Rosary, an out-numbered Christian fleet defeated a much larger Moslem navy, thus saving Christendom from the infidel. In honor of the miraculous victory, Pius V instituted the Feast of Our Lady of the Most Holy Rosary to commemorate her intercession. In one dramatic act, Paul VI renounced not only a remarkable Christian victory, but the prayers and sacrifices of a great pope and saint." (Mark Fellows, *Fatima in Twilight,* Niagara Falls, NY: Marmion Publications, 2003, p. 193)

·Under Paul VI, the Holy Office was reformed: its primary function now was research, not defending the Catholic Faith. (Mark Fellows, *Fatima in Twilight,* p. 193)

·According to those who watched film of Paul VI's visit to Fatima, he did not pray one Hail Mary. (Mark Fellows, *Fatima in Twilight,* p. 206)

·In 1969, Paul VI removed forty saints from the official liturgical calendar. (Nino Lo Bello, *The Incredible Book of Vatican Facts and Papal Curiosities,* Ligouri, MO: Liguori Pub., 1998, p. 195)

·Paul VI removed solemn exorcisms from the baptismal rite. In the place of the solemn exorcisms, he substituted an optional prayer that makes only a passing reference to fighting the Devil. (*The Reign of Mary,* Vol. XXVIII, No. 90, p. 8)

·Paul VI granted more than 32,000 requests from priests to return to lay status. (Malachi Martin)

·Paul VI's disastrous influence was visible immediately. For example, in Holland not a single candidate applied for admission to the priesthood in 1970, and within 12 months every seminary there was closed. (Piers Compton, *The Broken Cross,* Cranbrook, Western Australia: Veritas Pub. Co. Ptd Ltd, 1984, p. 138)

·Paul VI, *Speech to Lombard Seminary,* Dec. 7, 1968: "The Church finds herself in an hour of disquiet, of self-criticism, one might say even of self-destruction... The Church is wounding herself." (*L'Osservatore Romano,* Dec. 19, 1968, p. 3)

·Paul VI, *General Audience,* Oct. 1, 1969: "On the other hand, She [the Church] is also trying to adapt herself and assimilate herself to the world's ways; She is taking off her distinctive sacral garment, for She wants to feel more human and earthly. "She is tending to let herself be absorbed by the social and temporal milieu. She has almost been seized by human respect at the thought that She is different in some way and obliged to have a style of thought and life which is not that of the world. She is undergoing the world's changes and degradations with conformist, almost *avantegarde* zeal." (*L'Osservatore Romano*, Oct. 9, 1969, p. 1)

- Paul VI, *Homily*, June 29, 1972: "Satan's smoke has made its way into the Temple of God through some crack..." (*L'Osservatore Romano*, July. 13, 1972, p. 6)

Pretty clever statements to keep the faithful aloof, as Paul VI was one opening up the crack created by John XXIII, to let the smoke of Satan in. Apocalypse 9:1-3: "And there was given to him the key of the bottomless pit. And he opened the bottomless pit: and the smoke of the pit arose, as the smoke of a great furnace..."

-Jean Guitton, an intimate friend of Paul VI, related what Paul VI said at the final session of Vatican II: "It was the final session of the Council," Guitton wrote, "the most essential, in which Paul VI was to bestow on all humanity the teachings of the Council. He announced this to me on that day with these words, 'I am about to blow the seven trumpets of the Apocalypse.'" (Jean Guitton, "*Nel segno dei Dodici*," interview by Maurizio Blondet, *Avvenire*, Oct. 11, 1992)

-Paul VI said, "All honour to Man, king of the earth and now prince of the heavens!" (*Documentation Catholique' no.1580)*

Does this sound like the antichrist speaking? Well, interestingly enough he writes his name in an upside down 666.

Paulus PP. VI

"Paul went so far once as to state that a pope – to be truly pope – must be acknowledged by the whole human race. One century before this, a French philosopher named Lamennais had been condemned as a heretic for saying just that. And every one of Paul's predecessors, including Roncalli, would have unhesitatingly condemned Paul VI for saying so.

"Paul's new view meant recognizing the autonomy of the individual person and therefore accommodating all possible views. It meant that anyone had a right to be wrong. It meant the Catholic Church was no longer "the one true church of Christ." It meant embracing the concept of religious pluralism, and abstention from all "missionary activity." It meant that the people would decide for themselves what to believe and how to behave. Meanwhile, the church was there to minister to their social and physical needs.

'Paul consented, further, to abandon the age-old Catholic belief that the Mass was a sacrifice. It was, he propounded in an official document, a sacred memorial meal presided over by a "priest"; and only threats by the powerful cardinals Ottaviani and Bacci, saved Paul from proclaiming what would have been this formal heresy."

"...He gave moral support to terrorists in Spain and left-wing parties in Latin America. He allowed himself and his office to be used by the Communist government of North Vietnam in order to make the Tet offensive of 1968 possible. He favored Castro's Cuba, and gave free rein to Marxist bishops and priests and nuns in his church of the Americas and Europe and Africa. But Paul never uttered one syllable to protest the crucifixion of Lithuanian Catholics by the Soviets, the persecution of all believers in Hungary, Romania, Czechoslovakia, the tortured prisoners of Castro's Cuba; no more than he did about the planned destruction of the faith he was elected to protect and spread." (Malachi Martin, *The Decline and Fall of the Catholic Church*, Putnam: N.Y. 1981, p. 275) Fr Malachi said in interviews that Paul VI was not an intellectual, and was a weak man.

·Fr Malachi Martin goes on to say in later interviews (when John Paul II claimed to be pope) that the organization of the Roman Catholic Church is dead and in entombment waiting to be resurrected by Her Lord. Fr Malachi wasn't saying the gates of hell had prevailed since the Church still exists on earth but that it no longer exists as an organization. In that aspect, it was over for the Church as he stated, "following Her Lord in death and burial to be resurrected by Christ."

All the false claimants to papacy since 1958 were very clever. They all vigorously state orthodox teachings to keep good Catholics at bay, but then contradict themselves while practicing the opposite of what they preach so that apologists will cite the orthodox teachings in their defense. Even *Humanae Vitae* of Paul VI is the most noted document of his papacy. In it, he rejects artificial birth control, yet Pope Pius XI already solemnly condemned it in *Casti Cannubi* as did Pope Pius XII. *Novus Ordo* Vatican 2 "Catholics" never cite or recognize these prior statements but use *Humanae Vitae* as an argument for Paul VI great orthodoxy. Amazing!

One more thing: The so-called Catholic NAB or New American Bible was highly praised by Paul VI. Due to the modernism of its translators, the footnotes include clever but radically altered interpretations from the historical record.

For instance, it claims that author of Matthew may not be Matthew and that he borrowed as a source the Gospel of Mark. If this were true, then Matthew wouldn't truly be inspired but rather plagiarism. The NAB charges the Gospels as contradicting one another in reality rather than just appearance. The NAB implies some readings are fraudulent. The NAB implies Christ was mistaken. You can find all this and much more in the NAB's footnotes in the Gospel of Matthew alone, not to mention the whole of Scripture. The NAB is so bad that it would not at all be excessive to call it blasphemous. It's not surprising that Paul VI approved it.

John Paul I Highlights

In 1978, Albino Luciani was elected and chose the name, John Paul. Never before in history did a pope attempt take a double name.

He took the two names of his predecessors as if they were his mentors approving of the disaster that had taken place the last 20 years.

He was made bishop by John in 1958, and a cardinal by Paul.

Cardinals over eighty years of age were deprived not only of their right to vote, but to possibly be elected to the papal office. The 78' conclave was stacked. John had appointed 8 cardinals and Paul had appointed 100 cardinals out of 111 that voted. Since John and Paul were really antipopes, their cardinals were not valid cardinals. Therefore, Wyszinski, Leger, and Siri who were appointed by Pope Pius XII were the only valid cardinals in the conclave. Paul barred over 80 cardinals from voting in the next conclave and they were barred.

As for the name John Paul that was taken by Luciani, "the special significance of that name can be found in the thick book on Masonic Morals and Dogma, in which only two Saints' names are honored --- John and Paul. According to the doctrine expressed in this book, the Masons pretend that John the Baptist taught an esoteric doctrine of the Essenes; and they favor "Paul" because of his supposed "leniency," what the opponents of the Papacy have made of Paul's apparent opposition to Peter on one point. I have often mentioned Montini's wearing of the emblem of the high priesthood of Royal Arch Masonry, and I have on file a photo of John XXIII wearing a white glove which prominently displays the sun symbol of the Gnostics. By a top French Mason, Yves Maursodon, John XXIII and Paul VI were praised in the foreword of a book on Freemasonic ecumenism. Despite what was quoted from Paul VI in "Counter-Reformation," which I repeated on another page, there is no mystery at all about Montini's ecumenism." (Excerpt from W.F. Strojie Letter No. 21, May 25 1977)

-John Paul was a radical feminist as seen from his book '*Humbly Yours*'.

-He often made statements such as in his *Angelus Message*, Sept. 10, 1978: "He (God) is our father; even more he is our mother." (*L' Osservatore Romano,* September 21, 1978, p. 2)

-In Sept. 1978, he held up as a classical example of self-abnegation and devotion to duty, one Giosue Carducci, a Professor at the University of Bologna who founded two Masonic lodges and was the author of a long and blasphemous "Hymn to Satan." (*The Destruction of the Christian Tradition,* updated and revised, 2006, Rama P. Coomaraswamy p. 156)

-In 1968, he had recommended that the Catholic Church should approve of the use of the pill for artificial contraception. He rejected *Humanae Vitae* because it was against the pill.

-John Paul was a promoter of the Second Vatican Council as he stated: "...the Second Vatican Council (to whose teachings we wish to commit our total ministry)...We wish to continue to put into effect the heritage of the Second Vatican Council. Its wise norms should be followed out and perfected...We wish to continue the ecumenical thrust, which we consider a final directive from our immediate Predecessors." (*L' Osservatore Romano*, Aug. 31, 1978, p. 6)

He died 33 days after his invalid election in 1978. His death is highly suspicious as two accounts were given for his death.

John Paul II Highlights

Karol Jozef Wojtyla was the next in line after the short reign of John Paul I. He would take the same name as his predecessor and for the same reason.

John Paul II was also not a Catholic and therefore not a true pope, not to mention his election would have been invalid regardless. His reign was filled with very disturbing words and acts.

He was an extreme modernist making him the synthesis of all heretics.

He refused to take the papal oath, which the Council of Florence required as the form of accepting the papacy without which the papal election should be considered null and void.

He held two doctorates in theology, meaning he was not ignorant to theology.

Some things that will be mentioned, as with all five of the false claimants, do not make one an antipope. Only those things involving the elections such as rules and requirements, heresy and or apostasy, involvement with forbidden organizations, and establishing harmful and evil church disciplines make one an antipope. One could quite literally write a large book and fill it with pictures with all the things John Paul II did that were contrary to Christianity. Only a very brief description will be given as to why he is not recognized as a true pope.

·In October 1962, Bishop Wojtyła made two influential contributions to the Second Vatican Council, the *Decree on Religious Freedom* (*Dignitatis Humanae*) and the *Pastoral Constitution on the Church in the Modern World* (*Gaudium et Spes*).

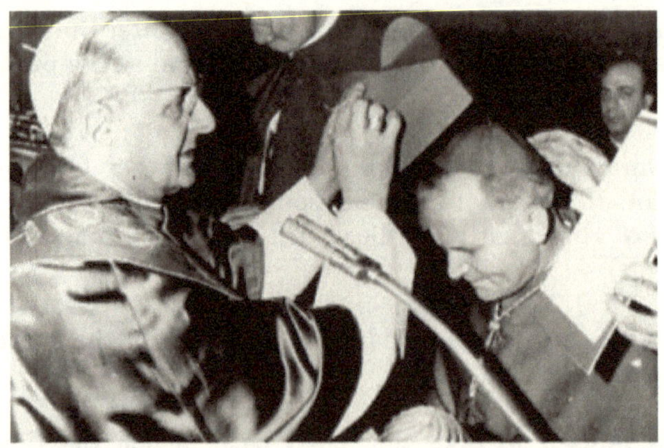

Wojtyla was made a cardinal by Paul VI

Since Paul VI was not a valid pope, then Wojtyla being made a cardinal would be invalid. Since he was an invalid cardinal, then his being elected was flawed by that fact alone, as the intent of the election was in electing what they thought was a cardinal. Of course, it didn't matter, since all but three in the conclave were invalid cardinals anyway just as it was in the case of the first John Paul when cardinals over eighty years of age were deprived not only of their right to vote, but to possibly be elected to the papal office.

·Like his immediate predecessor, "Pope" John Paul II dispensed with the traditional Papal coronation and instead received ecclesiastical investiture with the simplified Papal inauguration on 22 October 1978.

·He appointed to the College of Cardinals, Fr. Henry de Lubac, a known French heretical priest and one of the most influential and notorious modernist theologians at Vatican II.

·John Paul II kept the modernist heretic Fr. Raymond Brown as head of Pontifical Biblical Commission and never once censored him. Brown was responsible for the heretical New Jerome Biblical Commentary.

·He would at the end of his life add 5 new decades to the rosary. He apparently didn't think the Virgin Mary had perfected the form for the rosary as we had it for past 700 years. He called his new decades the luminous mysteries. These mysteries are now said by *Novus Ordo* Catholics on Thursdays in place of the traditional Joyful Mysteries.

·He participated in non-catholic worship services such as the Anglicans and Lutherans, which break the severe laws of God and Church.

·He also allowed the creation of the Anglican Use form of the Latin Rite, which incorporates the Anglican Book of Common Prayer.

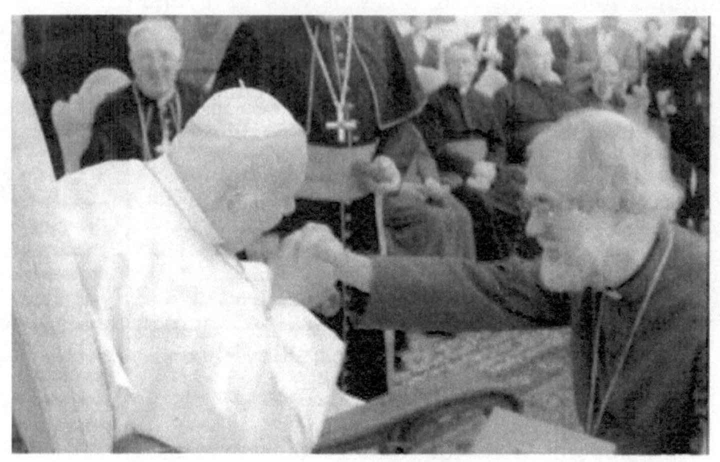

On October 4, 2003 at the Vatican, John Paul II kisses the ring of Rowan Williams, head of the Anglican sect. This means John Paul either rejected Leo's infallible document declaring Anglican orders invalid or put human respect above God and the Church.

John Paul II, the funny man. What a JOKER!

"...During the first day of voting last Sunday, Wojtyla nonchalantly read a quarterly review of Marxist theory as the time-consuming balloting dragged on. 'Don't you think it's sacrilegious to bring Marxist literature into the Sistine Chapel?' joked a Cardinal. Wojtyla smiled, 'My conscience is clear.'..." (*Time Magazine*, October 30, 1978, p. 87)

THE MASS ABOMINATIONS

Watching a dancer during Mass at World Youth Day in 2000

·Rev. Billy Graham said in the forward to Life Magazine's 2005 Commemorative Edition on John Paul II that John Paul II invited him to preach in his church in Poland in 1978, but was called to the conclave.

At a Mass said by John Paul II (*third from left*)

He rejects the words of Holy Scripture and lets women speak in the churches of the holy ones. The Epistle is read by a bare-breasted woman in paint and native garb as her pagan heritage is accepted, when before the Church expects the wearing of clothing as part of conversion.

Nakedness is one of the first things Adam and Eve realized after Original Sin. Today, cultures lost in the world of sin are often found naked. Modesty being the fruit of the Holy Ghost becomes part of man's conversion to God and His Church.

This enculturation by the Vatican 2 Church either ignores or rejects this fact as it accepts a conversion to the faith without a real conversion. This is a clear sign that conversion to the Vatican 2 Church produces no real fruit of modesty, therefore, the Holy Ghost is not really found in the Vatican 2 Church. Come as you are is the new motto. Naked, casual, dress, clean, dirty, uncovered, just come and be united.

·Nov. 7, 1999, in New Delhi, John Paul II celebrates mass with the performance of Hindu dancers. They were seated behind the altar during the rest of service. (*Inside the Vatican - Special Issue* p. 23)

When it comes to altar girls and girl acolytes we have that women should not have a place of prominence in the church According to the Sacred Scriptures in I Tim. 2:12; I Cor. 14:34-5, and the *Code of Canon Law* of 1917 by St. Pius X and Benedict XV formally forbade women to be acolytes at Mass or have access to the altar (Canon 813, # 2).

And Pope Benedict XIV stating in his, *Encyclical,* July 26, 1755: "Pope Gelasius in his ninth letter to the bishops of Lucania condemned *the evil* practice which had been introduced of women serving the priest at the celebration of Mass. Since this abuse had spread to the Greeks, Innocent IV strictly forbade it in his letter to the bishop of Tusculum: 'Women should not dare to serve at the altar; they should be altogether refused this ministry.' We too have forbidden this practice in the same words in Our oft-repeated constitution..." (*The Papal Encyclicals,* Vol. 1 (1740-1878), p. 64)

Pope Gelasius called the practice evil which was introduced in his time. He stated, "We have heard with sorrow of the great contempt [*mépris*] with which the sacred mysteries have been treated. It has reached the point where women have been encouraged to serve at the altar, and to carry out roles that are not suited to their sex, having been assigned exclusively to those of masculine gender."

However, John Paul II thought differently... he says altar girls enrich the liturgy and has no problem with them as acolytes.

The Holy Office on June 22, 1859 declared:

Communication with heretics can be either in a condemned doctrine, or in rites and other signs indicative of adherence to a false sect, with the accompanying scandal of the faithful, to whom the Church therefore forbids this communion, lest the faith be lost or endangered. Whence St. John the Evangelist strictly commands: "if anyone comes to you and does not bring this (i.e. the Catholic) doctrine, do not receive him into the house, or say to him, Welcome. For he who says to him, Welcome, is sharer in his evil works." II John 20. These words evidently imply that everything is forbidden that is expressed by a welcome, in so far as it constitutes liturgical actions instituted to signify ecclesiastical unity. Wherefore we read that a law was enacted by the Fathers of the Council of Carthage 'against praying or singing with heretics' as is cited by Benedict XIV. It is therefore illicit to invite heretics to a choir during sacred services, to sing alternately with them, to give them peace or sacred ashes and other such tokens of external worship, which are rightly and reasonably regarded as signs of interior bond and agreement. This is to be done neither in the active sense, namely by giving them such things, or in the passive sense, by accepting from them in their sacred services.

The decree of the Holy Office of June 19, 1889, strongly supported by Pope Leo XIII, describes the worship of the heretics as a "*cultus falsus*" (illegitimate worship).

ACTS OF APOSTASY BY JOHN PAUL II

John Paul II filled his life with total acts of apostasy, which by itself would deprive any true pope from his papal office.

The case of Pope Marcellinus illustrates an interesting point on this subject. The Donatist Bishop Petilianus of Constantine claimed in a letter that Marcellinus and his priests Melchiades, Marcellus, and Sylvester (his papal successors) had given up the sacred books, and offered incense to the pagan gods. In doing so, these men saved their lives. It was done under extreme duress and not voluntary or coerced.

It was never proven, but because of these acts, Marcellinus was considered to have lost his papacy because of it.

St. Augustine appears to have demonstrated that it never happened. However, he had to do so to protect the papacy presuming that such acts would indeed entail the loss of the papacy even when done under duress.

Whether or not these men actually did offer incense or not does not matter. The point is that we have a precedent in history that demonstrates that acts of apostasy would cause a pope to lose his office. A sound argument could be made that acts of apostasy done under duress would not cause one to lose the office. However, what you will see next is not only voluntary but approved, promoted, and praised by one claiming to be pope.

John Paul II concelebrating with a Monophysite Armenian patriarch Karekin II at St. Peter's Basilica on Nov. 11, 2000

This is severely condemned in The Canon Law of 1917 - *communicatio in sacris* - as suspect of heresy (Canons 1258, 2259, 2261, 2315, 2316, 2338, par. 3).

Canon 1258: It is unlawful for the faithful to assist in any active manner, or to take part in the sacred services of non-Catholics.

On February 5, 1986, in the city of Chennai (Madras for the Zoroastrians) India, John Paul II, alongside Dr. Meher Master Moos, actively participated in a Zoroastrian ceremony by lighting a candle as he wore a stole with the symbols of the pagan religion.

Zoroastrianism, founded by Zoroaster, which adores the sun and fire was the religion of Babylon when the Hebrews were her captives.

When 25 priests adored the sun inside the Temple, God reckoned it as an abomination and severely punished the Hebrews for participating. (Ezechiel 8:16)

The above picture is Zoroaster giving adoration to Adar, or the divination of fire. This fire is always burning on the altar inside the religion's temples.

·John Paul II invited the leaders of Zorastrianism to Assisi Italy to pray to their pagan god for world peace in 1986 and again in 2002. Later Benedict XVI would celebrate the events.

One of the big problems with the new age Vatican 2 sect is that they believe all religions that worship a single god, are really worshipping the one true God.

If one were to follow this logic, the pagan god BAAL of the Canaanites is the same true God Catholics believe in, they just had a false understanding of Him. RA of the Egyptians is the same true God Catholics believe in, they just had a false understanding of Him. DAGON of the Philistines is the same true God Catholics believe in, they just had a false understanding of Him.

It is so ridiculous, yet they have fooled millions into believing such nonsense.

John Paul II taking part in a Jewish worship service in a Jewish Synagogue, April 13, 1986

·John Paul II took part in several such services. Gilbert Levine, a Jewish music conductor and friend of John Paul II, was invited to the Vatican to commemorate the Holocaust. So as not to offend the Jews, the Vatican covered all the crucifixes. Levine would later reveal that John Paul II told him to be proud of his Jewish heritage and to live it out to the full. (Larry King Live, 4/4/1005)

Jesus said, "Whoever denies me before men, I also will deny before my Father who is in heaven." (Matthew 10:33, Luke 12:9)

John Paul II praying at the Wailing or Western Wall in Jerusalem

The Western Wall is all that was left after the complete and total destruction of the temple in Jerusalem as foretold by Our Lord. The Wall was not part of the temple. Christ spoke of the destruction of the temple as a punishment for not accepting Him as Lord and Messiah. John Paul II's prayer was an apology to the Jewish people. It would seem the John Paul II wasn't in agreement with God's ways as he rejected the just punishment God inflicted on the rebellious Jewish people. John Paul II has repeatedly stated that the Old Covenant with the Jews has not been revoked.

THE ASSISI EVENTS

·In 1986 and 2002, John Paul II invited all the world's religious leaders to come to Assisi, Italy and pray and offer sacrifices to each of their individual gods for world peace. Leaders from Eastern Orthodoxy, Protestantism, Judaism, Islam, Buddhism, Hinduism, Tenrikyo, Shintoism, Sikhism, Zoroastrianism, and Voodoo attended with prayers and even with animal sacrifices from the Voodooists all in the name of peace.

These Events were praised by Mother Theresa and were defended and justified by theologians around the world using the writings of great saints such as St. Thomas Aquinas.

Such is the New World Religion of the New World Order; butchering the very meaning of the great saints to justify evil.

In 2006, Benedict XVI celebrated the 20th anniversary of the first Assisi Events.

Throughout Catholic history, we see the Church condemn false beliefs and proselytize pagans, Protestants, and all infidels. In looking at these Events in the modern world, we see a clear-cut contradiction to the teachings of the Catholic Church and Her practice. To demonstrate this, we could look at *Mortalium Animos* by Pius XI as a recent example, or go back to the Apocalypse of Holy Writ on Babylon's Harlotry. However, the following anecdotes will best illustrate the contradiction between the Assisi Events and historic Christianity.

The Assisi Events are like:

-St. Peter and St. Paul inviting pagan Romans to come to the catacombs and pray to Jupiter, Saturn, and Mercury for world peace rather than seeing them as antichrists.

-St. John inviting over Cerinthus to pray instead of refusing even to use the same bathhouse as John did.

-St. Thomas inviting Hindus to pray to Vishnu for guidance and peace rather than telling them that only Christ can save them.

-St. Athanasius inviting Arians to pray to their anti-Trinitarian god for peace and reconciliation rather than slap them in their face as St. Nicholas did at Nicea.

-St. Ambrose and St. Augustine inviting Pelagians and Manicheans to come and pray with them rather than calling them agents of the devil.

-St. Patrick inviting the Druids of Ireland to offer sacrifices to their gods rather than proselytizing them to become faithful followers of Holy Trinity.

-St. Leo the Great inviting Attila and the rest of the Huns to come inside St. Peter's so they can pray to all their gods so that there will be peace rather than telling them to leave Rome.

-St. Francis of Assisi praying with the Muslims rather than telling them to believe in Jesus and convert to Catholicism.

-St. Anthony of Padua inviting Cathars to come in the local Catholic Church and pray for unity and peace, not tell them they are on the road to perdition unless they repent and be reunited to the faith.

-St. Francis Xavier inviting the local Buddhists to chant and pray their beads while he prayed his Rosary by demonstrating that it's okay to be Buddhists.

-Hernando Cortez and Bishop Zumarraga recognizing as a religion deserving of respect and honor Aztec Paganism and inviting the Aztecs to pray to Quetzelcoatl and Huitzilopochtli rather than seeing it as devil worship.

-Pope St. Pius V inviting all the new Protestants to come to Rome and pray with Catholics rather than condemning them for holding to heretical beliefs and practices.

-Pope St. Pius X inviting all the Modernists to come and pray that we all get along rather than anathematizing and saying that modernism is the synthesis of all heresies. Yea, right!

That's what the Assisi Events are like but anybody of goodwill can see they are so far off the mark of true Christianity.

The Catholic Church has decreed in her canons: "If any bishop, or priest, or deacon, shall join in prayers with heretics, let him be suspended from Communion." "If any clergyman or laic shall go into the synagogue of the Jews, or the meetings of heretics, to join in prayer with them, let him be deposed, and deprived of communion". (Canons 44 and 63 - of Bishop George Hay (1729-1811 in GENERAL LAWS OF GOD, FORBIDDING ALL COMMUNICATION IN RELIGION WITH THOSE OF A FALSE RELIGION) A general law of God is the Divine Law.

Also, in one of her most respected councils, held in the year 398, at which the great St. Augustine was present, she speaks thus: "None must either pray or sing psalms with heretics; and whosoever shall communicate with those who are cut off from the Communion of the Church, whether clergyman or laic, let him be excommunicated." (Council of Carthage. iv. 72 and 73)

THE SECOND ECUMENICAL COUNCIL OF CONSTANTINOPLE

(553 A.D. ratified by Pope Vigilius, and Pope St. Gregory the Great confirmed the teachings of the council)

For we are taught, "What fellowship hath righteousness with unrighteousness? and what communion hath light with darkness? And what concord hath Christ with Belial? Or what part hath he that believeth with an infidel? And what agreement hath the temple of God with idols."

Having thus detailed all that has been done by us, we again confess that we receive the four holy Synods, that is, the Nicene, the Constantinopolitan, the first of Ephesus, and that of Chalcedon, and we have taught, and do teach all that they defined respecting the one faith. And we account those who do not receive these things aliens from the Catholic Church. Moreover we condemn and anathematize, together with all the other heretics who have been condemned and anathematized by the before-mentioned four holy Synods, and by the holy Catholic and Apostolic Church,....These things therefore being settled with all accuracy, we, bearing in remembrance the promises made respecting the holy Church, and who it was that said that the gates of hell should not prevail against her, that is, **the deadly tongues of heretics**; remembering also what was prophesied respecting it by Hosea, saying, "I will betroth thee unto me in faithfulness, and thou shalt know the Lord," **and numbering together with the devil, the father of lies, the unbridled tongues of heretics who persevered in their impiety unto death, and their most impious writings,** will say to them, "Behold, all ye kindle a fire, and cause the flame of the fire to grow strong, ye shall walk in the light of your fire, and the flame which ye kindle." But we, having a commandment to exhort the people with right doctrine, and to speak to the heart of Jerusalem, that is, the Church of God, do rightly make haste to sow in righteousness, and to reap the fruit of life; and kindling for ourselves the light of knowledge from the holy Scriptures, and the doctrine of the Fathers, we have considered it necessary to comprehend in certain Capitula, both the declaration of the truth, and the condemnation of heretics, and of their wickedness.

Pope Pius XI, *Mortalium Animos*: "8 This being so, it is clear that the Apostolic See cannot on any terms take part in their assemblies, nor is it anyway lawful for Catholics either to support or to work for such enterprises; for if they do so they will be giving countenance to a false Christianity, quite alien to the one Church of Christ."

"9 Everyone knows that John himself, the Apostle of love, who seems to reveal in his Gospel the secrets of the Sacred Heart of Jesus, and who never ceased to impress on the memories of his followers the new commandment 'Love one another,' **altogether forbade any intercourse with those who professed a mutilated and corrupt form of Christ's teaching: 'If any man come to you and bring not this doctrine, receive him not into the house nor say to him: God speed you'** (II John 10)."

In 1986, the Dalai Lama placed a statue of Buddha on the tabernacle in the church of St Francis.

Many Catholics think the Events were scandalous, but the fact is the Assisi Events within themselves are more than scandalous. They are acts of apostasy.

John Paul II arranged for all crucifixes to be removed or covered. He gave each false religion their own special room they asked for such as an unblessed room for the Jews where Christ had no part, or one with windows for the Zoroastrians as the smoke of their god Adar could escape. John Paul provided all the pagans and infidels the special rooms to aid in their worship.

It is a total and disgusting lie that there were underlying theological principles keeping the Events from being heretical. In fact, they were Masonic and are not backed by any Catholic theology whatsoever. Again, some even go so far as to use statements of St. Thomas Aquinas to justify these abominable events.

Holy Writ says:

"For all the gods of the Gentiles are devils…" (Psalm 95)

"But the things which the heathens sacrifice, they sacrifice to devils, and not to God. And I would not that you should be partakers with devils." (I Cor. 10:20)

The Assisi Events are unspeakable crimes because they tell us that Masonic Rome wants us to be partakers with devils.

Note again, that even Voodoo priests were invited by Rome to sacrifice animals to their demons and it happened not once but twice.

Anyone who acted, promoted or defends these diabolical acts is in no way Catholic but rather apostates.

The Assisi Events are proofs that John Paul II and Benedict XVI who recently celebrated the 20th anniversary of the events are both non-Catholic apostates much less heretics which makes them both antipopes. They both reject the Gospel of Jesus Christ and accept the gospel of Masonry (antichrist).

Pope Pius XI, *Ad Salutem* (# 27), April 20, 1930: "...all the compulsion and folly, all the outrages and lust, introduced into man's life by the demons through the worship of false gods." (*The Papal Encyclicals*, Vol. 3 (1903-1939), p. 381)

The Assisi Events were by no means the only interreligious events. There were many more on a smaller scale.

There was the Pan-Christian Encounter

On Nov. 7, 1999, John Paul II praised the false religions of paganism.

The "Pan Encounter" took place in the center of St. Peter's Square.

Again, call to mind the Holy Scriptures... "For all the gods of the Gentiles are devils..." (Psalm 95)

"But the things which the heathens sacrifice, they sacrifice to devils, and not to god. And I would not that you should be partakers with devils." (I Cor. 10:20)

Pope Leo X, *Fifth Lateran Council*, Session 9, May 5, 1514: "Sorcery, by means of enchantments, divinations, superstitions and the invoking of demons, is prohibited by both civil laws and the sanctions of the sacred canons." (*Decrees of the Ecumenical Councils*, Vol. 1, p. 625)

-John Paul II has promoted what God Himself prohibits.

John Paul II also promoted Islamic culture

-John Paul II, Message to "Grand Sheikh Mohammed," Feb. 24, 2000: "Islam is a religion. Christianity is a religion. Islam has become a culture. Christianity has become also a culture... I thank your university, the biggest center of Islamic culture. I thank those who are developing Islamic culture..." (*L'Osservatore Romano*, March 1, 2000, p. 5)

This is a stunning remark coming from a supposed pope. Thanking those who are developing Islamic Culture? This is a culture that blasphemes the Most Holy Trinity while misleading literally a billion people away from the Gospel of Jesus Christ.

Pope Callixtus III: "I vow to... exalt the true Faith, and to extirpate the diabolical sect of the reprobate and faithless Mahomet [Islam] in the East."Von Pastor, (*History of the Popes*, II, 346; quoted by Warren H. Carroll, *A History of Christendom*, Vol. 3 *The Glory of Christendom*), Front Royal, VA: Christendom Press, 1993, p. 571)

-John Paul II, on March 21, 2000, stated: "May Saint John the Baptist protect Islam and all the people of Jordan..." (*L' Osservatore Romano*, March 29, 2000, p. 2)

This is an absolute stunning statement for John Paul II did not just say, may St. John protect a people but a false religion that denies the divinity of Christ. THIS IS BLASPHEMY!

Following Paul VI and Vatican 2 on Islam and Muslims, John Paul II states:

-*Encyclical On Social Concerns* (# 47), Dec. 30, 1987: "... Muslims who, like us, believe in the just and merciful God." (*The Encyclicals of John Paul II*, p. 474)

-*Homily*, Oct. 13, 1989: "... *the followers of Islam* who believe in the same good and just God." (*L'Osservatore Romano*, Oct. 23, 1989, p. 12)

-*Homily*, Jan. 28, 1990: "... our Muslim brothers and sisters... who worship as we do the one and merciful God." (*L'Osservatore Romano*, Feb. 19, 1990, p. 12)

-*General Audience*, May 16, 2001: "... the believers of Islam, to whom we are united by the adoration of the one God." (*L'Osservatore Romano,* May 23, 2001, p. 11)

-*General Audience*, May 5, 1999: "Today I would like to repeat what I said to young Muslims some years ago in Casablanca: 'We believe in the same God...'" (*L'Osservatore Romano,* May 12, 1999, p. 11)

John Paul II prayed with African Animists known as "witch doctors." He stated, "The prayer meeting in the sanctuary at Lake Togo was particularly striking. There I prayed for the first time with animists" (Prayer with an African Animist on August 8, 1985). *L'Osservatore Romano*, August 26, 1985, p. 9.

In Cotonou, Africa on Feb. 4, 1993, John Paul II was entertained with a "trance inducing" voodoo dance by chanting women.

-John Paul II actually promoted the African religion of Voodooism. Following Paul VI's lead, John Paul II in his February 4, 1993 address to the Voodoo representative of Benin at Cotonou, told them that their religion contained the "seed of the Word" (semina verbi) which elsewhere he has explained as a "kind of common soteriological [salvation] root present in all religions." This means that man may be saved in Voodoo. This is a major heresy!

-In his Apostolic Exhortation Ecclesia in Africa, John Paul II said: The adherents of African traditional religion should therefore be treated with great respect and esteem, and all inaccurate and disrespectful language should be avoided. For this purpose, suitable course in African traditional religion should be given in houses of formation for priests and religious.

Voodoo priests saw this as an endorsement of their religion. In a paper by N. Adu Kwabena-Essem entitled "Pope's Apology to Africans," the Voodooist said, "African religions had their biggest boost two years ago when Pope John Paul II, on a visit to Benin, apologized for centuries of ridiculing African cultural beliefs by the Western world. Benin is the home of Voodoo...The crucial question is whether the Pope's 'penance' will force others to start respecting African cultures, in particular the belief in African religions."

In 1993, the *L'Osservatore Romano* estimated the adherents of Voodoo in Benin to comprise 25 percent and dying. Due to John Paul's visit, Voodoo grew a staggering 60 percent of the population, according to a January 1996 Associated Press report. Now, Benin celebrated the rebirth of voodoo as an officially recognized religion.

As Paul VI, John Paul II endorsed and blessed the UN in 1979 and 1995

Following the schema of the failed League of Nations, the UN was established as a government of Man without God with the same anti-Christian philosophy as the French Revolution and the Masonic doctrines, which are contrary to the Catholic Church.

·In his 1979 speech, JPII praised and said "The humanist vision you have proclaimed before the world is ours also." (John Paul II, 11/12/79, address to the UN)

On April 18, 1983, a meeting of the Trilateral Commission was held in the Vatican.

The Church is *"una cum"* the *Novus Ordo Seclorum.*

John Paul II receiving the B'nai B'rith (Freemasonic Lodge of New York) on March 22, 1982.

·On March 22, 1984 John Paul II received, in a private audience, representatives of the Jewish-Masonic organization B'nai B'rith. He stated, "Dear Friends: I am very happy to receive you in the Vatican... You are the league of the B'nai B'rith... you are also connected with the Commission for religious relations with Judaism, founded ten years ago by Paul VI, ... And just as the two parts of the Bible are distinct, and closely related, so are the Jewish people and the Catholic Church... Thank you again for coming here and for your involvement in dialogue and the aim it pursues. Let us acknowledge it before God, the Father of us all." (*Catholic Counter-Reformation* #1874, pp. 509-510)

Is God the Father of those who reject Christ? Not according to Jesus in St. John chapter 8, who stated that those who claim to hold the faith of Abraham but reject the truth of the Gospel has the devil as their father.

-In December of 1996, the Grand Orient Lodge of Italian Freemasonry offered John Paul II its greatest honor, the Order of Galilee, as an expression of thanks for the efforts that he made in support of Freemasonic ideals. The representative of Italian Freemasonry noted that John Paul II merited the honor because he had promoted "the values of universal Freemasonry: fraternity, respect for the dignity of man, and the spirit of tolerance, central points of the life of true masons."

John Paul II flew down the wide road that leads to destruction

The Great Heresy of John Paul II on the Dogma Descent into Hell, an Article of Faith

Excerpt from a General Audience given JPII on January 11, 1989 on articles of the Apostles' Creed specifically denying the dogma Descent into Hell.

4. As is evident from the texts quoted, the article of the Apostles' Creed, "he descended into hell", is based on the New Testament statements <on the descent of Christ>, after his death on the Cross, into the "region of death", into the a abode of the dead", which in Old Testament language was called the "abyss". If the Letter to the Ephesians speaks of "the lower parts of the earth", it is because the earth receives the human body after death, and so it received also the body of Christ who expired on Calvary, as described by the Evangelists (cf. Mt 27:59 f, and parallel passages; Jn 19:40-42). <Christ passed through> a real <experience of death>, including the final moment which is generally a part of the whole process: <he was placed in the tomb.> It is a confirmation that this was a real, and not merely an apparent, death. His soul, separated from the body, was glorified in God, but his body lay in the tomb as a <corpse.>

During the three (incomplete) days between the moment when he "expired" (cf. Mk 15:37) and the resurrection, ***Jesus experienced the state of death", that is, the <separation of body and soul>, as in the case of all people. This is the primary meaning of the words "he descended into hell";*** *they are linked to what Jesus himself had foretold when, in reference to the story of Jonah. he had said: "For as Jonah was three days and three nights in the belly of the whale, so <will the Son of man be three days and three nights in the heart of the earth>" (Mt 12:40).*

Comment: Notice what John Paul is saying Descent into hell means: "experience of death" - "placed in a tomb" - "separation of body and soul" - "as is the case of all people" and this is "the primary meaning."

For John Paul II there is no real and actual place for the abode of the dead but that it is merely an expression for dying and being buried with a separation of body and soul but the soul doesn't really go anywhere.

Also, he states this descent into hell is the case for all people. In other words, this descent into hell will, according to him, happen to each and every one of us.

Again, see what else he states:

Death and glorification

5. This is precisely what the words about the descent into hell meant: <the heart or the womb of the earth.> By <dying> on the cross, Jesus had delivered his spirit into the Father's hands: "Father, into thy hands I commit my spirit!" (Lk 23:46). If death implies the separation of the soul from the body, it follows that in Christ's case also there was, on the one hand, the body in the state of a corpse, and on the other, the <heavenly glorification of his soul from the very moment of his death.> The First Letter of Peter speaks of this duality when, in reference to Christ's death for sins, he says of him: "<Being put to death in the flesh but made alive in the spirit" (1 Pt 3:18). Soul and body are therefore in the final condition corresponding to their nature, although on the ontological plane the soul has a relationship to be reunited with its own body. The Apostle adds however: "<In spirit (Christ) went and preached to the spirits in prison>" (1 Pt 3:19). This seems to indicate metaphorically the extension of Christ's salvation to the just men and women who had died before him.

Comment: Again, Descent into hell is merely an expression of dying and giving the soul over to the Father but never do we see JPII saying anything about a real substantial place for the souls known as limbo. Even I Pt 3:19 is only metaphor since JPII is saying that Christ didn't really go into some place like a prison but only as figure of speech of Christ's extensive work of salvation.

6. Obscure as it is, the Petrine text confirms the others concerning the concept of the "descent into hell" <as the complete fulfillment of the gospel message of salvation>. It is Christ—laid in the tomb as regards the body, but glorified in his soul admitted <to the fullness of the beatific vision of God>—who communicates his state of beatitude to all the just whose state of death he shares in regard to the body.

The Letter to the Hebrews describes his freeing of the souls of the just: "Since... the children share in flesh and blood, he himself likewise partook of the same nature, that through death he might destroy him who has the power of death, that is, the devil, and deliver all those who through fear of death were subject to lifelong " (Heb 2:14-15). As dead—and at the same time as alive "forevermore"—Christ has a the keys of death and Hades" (cf. Rev 1:17-18). In this is manifested and put into effect <the salvific power> of Christ's sacrificial death which brought redemption to all, even to those who died before his coming and his "descent into hell", but who were contacted by his justifying grace.

Metaphors of space and time

7. In the First Letter of Peter we read further: "...the gospel was preached even to the dead, that though judged in the flesh like men, they might live in the spirit like God" (1 Pt 4:6). This verse also, though not easy to interpret, confirms the concept of the "<descent into hell" as the ultimate phase of the Messiah's mission>. It is a phase "condensed" into a few days by the texts which try to present in a comprehensible way to those accustomed to reason and to speak in metaphors of space and time, but immensely vast in its real meaning of the extension of redemption to all people of all times and places, even to those who in the days of Christ's death and burial were already in the "realm of the dead". The word of the Gospel and of the Cross reaches all, even those belonging to the most distant generations of the past, because all who have been saved have been made partakers in the Redemption, even before the historical event of Christ's sacrificial *death on Calvary took place. The concentration of their evangelization and redemption into the days of the burial emphasizes that in the <historical fact> of Christ's death there is contained the <super-historical mystery> of the redemptive causality of Christ's humanity, the "instrument" of the omnipotent divinity. With the entrance of Christ's soul into the beatific vision in the bosom of the Trinity, the "<freeing from imprisonment>" of the just who had descended to the realm of the dead before Christ, finds its point of reference and explanation. Through Christ and in Christ there opens up before them the definitive freedom of the life of the Spirit, as a participation in the Life of God (cf. St. Thomas, III, q. 52, a. 6). This is the "truth" that can be drawn from the biblical texts quoted and which is expressed in the article of the Creed which speaks of the "descent into hell".*

Comment: Even the part of the Gospel, which states, "the Gospel was preached even to the dead" is only a metaphor.

8. We can therefore say that the truth expressed by the Apostles' Creed in the words "he descended into hell", while <confirming the reality of Christ's death>, at the same time proclaims <the beginning of his glorification>; and not only of his glorification, but of all those who, by means of his redemptive sacrifice, have been prepared for the sharing in his glory in the happiness of God's Kingdom.

Comment: This is all completely contradicted by Papal teachings and the Catechism of Trent which states:

"we firmly believe and profess that when His soul was dissociated from His body, His Divinity continued always united both to His body in the sepulcher and to His soul in limbo."(p. 53)

"by the word hell is not here meant the sepulcher, as some have not less impiously than ignorantly imagined; for in the preceding Article we learned that Christ the Lord was buried, and there was no reason why the Apostles, in delivering an Article of

Faith, should repeat the same thing in other and more obscure terms.

Hell, then, here signifies those secret abodes in which are detained the souls that have not obtained the happiness of heaven. In this sense the word is frequently used in Scripture. Thus the Apostles says: *At the name of Jesus every knee shall bow. Of those that are in heaven, on earth, and in hell*; and in the Acts of the Apostles St. Peter says that Christ the Lord is again risen, *having loosed the sorrows of hell.* (p. 62-63)

Lastly, the third kind of abode is that into which the souls of the just before the coming of Christ the Lord, were received, and where, without experiencing any sort of pain, but supported by the blessed hope of redemption, they enjoyed peaceful repose. To liberate these souls , who, in the bosom of Abraham were expecting the Saviour, Christ the Lord descended into hell. (p. 63)

Christ the Lord descended into hell, in order that, ... he might liberate from prison those holy Fathers and the other just souls... (p. 64)

John Paul II said this descent into hell is the case for all people indicating that it is merely a metaphor for what the Catechism denounces as meant the sepulcher (death or died and buried). The Catechism of Trent says this abode of the dead is the bosom of Abraham. However, Christ has now opened the Gates of Heaven to free man and there is no need for us to enter into this abode of hell for we cannot enter it.

However, John Paul II is denying that this abode of the dead "hell" is even a place as the Catechism indicates when it uses the word "prison." For John Paul II, everyone before Christ who died, without time, was immediately after their own death seeing Our Lord in His death and therefore there is no need to have this real place of prison where souls were detained over all the years since Adam. This is the clear reading of his metaphors of space and time and his explanation of what the Descent into hell meant in his views.

Therefore, this is a complete rejection of the historical dogma making John Paul II a radical and manifest heretic.

See also Appendix III - *Evangelium vitae* and the Death Penalty

Benedict XVI Highlights

Joseph Alois Ratzinger, aka, Benedict XVI is the present false pope occupying Rome.

The world has moved so far to the extreme in liberalism and modernism that Benedict is considered theologically conservative.

He is an extreme modernist and admits to being liberal.

He refused to take the papal oath, which the Council of Florence required as the form of accepting the papacy without which the papal election should be considered null and void.

He holds a doctorate in theology and was a professor of theology. He has also received numerous honorary doctorates around the world. He is currently processing the canonization of the apostate John Paul II.

·Made a bishop in 1977 under the new rite of orders and Paul VI made him cardinal in the same year. Since the new rite of orders mirrors that of the invalid Anglican orders, the new rite is highly doubtful. Ratzinger is at best a highly doubtful bishop and most likely invalid. A true pope cannot be an invalid bishop or a highly doubtful bishop.

-Like John XXIII, Ratzinger is on record for suspect of heresy.

-Like John XXIII and Paul VI Ratzinger is recognized by some within the Vatican as a homosexual.

Joseph RATZINGER : Allemand, 45 ans ; théologie dogmatique, œcuménisme ; naguère suspecté par le Saint-Office ; membre de la commission Foi et Constitution du Conseil œcuménique ; ouvrage remarqué (en collaboration avec Karl Rahner) : « Primat et épiscopat ».

(French magazine *Informations Catholiques Internationales* (n. 336 - May 15, 1969, p. 9)

No doubt, for Ratzinger being a modernist makes him the synthesis of all heretics. The following will demonstrate his modernism.

-In his 1968 book *Introduction to Christianity*, he wrote that the pope has a duty to hear differing voices within the Church before making a decision, and he downplayed the centrality of the papacy.

***30 Dias* - July, 1990**

Father Ratzinger attends Vatican II in a suit and tie with the liberal Fr Karl Rahner, also in suit and tie

From 1962 to 1965 he made a notable contribution to Vatican II as an "expert", being present at the Council as theological advisor of Cardinal Joseph Frings, Archbishop of Cologne. He was viewed during the time of the Council as a reformer, cooperating with radical Modernist theologians like Hans Kung and Edward Schillebeeckx. Ratzinger was an admirer of Karl Rahner, a notorious liberal/modernist theologian and a proponent of church reform.

-Ratzinger admitted that he was liberal during the days of the Second Vatican Council and in 1993 said his views have not changed since the 1960's. He stated: "I see no break in my views as a theologian [over the years]" (*Time Magazine*, 6 December 1993)

-In 1972 together with Hans Urs von Balthasar, Henri de Lubac and other important theologians, he initiated the theological journal *"Communio"* which was the mouthpiece of the New Theology, officially condemned by Pope Pius XII, as being nothing but a heap of "false opinions, which threaten to overthrow the very foundations of Catholic doctrine," has now become "the official theology of Vatican II" (Fr. Henrici).

-Vittorio Messori, who calls Ratzinger a "balanced progressivist" interviewed Ratzinger and asked him about being "one of the founders of Concilium, a meeting place for the progressivest wing of theology."

"'Was it a sin of youth, Your Emminence, this engagement with *Concilium*?' I asked him, joshing.

"'Absolutely not,' he answered. 'I did not change; they changed.'"

(*Rapporto sulla Fede - Vittorio Messori a coloquio con Joseph Ratzinger*, Rome:Paoline, 1985, p. 14).

Again, when asked about his liberalism of the 1960's and the present, Ratzinger gives his answer in another interview. "What are the more significant differences between the Ratzinger of Vatican II and the Ratzinger of today? Who changed more: you or the Church?"

-Cardinal Ratzinger – "I do not see a real, profound difference between my work at Vatican Council II and my present day work. While preparing this course for Bishops, I went to review a course of ecclesiology that I taught for the first time in

1956. Naturally, I found elements that needed to be updated. But as for the fundamental vision, I found a profound similarity. What I proposed to the Bishops in Rio de Janeiro (in this trip) was the same fundamental vision that I set out (then)." (Interview with Cardinal Joseph Ratzinger by Walter Falceta, Jr, 'Acao pastoral requer espiritualidade' in *O Estado de S. Paulo*, July 29, 1990)

- "It is not an exaggeration to say that on that day the old Holy Office, as it presented itself then, was destroyed by Ratzinger in union with his Archbishop Card. Seper, a man full of goodness, initiated the renovation. Ratzinger, who did not change, continues it. It would be good to keep this episode in mind." (Henri de Lubac, *Entretien autour du Vatican II*, Paris: Cerf, 1985, p. 123).

Ratzinger wrote that Vatican 2 is contrary to the infallible teaching of Pope Pius IX. In other words, he admits that his religion is contrary to the historic Catholic Faith.

- "If it is desirable to offer a diagnosis of the text [of the Vatican II document, *Gaudium et Spes*] as a whole, we might say that (in conjunction with the texts on religious liberty and world religions) it is a revision of the *Syllabus* of Pius IX, a kind of counter *syllabus*... As a result, the one-sidedness of the position adopted by the Church under Pius IX and Pius X in response to the situation created by the new phase of history inaugurated by the French Revolution, was, to a large extent, corrected..." (Ratzinger, *Principles of Catholic Theology*, 1982, p. 381)

- "By a kind of inner necessity, therefore, the optimism of the countersyllabus gave way to a new cry that was far more intense and more dramatic than the former one." (Ratzinger, *Principles of Catholic Theology*, 1982, p. 385)

- "The task is not, therefore, to suppress the Council but to discover the real Council and to deepen its true intention in the light of present experience. That means that there can be no return to the *Syllabus*, which may have marked the first stage in the confrontation with liberalism and a newly conceived Marxism but cannot be the last stage." (Ratzinger, *Principles of Catholic Theology*, 1982, p. 391)

Ratzinger wrote that the teachings of Popes against Modernism are obsolete.

- "the declarations of Popes in the last century [19th century] about religious liberty, as well as the anti-Modernist decisions at the beginning of this century, above all, the decisions of the Biblical Commission of the time [on evolutionism]... in the details of the determinations they contain, they became obsolete after having fulfilled their pastoral mission at their proper time." (Joseph Ratzinger, "*Instruction on the Theologian's Ecclesial Vocation*," published with the title "*Rinnovato dialogo fra Magistero e Teologia*," in *L'Osservatore Romano*, June 27, 1990, p. 6)

-Ratzinger wrote that dogmatic formulas must constantly change, "the difficult problem of the relationship between language and thought is debated, which in post-conciliar discussions was the immediate departure point of the dispute.

-The identity of the Christian substance as such, the Christian 'thing' was not directly ... censured, but it was pointed out that no formula, no matter how valid and indispensable it may have been in its time, can fully express the thought mentioned in it and declare it unequivocally forever, since language is constantly in movement and the content of its meaning changes." (Joseph Ratzinger, "*Sobre la Question de la Validez Permanente de las Formulas Dogmaticas*," in *El Pluralismo Teologico*, Madrid: BAC, 1976, p. 62)

-After his "election", Ratzinger has maintained that he will give his full and complete support for Vatican II. This means that he is fully supporting the countersyllabus and the New Theology while at the same time the destroying of the historic Catholic Faith.

-His first appointment was San Francisco's Archbishop Levada to the head of the Congregation for the Doctrine of Faith.

-Levada is on record for supporting homosexual rights and benefits. (San Francisco's Catholic Mayor Shakes Up His Church on Gay Marriage," *Pacific News Service* online, March 3, 200.4)

-He was accused of covering two priests charged with molesting boys. ("Levada Takes Heat Over Abuse Inquiry," (*San Francisco Chronicle* online, November 12, 2004)

Ratzinger has made many staggering remarks in word and writing, but the next two statements are hard to believe.

-When addressing Protestants at *World Youth Day*, on August 19, 2005, Benedict stated:

"And we now ask: What does it mean to restore the unity of all Christians?... this unity does not mean what could be called ecumenism of the return: that is, to deny and to reject one's own faith history. Absolutely not!" (*L'Osservatore Romano*, August 24, 2005, p. 8)

Pope Pius XI taught in *Mortalium Animos* (# 10), Jan. 6, 1928, "the union of Christians can only be promoted by promoting the **return** to the one true Church of Christ of those who are separated from it..." (*The Papal Encyclicals*, Vol. 3 (1903-1939), p. 317)

This statement comes from his early liberal days, which he says and as we can see from which he has not departed.

- "Meantime the Catholic Church has no right to absorb other Churches. ... A basic unity – of Churches that remain Churches, yet become one Church – must replace the idea of conversion..." (Ratzinger, *Theological Highlights of Vatican II*, 1966, pp. 61, 68)

- "It means that the Catholic does not insist on the dissolution of the Protestant confessions and the demolishing of their churches but hopes, rather, that they will be strengthened in their confessions and in their ecclesial reality." (Ratzinger, *Principles of Catholic Theology,* 1982, p. 202)

Benedict is in direct contradiction with not only Pope Pius XI but in direct logic.

-Prior to his "election" Benedict implies that Christianity is not the only way to Heaven, which means Christ and the Gospel is not the only way to Heaven.

- "The question that really concerns us, the question that really oppresses us, is why it is necessary for us in particular to practice the Christian Faith in its totality; why, **when there are so many other ways that lead to heaven and salvation**, it should be required of us to bear day after day the whole burden of ecclesial dogmas and of the ecclesial ethos. And so we come again to the question: What exactly is Christian reality? What is the specific element in Christianity that not merely justifies it, but makes it compulsorily necessary for us? When we raise the question about the foundation and meaning of our Christian existence, there slips in a certain false hankering for the apparently more comfortable life of other people who are also going to heaven. We are too much like the laborers of the first hour in the parable of the workers in the vineyard (Mt. 20:1-16). Once they discovered that they could have earned their day's pay of one denarius in a much easier way, they could not understand why they had to labor the whole day. But what a strange attitude it is to find the duties of our Christian life unrewarding just because the denarius of salvation can be gained without them! It would seem that we – like the workers of the first hour – want to be paid not only with our own salvation, but more particularly with others' lack of salvation. That is at once very human and profoundly un-Christian." (Ratzinger, *Co-Workers of the Truth,* Ignatius Press, 1990, p. 217)

This Masonic way of believing is why we see Benedict in the next few pages promoting a New World Order. You can't have a New World Order if Christianity is the only way to absolute truth that alone leads to Heaven...

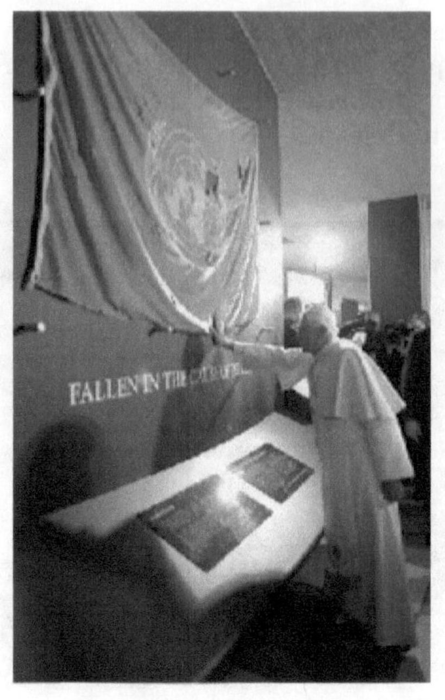

Reuters

Pope Benedict XVI blessed a United Nations flag that was damaged in the 2003 bombing of the U.N. headquarters in Baghdad.

April 2008, Benedict warned nations against undermining the authority of the United Nations. This warning would, of course, undermine the authority of pre-Vatican 2 Rome.

-The international community must be "capable of responding to the demands of the human family through binding international rules," said the pope. He said the notion of multilateral consensus was "in crisis because it is still subordinated to the decisions of a few, whereas the world's problems call for interventions in the form of collective action by the international community."

This is the Vatican with Benedict leading the charge blessing with total support for the New World Order.

Two Destroyers of the Catholic Faith enjoying their moment in time

ACTS OF APOSTASY BY BENEDICT XVI

Benedict XVI participates in an Jewish ceremony in a synagogue with Jews on Aug. 19, 2005.

·In section II, A, 5, *The Jewish People and their Sacred Scriptures in the Christian Bible* states: "Jewish messianic expectation is not in vain..."
www.vatican.va/roman_curia/congregations/cfaith/pcb_documents/rc_con_cfaith_doc_20020212_popoloebraico_en.html

·In section II, A, 7, *The Jewish People and their Sacred Scriptures in the Christian Bible* states: "...to read the Bible as Judaism does necessarily involves an implicit acceptance of all its presuppositions, that is, the full acceptance of what Judaism is, in particular, the authority of its writings and rabbinic traditions, which exclude faith in Jesus as Messiah and Son of God... Christians can and ought to admit that the Jewish reading of the Bible is a possible one..." (Vatican Website)

·Benedict XVI, *Address to Chief Rabbi of Rome*, Jan. 16, 2006: "Distinguished Chief Rabbi, you were recently entrusted with the spiritual guidance of Rome's Jewish Community; you have taken on this responsibility enriched by your experience as a scholar and a doctor who has shared in the joys and sufferings of a great many people. I offer you my heartfelt good wishes for your mission, and I assure you of my own and my collaborators' cordial esteem and friendship." (*L'Osservatore Romano,* Jan. 25, 2006, p. 2)

The mission of the Chief Rabbi is to promote Judaism, which rejects the Gospel of Jesus Christ. It is antichrist and Benedict wishes him well in it.

Imitating his predecessor

Benedict XVI celebrates the 20th anniversary of the abominable Assisi Events

-In his message on Sept. 2, 2006, Benedict states: "This year is the 20th anniversary of the *Interreligious Meeting of Prayer for Peace*, desired by my venerable Predecessor John Paul II on 27 October 1986 in Assisi. It is well known that he did not only invite Christians of various denominations to this Meeting but also the exponents of different religions. It constituted a vibrant message furthering peace and an event that left its mark on the history of our time... attestations of the close bond that exists between the relationship with God and the ethics of love are recorded in all great religious traditions. Among the features of the 1986 Meeting, it should be stressed that this value of prayer in building peace was testified to by the representatives of different religious traditions, and this did not happen at a distance but in the context of a meeting... We are in greater need of this dialogue than ever... I am glad, therefore, that the initiatives planned in Assisi this year are along these lines and, in particular, that the Pontifical Council for Interreligious Dialogue has had the idea of applying them in a special way for young people... I gladly take this opportunity to greet the representatives of other religions who are taking part in one or other of the Assisi commemorations. Like us Christians, they know that in prayer it is possible to have a special experience of God and to draw from it effective incentives for dedication to the cause of peace."

Bavaria, September 12, 2006 in Regensburg, Germany

-Benedict XVI, *Address during ecumenical Vespers service*, Sept. 12, 2006: "Dear Brothers and Sisters in Christ! We are gathered, Orthodox Christians, Catholics and Protestants – and together with us there are also some Jewish friends – to sing together the evening praise of God... This is an hour of gratitude for the fact that we can pray together in this way and, by turning to the Lord, at the same time grow in unity among ourselves... This is an hour of gratitude for the fact that we can pray together in this way and, by turning to the Lord, at the same time grow in unity among ourselves... Among those gathered for this evening's Vespers, I would like first to greet warmly the representatives of the Orthodox Church. I have always considered it a special gift of God's Providence that, as a professor at Bonn, I was able to come to know and to love the Orthodox Church, personally as it were, through two young Archimandrites, Stylianos Harkianakis and Damaskinos Papandreou, both of whom later became Metropolitans... Our koinonia [communion] is above all communion with the Father and with his Son Jesus Christ in the Holy Spirit; it is communion with the triune God, made possible by the Lord through his incarnation and the outpouring of the Spirit. This communion with God creates in turn koinonia among people, as a participation in the faith of the Apostles..." (*L'Osservatore Romano*, Sept. 20, 2006, p. 10)

On Nov. 30, 2006, Benedict XVI praying in a mosque with Muslims as Muslims (barefoot with arms crossed) towards Mecca

St. Thomas Aquinas, *Summa Theologica*, Pt. I-II, Q. 103., A. 4: "All ceremonies are professions of faith, in which the interior worship of God consists. Now man can make profession of his inward faith, by deeds as well as by words: and in either profession, if he make a false declaration, he sins mortally."

St. Thomas Aquinas, *Summa Theologica*, Pt. II, Q. 12, A. 1, Obj. 2: "... if anyone were to...worship at the tomb of Mahomet, he would be deemed an apostate."

Following in the footsteps of his predecessors and the teaching of *Lumen Gentium* of Vatican 2. Benedict declares that Islam and Christians have the same true God.

Ratzinger *Pilgrim Fellowship of Faith,* 2002, p. 273: "... Islam, too, ... has inherited from Israel and the Christians the same God..."

Benedict asks the Lord to promote Anglicanism

The second meeting with Rowan Williams, Archbishop of Canterbury, in 2008

- "It is our fervent hope that the Anglican Communion will remain grounded in the Gospels and the Apostolic Tradition which form our common patrimony... The world needs our witness... May the Lord continue to bless you and your family, and may he strengthen you in your ministry to the Anglican Communion!" (*L'Osservatore Romano*, Nov. 29, 2006, p. 6, Benedict XVI, *Address to Anglican "Archbishop of Canterbury,"* on Nov. 23, 2006)

1917 Code of Canon Law 2316 states: A person who of his own accord and knowingly helps in any manner to propagate heresy, or who communicates in sacred rites with heretics in violation of Canon 1258, incurs suspicion of heresy.

Canon 1325: The faithful are bound to profess their faith publicly, whenever silence, subterfuge, or their manner of acting would otherwise entail an implicit denial of their faith, a contempt of religion, an insult to God, or scandal to their neighbor. Any baptized person who, while retaining the name of Christian, obstinately denies or doubts any of the truths proposed for belief by the divine and Catholic faith, is a heretic; if he abandons the Christian faith entirely, he is called an apostate; if, finally, he refuses to be subject to the Supreme Pontiff, or to have communication with the members of the church subject to the Pope, he is a schismatic."

Canon 2315: If a person suspected of heresy, does not amend within six months... he shall be considered as a heretic and be liable to the penalties for heresy.

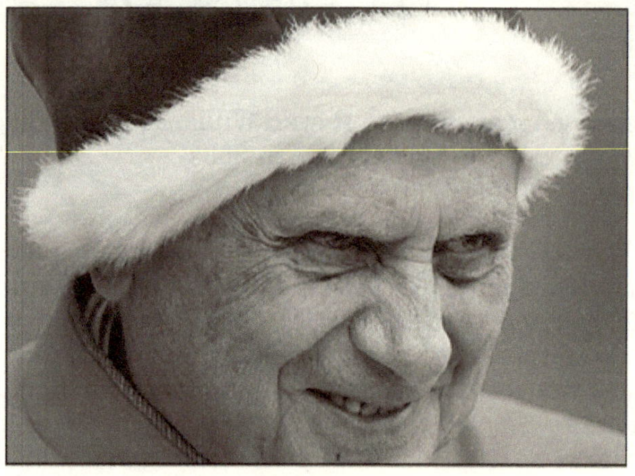

A Catholic Pope? Are you kidding?

As Paul VI reference non-Catholic churches as being part of the Church of Christ stemming from *Lumen Gentium* of Vatican 2, Benedict now does the same thing giving us the interpretation of Vatican 2...

-*Common Declaration* of Benedict XVI with Orthodox "H.B." Chrysostomos II, June 16, 2007: "We, Benedict XVI, Pope and Bishop of Rome, and Chrysostomos II, Archbishop of Nea Justiniana and All Cyprus... we assure our faithful of our fervent prayers as Pastors in the Church... among the human rights to be safeguarded, **freedom of religion should be at the top of the list**. Failure to respect this right constitutes a very serious offence to the dignity of the human being, who is struck deep within his heart where God dwells. Consequently, to profane, destroy or sack the places of worship **of any religion** is an act against humanity and the civilization of the peoples.

-Benedict XVI, *letter to* [schismatic/heretic] *Romanian Patriarchate*, published August 2, 2007: "Having received news of the death of His Beatitude Teoctist, Patriarch of the Romanian Orthodox Church, I hasten to express to you, to the Holy [schismatic/heretical "Orthodox"] Synod and all the members of the Church my heartfelt condolences, and to assure you of my spiritual union with all those who mourn the passing of this distinguished and highly regarded Church leader. I pray that the Romanian Orthodox Church will rejoice in the legacy of Patriarch Teoctist's many years of wise ministry, and that you will be sustained and comforted by the fruits of his apostolate as you commend his noble soul to the merciful love of our Heavenly Father. In conveying my closeness in prayer at this time of grief, I also wish to express my earnest good wishes for you and your brother Bishops as **you guide the Church** in this time of transition."

-Benedict XVI, *Joint Declaration with* [schismatic/heretic] *Patriarch Bartholomew*, Nov. 30, 2006: "This fraternal encounter which brings us together, Pope Benedict XVI of Rome and Ecumenical Patriarch Bartholomew I, is God's work, and in a certain sense his gift. We give thanks to the Author of all that is good, who allows us once again, in prayer and in dialogue, to express the joy we feel as brothers and to renew our commitment to move towards full communion. This commitment comes from the Lord's will and **from our responsibility as Pastors in the**

Church of Christ... As far as relations between the Church of Rome and the Church of Constantinople are concerned, we cannot fail to recall the solemn ecclesial act effacing the memory of the ancient anathemas which for centuries had a negative effect on our Churches." (www.zenit.org, *Zenit news report*, Nov. 30, 2006)

- "The rich patrimony of faith and the solid Christian tradition of our lands should spur **Catholics and Orthodox to a renewed impetus** in proclaiming the Gospel in our age, **in being faithful to our Christian vocation** and in responding to the demands of the contemporary world." (*L'Osservatore Romano*, July 4, 2007, pp. 6-7)

-Again, following in the footsteps of his predecessors and the teaching of Vatican 2 that man has a "right" to be wrong, Benedict states the following: "The Church also insists on the inalienable right of individuals to profess their own religious faith without hindrance, both publicly and privately, as well as the right of parents to have their children receive an education that complies with their values and beliefs without explicit or implicit discrimination." (*Address to ambassador of Spain*, May 20, 2006)

- "There were in fact Christian hotheads and fanatics who destroyed temples, who were unable to see paganism as anything more than idolatry that had to be radically eliminated." (Ratzinger, *God and the World*, 2000, p. 373)

This is quite interesting considering that our saints were the ones who did the very things Benedict characterizes as "hotheads and fanatics." Pope Pius XII praises the very actions that Benedict condemns.

- "he [St. Benedict] went south and arrived at a fort 'called Cassino situated on the side of a high mountain; on this stood an old temple where Apollo was worshipped by the foolish country people, according to the custom of the ancient heathens. Around it likewise grew groves, in which even till that time the mad multitude of infidels used to offer their idolatrous sacrifices. The man of God coming to that place broke the idol, overthrew the altar, burned the groves, and of the temple of Apollo made a chapel of St. Martin. Where the profane altar had stood he built a chapel of St. John; and by continual preaching he converted many of the people thereabout.'" (Pope Pius XII, *Fulgens Radiatur* (# 11), March 21, 1947)

"Saint" Antonio Margil

Fr. Antonio Margil (1657-1726), the great Central American Missionary, who had extraordinary miracles attributed to him such as bilocation, walking on water and over long distances over the desert in short time barefoot, would destroy all idols of the pagans in the Americas. When they heard that Antonio was going to show up they would try to hide their idols but to no avail. Antonio would still find and destroy them. Those he converted would destroy idols of their pagan brethren out of love for Christ.

St Francis Xavier, perhaps the greatest missionary of all time and whose body is still incorrupt

St. Francis Xavier stated that children he converted out of love for Christ would, "run at the idols, upset them, dash them down, break them to pieces, spit on them, trample on them, kick them about, and in short heap on them every possible outrage."

ASSISI EVENTS 2011

On October 27, 2011, Warlock Wande Abimbola from the Nigerian Yoruba Voodoo sect sang a hymn to the goddess Olokun at the Assisi Basilica of Holy Mary of the Angels. Benedict XVI promoted this event giving demons a place of honor in a Catholic Church, all in the name of love and peace.

Photos from Gloria TV, Reuters & Internet

Benedict XVI bows towards empty Lutheran altar

All photos from *CTV and Internet*

On March 14, 2010, in a Lutheran temple in Rome, Benedict XVI preaches on the anniversary of the joint declaration on justification which is a rejection of the Council of Trent. In 1983, John Paul II went to the same Protestant temple for the 500th anniversary of Luther's birth.

On September 23, 2011, Benedict XVI met with the Lutheran council in Erfurt and celebrated an ecumenical service in the chapel of the Lutheran monastery of St. Augustine.

Again, Benedict bowed towards their empty altar and prayed alongside a woman bishop.

Ratzinger's understanding of the sacraments is extremely erroneous and downright heretical.

- "we are witnesses today of a new integralism that may seem to support what is strictly Catholic but in reality corrupts it to the core. It produces a passion of suspicions, the animosity of which is far from the spirit of the gospel. There is an obsession with the letter that regards the liturgy of the Church as invalid and thus puts itself outside the Church. It is forgotten here that the validity of the liturgy depends primarily, not on specific words, but on the community of the Church..." (*Principles of Catholic Theology*, Joseph Ratzinger [Benedict XVI], 1982, p. 377)

This is an outright rejection of the infallible teachings of Pope Eugene IV and Pope St. Pius V who both teach that it is the specific words.

Ratzinger denies Articles of Faith

Catholics declare in the Credo that the Church is one. This oneness is the first mark of the Church, which means that the Catholic Church is unified and undivided.

The Dogmatic Constitution *Lumen Gentium* of Vatican 2 states that "Church of Christ...subsists in the Catholic Church." Vatican 2 defenders say that subsists means "is" and "only" as this is what the Congregation of the Doctrine of the Faith states is the correct interpretation.

However, the Vatican 2 document, *Unitatis Redintegratio* (Decree on Ecumenism), states, ""Yet almost all, though in different ways, **long for** the **one** visible **Church of God, that truly universal Church" and "**the divisions among Christians **prevent the Church from realizing in practice the fullness of Catholicity proper to her**, in those of her sons and daughters who, though attached to her by baptism, are yet separated from full communion with her. Furthermore, the **Church herself finds it more difficult to express in actual life her full Catholicity** in all its bearings" and "**significant elements and endowments** which together go to **build up and give life to the Church itself, can exist outside the visible boundaries of the Catholic Church**: the written word of God; **the life of grace**" and "separated churches and communities as such, though we believe them to be deficient in some respects, have by no means been deprived of significance and importance in the mystery of salvation. For the Spirit of Christ **has not refrained from using them as means of salvation."**

Obviously, Vatican 2 teaches that "subsists" includes other religions and the Church of Christ is not one or unified since non-Catholic churches are also part of this Church of Christ.

This writing just demonstrated how Benedict believes the schismatic Orthodox Churches form part of the Church of Christ.

This belief and teaching of Benedict leads to the denial of an article of Faith. This article is the first mark of the Catholic Church, which again means the Church is one and united.

-Benedict rejects the article of Faith by implying that the Church of Christ which is the Catholic Church is not one or unified when he stated:

Principles of Catholic Theology (1982), p. 147: "**The Fathers, we can now say, were the theological teachers of the undivided Church...**" pp. 145-146: "**The Fathers are the teachers of the yet undivided Church.**"

And *Co-Workers of the Truth,* (1990), p. 29: "...**This means that even in Catholic belief the unity of the Church is still in the process of formation; that it will be totally achieved only in the eschaton**..."

Principles of Catholic Theology (1982), p. 202: "**It means that the Catholic does not insist on the dissolution of the Protestant confessions** and the demolishing of their churches **but hopes, rather, that they will be strengthened in their confessions and in their ecclesial reality**."

Theological Highlights of Vatican II, (1966), pp. 61, 68: "... **Meantime the Catholic Church has no right to absorb other Churches**. ... **A basic unity – of Churches that remain Churches, yet become one Church – must replace the idea of conversion**..."

In other words, the Church is divided and needs to be united. The two articles of Faith that he denies is the Church of Christ is only the Catholic Church and that Church is one.

The Great Heresy of Benedict XVI on the Resurrection of the Body, an Article of Faith

Just as John Paul II rejected the dogma from the Apostles' Creed of Christ's Descent into Hell and espoused a metaphorical decent rather than literal descent, so also, Benedict XVI rejects the dogma from the Apostles' Creed on the Resurrection of the Body. This attack by Benedict is the natural flow from John Paul II's heresy on Christ's Descent.

Taken from Benedict XVI book, Introduction to Christianity, 2004, we see him speaking about the Apostles' Creed, "... Perhaps it will have to be admitted that the tendency to such a false development, which only sees the dangers of responsibility and no longer the freedom of love, is already present in the [Apostles'] Creed ..."(p. 326)

From here Benedict attacks the dogma on the Resurrection of the Body found in the Apostles' Creed. "It now becomes clear that the real heart of faith in **the resurrection does not consist at all in the idea of the restoration of bodies,** to which we have reduced it in our thinking; such is the case even though this is the pictorial image used throughout the Bible." (p. 349)

"The foregoing reflections may have clarified to some extent what is involved in the biblical pronouncements about the resurrection: **their essential content is not the conception of a restoration of bodies to souls after a long interval**..."(p. 353)

"To recapitulate, Paul teaches, **not the resurrection of physical bodies, but the resurrection of persons**..." (pp. 357-358)

Comment: This is a blatant contradiction to the dogma and word for word contrary to the Catechism of Trent which states: "Lest anyone, despite the fact that many passages of Scripture plainly teach that the soul is immortal, might imagine that it dies with the body, and that both are to be restored to life, the Creed speaks only of *the resurrection of the body.*

Although in Sacred Scripture the word *flesh* often signifies the whole man, ... yet in this place it is used to express the body only, thus giving us to understand that of the two constituent parts of man, soul and body, ..."

The word *body* is also mentioned, in order to confute **the heresy** of Hymeneus and Philetus, who, during the lifetime of the Apostle, **asserted that whenever the Scriptures speak of the Resurrection, they are to be understood to mean not the resurrection of the body, but that of the soul,** by which it rises from the death of sin to the life of grace. **The words of this Article, therefore, as is clear, exclude that error, and establish a real resurrection of the body."** (pp. 120-121)

"**The Body Shall Rise Substantially the Same**" (p. 125)

The Catechism spends 12 pages explaining the very thing Benedict denies.

Besides the Catechism, we have many dogmatic statements on the Resurrection of the Body. To give one example of many:

Pope Innocent III, 1215, *ex cathedra*: "...all of whom will rise with their bodies which they now bear..."

Since this is a major Article of Faith and must be believed to be a Catholic and be saved, we have a clear-cut example of Benedict XVI proving he to be a manifest heretic.

It is sometimes argued that Benedict is not really denying the dogma based on his other book "Eschatology and Principles of Catholic Theology." Those defenders of Benedict will say he is contradicting the false notion that when someone dies their "body" dies, not the person. He is combating a false Cartesian notion of "ghost in the machine" anthropology and presenting the Thomistic notion, as the Council of Vienne would later define it that the human person is a body/soul composite. St. Paul was not Plato. He was not teaching the resurrection of physical bodies as if there could be such a thing apart from human persons.

The problem is this is simply not the case at all. Ratzinger is not combating anything but historic Catholic dogma. There is no context from his writing that one could draw such a conclusion. They have to come up with something in his defense but where do they go with it? Another heresy...Are bodies only resurrected or is it the whole person?

Since Ratzinger's defenders are defending his position, then they must conclude the whole person and not the just the body, which means "souls", are resurrected with the bodies. But wait a second, souls are already in Heaven or Hell and some have been there for long intervals, such as Adam and Eve.

Look again at Ratzinger's statement: "The foregoing reflections may have clarified to some extent what is involved in the biblical pronouncements about the resurrection: **their essential content is not the conception of a restoration of bodies to souls after a long interval**..."(p. 353)

The Catechism of Trent, indeed the whole history of Christianity, says, "Lest anyone, despite the fact that many passages of Scripture plainly teach that the soul is immortal, might imagine that it dies with the body, and that both are to be restored to life, the Creed speaks only of *the resurrection of the body.* Although in Sacred Scripture the word *flesh* often signifies the whole man, ... yet in this place it is used to express the **body only, thus giving us to understand that of the two constituent parts of man, soul and body,** ..."

The Catechism is the one who is debunking the false Cartesian notion not Ratzinger. He just takes the issue and swings the other way but the Catechism debunks both positions.

It is not the whole person that is resurrected but the BODY ONLY.

Again, Ratzinger says, ""It now becomes clear that the real heart of faith in **the resurrection does not consist at all in the idea of the restoration of bodies,** to which we have reduced it in our thinking; such is the case even though this is the pictorial image used throughout the Bible."(p. 349) To recapitulate, Paul teaches, **not the resurrection of physical bodies, but the resurrection of persons**..." (pp. 357-358)

Trent's Catechism says: The words of this Article, therefore, as is clear, exclude that error, and establish a real resurrection of the body."(pp. 120-121) "**The Body Shall Rise Substantially the Same**" (p. 125)

Is not the pictorial image of bodies resurrecting more accurately describing pages 120-125 than Ratzinger saying that it is not physical bodies?

Ratzinger's defenders, who use the silly argument about Christ and St. Paul not using the word only, is not at all the same as this. Ratzinger does not believe in the Resurrection of the Body, as it has always been understood. He clearly denies it and apparently his defenders do also. The reason is they all are modernists or the synthesis of all heretics.

Why is Ratzinger even discussing the issue to begin with in his book? He wants us to believe differently than the historic Faith and says as much by saying it is not the way we've always seen it depicted.

Read Pius IX: **Vatican I**, Session 3, April 24, 1870 Chapter 4 "On Faith and Reason"

For the doctrine of the faith which God has revealed is put forward not as some philosophical discovery capable of being perfected by human intelligence, but as a divine deposit committed to the spouse of Christ to be faithfully protected and infallibly promulgated. Hence, too, that meaning of **the sacred dogmas is ever to be maintained which has once been declared by holy mother church, and there must never be any abandonment of this sense** under the pretext or **in the name of a more profound understanding.** May understanding, knowledge and wisdom increase as ages and centuries roll along, and greatly and vigorously flourish, in each and all, in the individual and the whole church: but this **only in its own proper kind,** that is to say, in the same doctrine, **the same sense, and the same understanding.**

Notice Pius X condemnation of modernists below:

62. The principal articles of the Apostles' Creed did not have the same meaning for the Christians of the earliest times as they have for the Christians of our time. CONDEMNED as an error of the Modernists, by Pope St. Pius X in Lamentabili, July 3, 1907

Ratzinger's defenders do not believe his position is contrary to historic Christianity, but we know that he does believe it is contrary or else he wouldn't be giving us an interpretation completely unheard of and without any cause except to what Vatican 1 condemns. Even the explanation from his defenders is modernist, since nobody says that it is the person that is resurrected.

Why does the Creed say body when it is not the body but the person?

According to Ratzinger and his defenders, we need to reject Vatican I and abandon the dogmas for a **more profound understanding, with a different sense.**

They all deny the Article of Faith on the Resurrection of the Body, since they say that it is not "physical bodies" that is resurrected despite the fact that Christ's own Body was physical after His Resurrection, which gives the example for our glorified bodies at the end of time.

Ratzinger rejects another infallible dogma of the Catholic Church

When Benedict was "Cardinal" Ratzinger he wrote that Limbo was only a hypothesis.

"Limbo was never a defined truth of faith...I would abandon it since it was only a theological hypothesis. It formed part of a secondary thesis in support of a truth which is absolutely of first significance for faith, namely, the importance of baptism. To put it in words of Jesus to Nicodemus: "Truly, truly I say to you, unless one is born of water and the Spirit, he cannot enter the Kingdom of God: (Jn 3:5). One should not hesitate to give up the idea of "limbo" if need be (and it is worth noting that the very theologians who proposed 'limbo' also said that parents could spare the child limbo by desiring its baptism and through prayer); but the concern behind it must not be surrendered. Baptism has never been a side issue for faith; it is not now, nor will it ever be." (Joseph Ratzinger, *The Ratzinger Report*, San Francisco: Ignatius Press, 1985, pp. 147-148)

In 2007, Ratzinger got his wish. The Holy See has done away with the doctrine of Limbo and now teach, "*THE HOPE OF SALVATION FOR INFANTS WHO DIE WITHOUT BEING BAPTISED*" (Vatican Website under documents – un-baptized-infants)

In fact, this is an implied heresy.

The Councils of Florence and Lyons II both taught as de fide that those who die in original sin only (which would necessarily include unbaptized infants) go to hell. There are exceptions but they don't go across the board.

Now, Ratzinger is saying that you may hope against this dogma.

A Catholic cannot hope against this dogma anymore than he can hope against the Church that the Calvinists were right about justification or that the pope is not infallible.

As for limbo, it is a theory about that place in hell where unbaptized infants go.

In his decree against the Synod of Pistoia in 1794, Pius VI alludes to "that place of the lower regions which the faithful generally designate as the limbo of the children" in which the souls of those dying "with the sole guilt of original sin" go. Nevertheless, the view which the Holy Father adopts in no way holds either for a parental or infantile 'baptism of desire' nor for the rewards of the Beatific Vision for unbaptized souls (Denzinger 1526).

This limbo of the children amounts to merely the 'highest place' in the abode of Hell, as explained by St. Vincent Ferrer in his sermon preached on the Octave of the Epiphany (*Sermons,* London: Blackfriars, 1954, p. 82-83).

In other words, Limbo is Hell but with a different degree of suffering. To say Limbo doesn't exist is to say part of Hell doesn't exist, and that part of Hell has been infallibly defined to exist at Florence by Pope Eugene IV. Those parts of Hell are where those who die in mortal sin or original sin only "undergo punishments of different kinds." (Steven Speray, *Baptism of Desire or Blood,* Appendix 8)

Ratzinger was in error by not telling the whole truth when he stated, "it is worth noting that the very theologians who proposed 'limbo' also said that parents could spare the child limbo by desiring its baptism and through prayer."

St. Alphonsus Maria Liguori responded with: "Calvin says that infants born of parents who have the faith are saved, even though they should die without Baptism. But this is false: for David was born of parents who had the faith, and he confessed that he was born in sin. This was also taught by the Council of Trent in the Fifth Session, number Four: there the fathers declared that infants dying without Baptism, although born of baptized parents, are not saved, and are lost, not on account of the sin of their parents, but for the sin of Adam in whom all have sinned" (*Explanation of Trent*, Duffy Co., 1845, p.56).

A Flemish Jesuit named Cornelius Van Den Steen declared in his Commentaria: "Calvin, in order to detract from the necessity of Baptism, maintains that the children of believers are justified in the womb simply because they are children of believers. But this is absurd and perverse, and condemned by the Church as heretical. If it be lawful to wrest this passage with Calvin, then we may do the same with every other passage, and thus pervert; the entirety of Scripture. No commandment will survive, not even the institution of Baptism itself!" (In John III).

The Council of Florence states, "With regard to children, since the danger of death is often present and **the only remedy available to them is the sacrament of baptism by which they are snatched away from the dominion of the devil** and adopted as children of God, it admonishes that sacred baptism is not to be deferred for forty or eighty days or any other period of time in accordance with the usage of some people, but it should be conferred as soon as it conveniently can; and if there is imminent danger of death, the child should be baptized straightaway without any delay, even by a lay man or a woman in the form of the church, if there is no priest" (Decrees of the Ecumenical Councils Vol.1, p. 576)

The Catechism of Trent says baptism for infants should not be delayed "**Since infant children have no other means of SALVATION except Baptism**..." (p. 178)

Again, the Catechism of Trent also says adults "are not baptized at once....The delay is not attended the same danger as in the case of infants, which we have already mentioned..." (p. 179)

Notice: The implication is the infants already come from adults who have the Faith, and it is those children that need to be baptized without delay.

Pope Martin V, Council of Constance, Session 15, July 6, 1415. Condemning the articles of John Wycliffe Proposition 6:

"Those who claim that the children of the faithful dying without sacramental baptism will not be saved, are stupid and presumptuous in saying this." Condemned

(Steven Speray, *Baptism of Desire or Blood*, Appendix 8)

33 Objections and Answers to Sedevacantism

1. A (formal) heretic could be pope but he could never teach a heresy formally.

This is an argument used against sedevacantists so that sedevacantism would be an invalid position. Actually, sedevacantism has three foundations to fall back on:

a. heretical or Masonic claimant to the papacy,
b. formal heretical teaching, and
c. harmful laws and disciplines.

All of these could be used separately to justify sedevacantism. Again, sedevacantism is a position, not a religion in and of itself unlike the Vatican 2 Church, which is a new religion.

The argument that a pope could be a formal heretic is illogical.

A simple definition of heretic is a baptized non-Catholic. He is one who knowingly recedes in the least degree any point of doctrine of the Catholic Church. Therefore, heretics being non-Catholics are outside the Church.

The Pope is head of the Catholic Church in union with Christ. One cannot be the head of a body which he not a member.

Pope Innocent III, *Eius exemplo*, Dec. 18, 1208: "By the heart we believe and by the mouth we confess the **one Church, not of heretics**, but the Holy Roman, Catholic, and Apostolic Church."

Pope Eugene IV, Council of Florence, "*Cantate Domino*," 1441: "The Holy Roman Church firmly believes, professes and preaches that all those who **are outside the Catholic Church**, not only pagans **but also** Jews or **heretics and schismatics**..."

Pope Leo XIII, *Satis Cognitum* (# 9), June 29, 1896: "The practice of the Church has always been the same, as is shown by the unanimous teaching of the Fathers, who were wont to hold as outside Catholic communion, and alien to the Church, whoever would recede in the least degree from any point of doctrine proposed by her authoritative Magisterium." (#15) Bishops Separated from Peter and his Successors Lose All Jurisdiction: "From this it must be clearly understood that Bishops are deprived of the right and power of ruling, if they deliberately secede from Peter and his successors; because, by this secession, they are separated from the foundation on which the whole edifice must rest. They are therefore outside the edifice itself; and for this very reason they are separated from the fold, whose leader is the Chief Pastor; they are exiled from that Kingdom, the keys of which were given by Christ to Peter alone... No one, therefore, unless in communion with Peter can share in his authority, since it is absurd to imagine that he who is outside can command in the Church."

This is meant to imply bishops other than the papacy, however, it still applies to the popes themselves, since popes are also bishops and they too must be in union with Peter and his other successors.

Pope Pius XII, *Mystici Corporis Christi* (# 23), June 29, 1943: "For not every sin, however grave it may be, is such as of its own nature to sever a man from the Body of the Church, as does schism or heresy or apostasy."

As we see in all these papal statements, heresy and heretics are non-Catholic. Therefore, a heretic cannot also be a Catholic Pope.

This is a Divine Law and cannot be altered by anybody whosoever.

The Saints and Doctors of the Church also testify to this truth:

St. Vincent of Lerins (ca. 400-ca. 450) "What then should a Catholic do if some part of the Church were to separate itself from communion with the universal Faith? What other choice can he make but to prefer to the gangrenous and corrupted member the whole of the body that is sound. And if some new contagion were to try to poison no longer a small part of the Church, but all of the Church at the same time, then **he will take the greatest care to attach himself to antiquity** which, obviously, can no longer be seduced by any lying novelty." *(Commonitorium)*

Pope Innocent III (ca. 1160-1216) "The pope should not flatter himself about his power, nor should he rashly glory in his honour and high estate, because the less he is judged by man, the more he is judged by God. Still the less can the Roman Pontiff glory, because he can be judged by men, or rather, can be shown to be already judged, if for example he should wither away into heresy, because he who does not believe is already judged. In such a case it should be said of him: 'If salt should lose its savour, it is good for nothing but to be cast out and trampled under foot by men.'" (*Sermo 4*)

St. Antoninus, O.P. (1389-1459) "In the case in which the pope would become a heretic, he would find himself, by that fact alone and without any other sentence, separated from the Church. A head separated from a body cannot, as long as it remains separated, be head of the same body from which it was cut off. 'A pope who would be separated from the Church by heresy, therefore, would by that very fact itself cease to be head of the Church. He could not be a heretic and remain pope, because, since he is outside of the Church, he cannot possess the keys of the Church.'" (*Summa Theologica* cited in *Actes de Vatican I.* V. Frond pub.)

St. Giacomo Tommaso de Vio Gaetani O.P. (1469-1534) "'Where the Pope is, there is also the Church' holds true only when the pope acts and behaves as the pope, because Peter 'is subject to the duties of the Office'; otherwise, 'neither is the Church in him, nor is he in the Church.'" (Apud St. Thomas Aquinas, *Summa Theologica*, IIa IIae, Q. 39, Art. 1, ad 6)

St. Robert Bellarmine, S.J. (1542-1621) "A pope who is a manifest heretic automatically (per se) ceases to be pope and head of the Church, just as he ceases automatically to be a Christian and a member of the Church. Wherefore, he can be judged and punished by the Church. All the early Fathers are unanimous in teaching that manifest heretics immediately lose all jurisdiction. St. Cyprian, in particular, laid great stress on this point." (*De Romano Pontifice*, II. 30)

St. Francis de Sales (1567-1622) "Thus we do not say that the Pope cannot err in his private opinions, as did John XXII; or be altogether a heretic, as perhaps Honorius was. Now when he (the Pope) is explicitly a heretic, he falls ipso facto from his dignity and out of the Church, and the Church must either deprive him, or, as some say, declare him deprived, of his Apostolic See." (*The Catholic Controversy*, Tan Books, pp. 305-306)

St. Alphonsus Liguori, C.S.S.R. (1696-1787) "If ever a pope, as a private person, should fall into heresy, he would at once fall from the pontificate. If, however, God were to permit a pope to become a notoriously and contumacious heretic, he would by such fact cease to be pope, and the apostolic chair would be vacant." (*Verita della Fede*, Pt. III, Ch. VIII. 9-10)

Serapius Iragui (1959): "What would be said if the Roman Pontiff were to become a heretic? In the First Vatican Council, the following question was proposed: Whether or not the Roman Pontiff as a private person could fall into manifest heresy?

"The response was thus: 'Firmly trusting in supernatural providence, we think that such things quite probably will never occur. But God does not fail in times of need. Wherefore, if He Himself would permit such an evil, the means to deal with it would not be lacking.' [Mansi 52:1109]

"Theologians respond the same way. We cannot prove the absolute impossibility of such an event [*absolutam repugnatiam facti*]. For this reason, theologians commonly concede that the Roman Pontiff, if he should fall into manifest heresy, would no longer be a member of the Church, and therefore could neither be called its visible head." (*Manuale Theologiae Dogmaticae.* Madrid: Ediciones Studium 1959. 371)

J. Wilhelm (1913): "The pope himself, if notoriously guilty of heresy, would cease to be pope because he would cease to be a member of the Church." (*Catholic Encyclopedia.* New York: Encyclopedia Press 1913. 7:261)

Caesar Badii (1921): "*Cessation of pontifical power.* This power ceases: . (d) Through notorious and openly divulged *heresy.* A publicly heretical pope would no longer be a member of the Church; for this reason, he could no longer be its head." (*Institutiones Iuris Canonici.* Florence: Fiorentina 1921. 160, 165. His emphasis)

Dominic Prümmer (1927): "*The power of the Roman Pontiff is lost:* . (c) *By his perpetual insanity or by formal heresy.* And this at least probably.

"The authors indeed commonly teach that a pope loses his power through certain and notorious heresy, but whether this case is really possible is rightly doubted.

"Based on the supposition, however, that a pope could fall into heresy as a *private* person (for as pope he could not err in faith, because he would be infallible), various authors have worked out different answers as to how he would then be deprived of his power. None of the answers, nevertheless, exceed the limits of probability." (*Manuale Iuris Canonci.* Freiburg im Briesgau: Herder 1927. 95. His emphasis)

F.X. Wernz, P. Vidal (1943): "Through notorious and openly revealed heresy, the Roman Pontiff, should he fall into heresy, by that very fact is deemed to be deprived of the power of jurisdiction even before any declaratory judgment of the Church..." (*Ius Canonicum.* Rome: Gregorian 1943. 2:453)

Udalricus Beste (1946): "Not a few canonists teach that, outside of death and abdication, the pontifical dignity can also be lost by falling into certain insanity, which is legally equivalent to death, as well as through manifest and notorious heresy. In the latter case, a pope would automatically fall from his power, and this indeed without the issuance of any sentence, for the first See [i.e., the See of Peter] is judged by no one.

"The reason is that, by falling into heresy, the pope ceases to be a member of the Church. He who is not a member of a society, obviously, cannot be its head. We can find no example of this in history." (*Introductio in Codicem.* 3rd ed. Collegeville: St. John's Abbey Press 1946. Canon 221)

A. Vermeersch, I. Creusen (1949): "The power of the Roman Pontiff ceases by death, free resignation (which is valid without need for any acceptance, c. 221), certain and unquestionably perpetual insanity, and notorious heresy.

"At least according to the more common teaching, the Roman Pontiff as a private teacher can fall into manifest heresy. Then, without any declaratory sentence (for the supreme See is judged by no one), he would automatically [*ipso facto*] fall from a power which he who is no longer a member of the Church is unable to possess." (*Epitome Iuris Canonici.* Rome: Dessain 1949. 340)

Eduardus F. Regatillo (1956): "The Roman Pontiff ceases in office: (4) *Through notorious public heresy?* Five answers have been given:

"1. 'The pope cannot be a heretic even as a private teacher.' A pious thought, but essentially unfounded.

"2. 'The pope loses office even through secret heresy.' False, because a secret heretic can be a member of the Church.

"3. 'The pope does not lose office because of public heresy.' Objectionable.

"4. 'The pope loses office by a judicial sentence because of public heresy.' But who would issue the sentence? The See of Peter is judged by no one (Canon 1556).

"5. 'The pope loses office *ipso facto* because of public heresy.' This is the more common teaching, because a pope would not be a member of the Church, and hence far less could he be its head." "*Institutiones Iuris Canonici.* 5th ed. Santander: Sal Terrae, 1956. 1:396. His emphasis)

Heretics and Schismatics are barred from the election to the papacy by Divine Law.

The conciliar popes all held to their heresies long before their *"elections"* to the papacy. Therefore, the following teaching applies to each of them. Pope Pius XII lifted ecclesiastical penalties in his new legislation on papal elections but he did not, could not dispense from Divine Law

Pope Paul IV [16 Feb. 1559]: "Further, if ever it should appear that any bishop (even one acting as an archbishop, patriarch or primate), or a cardinal of the Roman Church, or a legate (as mentioned above), or even the Roman Pontiff (whether prior to his promotion to cardinal, or prior to his election as Roman Pontiff), has beforehand deviated from the Catholic faith or fallen into any heresy, We enact, decree, determine and define:

"Such promotion or election in and of itself, even with the agreement and unanimous consent of all the cardinals, shall be null, legally invalid and void.

"It shall not be possible for such a promotion or election to be deemed valid or to be valid, neither through reception of office, consecration, subsequent administration, or possession, nor even through the putative enthronement of a Roman Pontiff himself, together with the veneration and obedience accorded him by all.

"Such promotion or election, shall not through any lapse of time in the foregoing situation, be considered even partially legitimate in any way....

"Each and all of their words, acts, laws, appointments of those so promoted or elected — and indeed, whatsoever flows therefrom — shall be lacking in force, and shall grant no stability and legal power to anyone whatsoever.

"Those so promoted or elected, by that very fact and without the need to make any further declaration, shall be deprived of any dignity, position, honor, title, authority, office and power." (*Bull Cum Ex Apostolatus,* 16 February 1559)

Caesar Baldii [1921]: "c) *The law now in force for the election of the Roman Pontiff is reduced to these points:*.

"Barred as *incapable* of being validly elected are the following: women, children who have not reached the age of reason, those suffering from habitual insanity, the unbaptized, heretics and schismatics..." (*Institutiones Iuris Canonici*)

Marato [1921]: "Heretics and schismatics are barred from the Supreme Pontificate by the Divine Law itself, because, although by divine law they are not considered incapable of participating in a certain type of ecclesiastical jurisdiction, nevertheless, they must certainly be regarded as excluded from occupying the throne of the Apostolic See, which is the infallible teacher of the truth of the faith and the center of ecclesiastical unity. (*Institutiones Iuris Canonici*)

Matthaeus Conte a Coronata (1950): "*III. Appointment to the office of the Primacy* [i.e. papacy]. 1 ° What is required by divine law for this appointment: (a) The person appointed must be a man who possesses the use of reason, due to the ordination the Primate must receive to possess the power of Holy Orders. This is required for the validity of the appointment.

"Also required for validity is that the man appointed be member of the Church. Heretics and apostates (at least public ones) are therefore excluded.".

"2 ° *Loss of office of the Roman Pontiff.* This can occur in various ways:. "

c) *Notorious heresy.* Certain authors deny the supposition that the Roman Pontiff can become a heretic.

"It cannot be proven however that the Roman Pontiff, as a private teacher, *cannot* become a heretic - if, for example, he would contumaciously deny a previously defined dogma. Such impeccability was never promised by God. Indeed, Pope Innocent III expressly admits such a case is possible.

"If indeed such a situation would happen, he [the Roman Pontiff] would, by divine law, fall from office without any sentence, indeed, without even a declaratory one. He who openly professes heresy places himself outside the Church, and it is not likely that Christ would preserve the Primacy of His Church in one so unworthy. Wherefore, if the Roman Pontiff were to profess heresy, before any condemnatory sentence (which would be impossible anyway) he would lose his authority." (*Institutiones Iuris Canonici.* Rome: Marietti 1950. 1:312, 316. My emphasis)

Suspected Heresy

Canon 2315: If a person suspected of heresy, does not amend within six months... he shall be considered as a heretic and be liable to the penalties for heresy.

Vatican approved Professor of Canon Law, Rev. P. Charles Augustine, O.S.B., D.D explained in Canon 2315 that there are three types of suspicion for heretics.

*"Violent suspicion amounts to morally certain proof...*and *is to be considered as a positive proof and therefore rather falls under can. 2314."*

Canon 2314.1 states that all heretics incur **ipso facto excommunication**.

Augustine explained can. 2314:

"2) The penalties here enunciated are twofold: censure and vindictive penalties; besides, a distinction is drawn, according to can. 2207, n. 1, by reason of dignity, between laymen and clerics.

a) *The censure inflicted is excommunication incurred **ipso facto**, which per se requires **not even a declaratory sentence**... Note that the term moniti* [warnings] *(2314 Â§1, n. 2) does not refer to the incurring of the censure. **Consequently, no canonical warning or admonition is required."*** (A COMMENTARY ON THE NEW CODE OF CANON LAW, Volume VIII, Book V, Penal Code, Canon 2314, pp. 275-276; B. Herder Book Company, Imprimatur by John J. Glennon, Archbishop of Saint Louis, Friday, August 25, 1922)

Obstinacy

The Law doesn't require internal knowledge or intention. To be found guilty of heresy, obstinacy only needs to be observed in the external forum, even if subjectively one isn't actually obstinate. No one can judge hearts, not even the Church. According to the Law (both Divine and Church), the pope must in the external forum manifestly demonstrate that he knows and believes in the Catholic Church. He can't be a dummy (ignorant), and he can't only have an internal intention of following the Faith. According to the Law, there are no excuses for the man claiming to be pope. If he goes astray from defined truth or Divine law, he must be considered a non-Catholic and a non-member of the

Church, no matter what! This is universally taught by the Church through the popes, saints, and theologians.

Canon 2200.2, 1917 Code of Canon Law: "**When an external violation of the law has been committed, malice is presumed** in the external forum until the contrary is proven."

"**The very commission of any act which signifies heresy, e.g., the statement of some doctrine contrary or contradictory to a revealed and defined dogma, gives sufficient ground for juridical presumption of heretical depravity...** Excusing circumstances have to be proved in the external forum, and **the burden of proof is on the person whose action has given rise to the imputation of heresy. In the absence of such proof, all such excuses are presumed not to exist."** (Eric F. Mackenzie, A.M., S.T.L., J.C.L. Rev., The Delict of Heresy, Washington, D.C.: The Catholic Univ. of America, 1932, p. 35. (Cf. Canon 2200.2).

Another canon law manual states: "**If the delinquent making this claim be a cleric, his plea for mitigation must be dismissed,** either as untrue, or else as indicating ignorance which is affected, or at least crass and supine... His ecclesiastical training in the seminary, with its moral and dogmatic theology, its ecclesiastical history, not to mention its canon law, all insure that the Church's attitude towards heresy was imparted to him." (G. McDevitt, *The Delict of Heresy*, 48, CU, Canon Law Studies 77. Washington: 1932)

The Faithful are not required to read the mind of a delinquent even if that person claims to be pope. The Faithful are not required to presume innocence of a cleric, especially the pope, before concluding that he is a heretic.

Pope Leo XIII, *Satis Cognitum* (# 13), June 29, 1896: "**You are not to be looked upon as holding the true Catholic faith if you do not teach that the faith of Rome is to be held.**"

Pope Pius VI, *Auctorem fidei*, Aug. 28, 1794: "47. Likewise, the proposition which teaches that it is necessary, according to the natural and divine laws, **for either excommunication or for suspension, that a personal examination should precede,** and that, therefore, sentences called 'ipso facto' have no other force than that of a serious threat without any actual effect" – false, rash, pernicious, injurious to the power of the Church, erroneous.

St. Robert Bellarmine, *De Romano Pontifice, II, 30*: "... for men are not bound, or able to read hearts; but **when they see that someone is a heretic by his external works, they judge him to be a heretic pure and simple, and condemn him as a heretic."**

He continues...

"In addition to this, what finds itself in the ultimate disposition to death, immediately thereafter ceases to exist, without the intervention of any other external force, as is obvious; therefore, also the Pope heretic ceases to be Pope by himself, **without any deposition.**

Also:

Canon 192, 1917 Code of Canon Law: "A person may be **unwillingly deprived** of, **or removed from, an office, either by operation of law** or an act of the lawful superior."

Canon 188.4, 1917 Code of Canon Law: "There are certain causes which effect the tacit (silent) resignation of an office, **which resignation is accepted in advance by operation of the law, and hence is effective without any declaration**. These causes are... (4) if he has publicly fallen away from the faith."

Publicly fallen away can be determined...

Canon 2197.1, 1917 Code of Canon Law: "A Crime is public: (1) if it is already commonly known or the circumstances are such as to lead to the conclusion that it can and will easily become so..."

Today's sedevacantists hold that John XXIII through Benedict XVI were never validly elected precisely because they all were heretics beforehand. Pope Paul IV tells us that such a man cannot be validly elected.

Cum ex Apostolatus Officio, (Feb. 15. 1559) Pope Paul IV stated, "1. In assessing Our duty and the situation now prevailing, We have been weighed upon by the thought that a matter of this kind [i.e. error in respect of the Faith] is so grave and so dangerous that **the Roman Pontiff, who is the representative upon earth of God and our God and Lord Jesus Christ, who holds the fullness of power over peoples and kingdoms, who may judge all and be judged by none in this world, may nonetheless be contradicted if he be found to have deviated from the faith...**

6. In addition, [by this Our Constitution, **which is to remain valid in perpetuity** We enact, determine, decree and define:-] **that if ever at any time it shall appear** that any Bishop, even if he be acting as an Archbishop, Patriarch or Primate; or any Cardinal of the aforesaid Roman Church, or, as has already been mentioned, any legate, or even the **Roman Pontiff, prior to his promotion or his elevation as Cardinal or Roman Pontiff, has deviated from the Catholic Faith or fallen into some heresy: the promotion or elevation, even if it shall have been uncontested and by the unanimous assent of all the Cardinals, shall be null, void and worthless;** it shall not be possible for it to acquire validity (nor for it to be said that it has thus acquired validity) through the acceptance of the office, of consecration, of subsequent authority, nor through possession of administration, nor through the putative enthronement of a Roman Pontiff, or Veneration, or obedience accorded to such by all, nor through the lapse of any period of time in the foregoing situation; it shall not be held as partially legitimate in any way...**those thus promoted or elevated shall be deprived automatically, and without need for any further declaration, of all dignity, position, honour, title, authority, office and power...**

10. No one at all, therefore, may infringe this document of our approbation, re-introduction, sanction, statute and derogation of

wills and decrees, or by rash presumption contradict it. **If anyone, however, should presume to attempt this, let him know that he is destined to incur the wrath of Almighty God and of the blessed Apostles, Peter and Paul."**

Of course, this leads to Objection 8.

2. The promise of Christ that the Gates of Hell would not prevail against His Church would have proved false if sedevacantism were true.

The single most common argument used by Vatican 2 Catholics against sedevacantism is, *"it is impossible to go 50 plus years without a pope because Christ promised that the gates of hell would not prevail against His Church."* (See Objection 26) The typical *Novus Ordo* Catholic will accept this argument without any thought as to how anyone calling himself a Catholic could hold to sedevacantism.

One would think that sedevacantists must have thought about this before coming to this conclusion, right? Why on earth would sedevacantists not believe in Christ's promise?

This argument is used in three ways:

a. The Church failed by the Vatican I declaration of perpetual successors. See also Objection 7.

b. The Church failed by not having a visible church with a visible head and apostolic authority. See also Objection 26.

c. True popes taught heresy and are heretics therefore the gates of hell prevailed because error is now in, through, and part of the Church.

However, this argument is a misunderstanding of Vatican I, the nature of the Church, and specifically indefectibility.

What are the gates of hell?

Pope Vigilius at the Second Council of Constantinople, in 553 called *"the tongues of heretics"* the *"gates of hell."* Pope St. Leo IX, *In terra pax hominibus*, Sept. 2, 1053, said to Michael Cerularius that *"the gates of Hell"* are the *"disputations of heretics."*

Based on Christ's promise that the gates of hell will not prevail, Popes Vigilius and St. Leo statements imply that heretics and their heresies will never overcome the Church. The Church will always exist without error.

The very Scripture verse of Christ's promise, used as the most common argument against sedevacantism, is precisely the verse on which sedevacantism rests.

Since the Second Vatican Council, the Catholic Church had to go underground because the last 5 claimants to the papacy have been those heretics with death-dealing tongues as they have led astray many of the faithful with their heresies and acts of apostasy.

The gates of hell have not prevailed against the Church but it has prevailed against particular churches such as Rome today as it did with England in the 16th century.

Rome is not *"the"* Church as the Vatican 2 apologists would like to have us believe. It is only one part of the Church. No doubt, the pope is the head of the Church on earth, but Christ is always the Head of the Church. Every time a pope dies, the visible head is absent but Christ (the invisible Head) remains.

If the papacy could be filled with a death-dealing tongue of a heretic, then the head of the church would be counted along with the devil, the father of lies.

This is impossible since Christ with the pope is the Head of the Church. Christ is not in union with the devil, but a heretic is. Therefore, the pope cannot be a heretic nor formally teach heresy.

This is what Christ meant when He said the gates of hell will not prevail.

Pope Leo XIII called the Roman Pontiffs *"the Gates of the Church"* in his 1894 encyclical letter *Praeclara Gratulationis Publicae.*

Therefore, the gates of the Church cannot be one and the same as the gates of hell.

By claiming that popes can be formal heretics, Vatican 2 apologists are actually claiming the Gates of Hell have indeed prevailed without realizing it. This also means they are calling Christ a liar and worse, they are saying this is the law of the Church given by the Holy Ghost.

Cardinal Manning of Rome said in 1861 that it is the universal testimony of the Church fathers that Rome will lose the faith in the end. He was speaking about the great apostasy, and sedevacantists are following this universal testimony. If sedevacantists don't believe in Christ's promise then neither did all the Church fathers. However, they knew what Christ meant when He said the gates of hell would not prevail.

As long as one person holds the faith, the church exists in that one person.

We know that the Church does not exist for the sake of the papacy or the rest of the hierarchy, but rather, it is the hierarchy that exists for the sake of the Church.

We have seen in history Catholics living for centuries without any hierarchy. Japan is a prime example. The Church can and will survive till the very end. This is the promise.

The great apostasy foretold in Scripture will surely be disastrous, and it happens around the time of the final antichrist just before the Second Coming.

Christ said, ***"I tell you that he will avenge them quickly. Yet when the Son of Man comes, will he find, do you think, faith on the earth?"***

We know He was using hyperbole, but He was clearly emphasizing that it will be so bad that very few will actually profess the true faith. Christ never promised a pope in every generation. When He built the Church on Peter, it was on him and his faith, not necessarily his office. The Church has never stated otherwise. All of Peter's successors must be in union with Christ, Peter, and Peter's Faith to be part of the Church.

There have been over 40 antipopes in history, and never were Catholics expected to be union with them just because these men claimed to be popes. Catholics had to make a judgment call whether or not these men were true popes or not. Some made the right call, some didn't.

St. Vincent Ferrer made the wrong call if Benedict XIII were not a true pope. He even declared the papacy vacant because things were so confusing, it didn't matter whether there was a true pope or not.

Today, it is not as confusing as in St. Vincent's time. Never before in history has it been clearer than now. The last 5 claimants to the papacy are not true popes because of their extreme modernism and anti-Catholic practices.

They reject over 5 dogmas found right in the Apostles' and Nicene Creeds. Benedict XVI has even criticized the Creed, but that should not come to any surprise since he doesn't believe it as it has historically been understood. Being an extreme modernist, he, like his 4 predecessors, understands the Creed precisely as the Protestants who profess the same Creed.

Anyway, the point is made that Christ's promise is the reason for sedevacantism, not the proof against it.

I suspect there are two reasons psuedo-catholics keep using this straw-man argument.

The first reason is the belief in the nonexistent dogma that there must always be a pope in every generation.

Just like the nonexistent Scripture teaching that the Scriptures alone are the sole authority for Christians, the psuedo-catholic rejects the historic Catholic Faith by ignoring clear and unambiguous papal teachings on what constitutes Catholicism and the gates of hell.

Just as the Protestant will, in vain, give his personal interpretation of this and that Bible verse to demonstrate why Sola Scriptura is biblical, the psuedo-Catholic will, in vain, give his personal interpretation of this or that council and canon law to demonstrate how a papal interregnum cannot last more than a generation.

In the end, it always comes back to Christ's promise.

The second reason is the good-ole-fashion bearing false witness against thy neighbor, because of the intense hatred of us Catholics who hold fast to the Catholic Faith.

Notice how Vatican 2 *"Catholics"* are so very kind, considerate and understanding with the Muslims, Jews, and Protestants, but when it comes to traditional Catholics, watch-out!

Those Vatican 2 *"Catholics"* are not so kind, considerate and understanding. They get downright nasty and look downward on the traditionalists.

It's not hard to figure out. Holding fast to Catholic Tradition means being more orthodox and conservative than those who like to pride themselves as being orthodox and conservative while accepting every modernist novelty that comes down from Rome.

Sedevacantists follow the much more stricter 1917 Code of Law, with over 50 days of fasting throughout the year compared to 2 days in the Vatican 2 *Novus Ordo* church.

Sedevacantists are just viewed as weird or loony for being so completely counter-cultural.

Lastly, it would appear, contrary to their claim, psuedo-catholics don't really believe in the great apostasy, antichrist, and Christ's return.

Whenever that time should happen, there surely will be men warning the faithful about the antichrist and the great apostasy, as sedevacantists are doing now and being ridiculed and persecuted for it.

However, pseudo-Catholics will keep disregarding the warning for it means the Second Coming would be imminent. The psuedo-catholic will take the Bible out of context and say, *"no one knows the day or hour."*

The problem with this position is how can anyone be told and warned about the appearance of antichrist or the great apostasy once we're in that time? The psuedo-catholic position is illogical.

Sedevacantists don't claim to know the hour or day of Christ's return, but do know that it must be imminent because we are now in that period of the great apostasy.

3. A Freemason could be pope.

This argument presumes that a Mason can also be a Catholic. However, the 1917 Code of Canon Law has an automatic excommunication for those who belong to Masonry.

Can 2335 states: *"Persons joining associations of the Masonic sect or any others of the same kind which plot against the Church* *and legitimate civil authorities contract <ipso facto> excommunication simply reserved to the Apostolic See."*

Masonry is form of another religion regardless if Masonry itself denies it.

If a secret Mason fooled the Church by being elected to the papacy he would no more be pope then if a woman fooled the Church as a man and was elected pope.

Once discovered that a claimant to the papacy were in fact a Freemason, the conclusion would be he was not a secret heretic anymore and everything he did would be null and void.

This objection continues in Objections 10 and 13 because if we admit we had antipopes for the past 50 plus years we would be unable to tell what is valid and what is not and there would be chaos.

This objection fails to deal with the question what if the majority of Cardinals as secret Masons elected a Mason as pope and that pope converted the church into Masonry?

This is precisely what has happened to the Vatican 2 Church but her apologists deny that many teachings are in fact Masonic.

If a secret Mason fooled the Church and was never found out, it wouldn't matter unless he taught an error, gave the Church a harmful law or discipline, or attempted in any way to change the organic constitution of the Church.

Such an act would expose him as an imposter to those faithful willing to stand-up just as sedevacantists today.

4. Most Catholics, including Padre Pio, indeed the whole world, recognize John XXIII through Benedict XVI as true popes, therefore they are true popes.

This is a false argument and does not stand-up against history.

Boniface VII was recognized by the whole world but was not a true pope. The Catholic Church had him on the official list of popes for a thousand years before removing him in 1904.

Pope Benedict X (reigned 1058-1059, died 1073) is considered to be an antipope by the Catholic Encyclopedia but he functioned as a pope for 9 months and was considered pope by many of the faithful. He was forced to the papacy but resigned.

Anacletus II was elected Feb. 14, 1130 despite the fact that Innocent II was reigning as pope at the time. Anacletus gained control of Rome and the majority of cardinals recognized him as the true pope.

St. Bernard of Clairvaux sided with Innocent and convinced the faithful to join him. The two popes debated their cases before Roger at Salerno in Nov. through Dec. of 1137, but Innocent gained the upper hand. Anacletus died Jan 25, 1138 and his successor Victor IV submitted to Innocent thus ending the schism.

The majority doesn't always mean right.

It is argued that Padre Pio believed it, and because he was in touch with the supernatural, he would have known if John XXIII and Paul VI were not popes. It is said that Padre Pio prophesied John Paul II as becoming the future pope.

Padre Pio

It is argued that Padre Pio believed it, and because he was in touch with the supernatural, he would have known if John XXIII and Paul VI were not popes. It is said that Padre Pio prophesied John Paul II as becoming the future pope.

This fabrication comes from a false interpretation of what Cardinal Alfons Stickler reported. The Cardinal said Wojtyla confided to him that during this meeting (after a private confession in 1947) Padre Pio told him he would one day ascend to *"the highest post in the Church."* (*Man of the Century: The Life and Times of Pope John Paul II*, Jonathan Kwitny; Henry Holt and Company, New York, page 101)

Cardinal Sticker further went on to say that Wojtyla believed that the prophecy was fulfilled when he became a Cardinal, not Pope, as has been reported in works of piety.

The only man allowed to interview Padre Pio more than once, Antonio Pandiscia, also reported the same meeting in 1947. He said: *"The current Pope went to San Giovanni Rotondo for the first time in 1947 shortly after his ordination."*

A witness, who has since passed away, told me that Padre Pio was brusque with the young Polish priest on that occasion. *"I think he could not accept the fact that the young Wojtyla (John Paul II) had worked in the theater before becoming a priest." (Inside the Vatican,* August/September 1996 (3050 Gap Knob Rd. New Hope, KY) p. 12)

However, even if Padre Pio had actually prophesied the statement that John Paul II were to become pope, it would only mean Padre Pio was wrong just as many saints have been wrong in prophetic statements. As a matter of fact, Wojtyla wasn't even a true Cardinal, therefore, Padre Pio was indeed wrong.

Padre Pio affirmed Garabadal, which said John Paul II would be the last pope of Catholic times. This means Padre Pio was very wrong about a false apparition since Garabandal has now proven to be untrue since John Paul II was to be the last *"pope"* of Catholic times according to the visionaries but times are no different now than when John Paul claimed (falsely) the papacy.

Padre Pio believed in the Three Days of Darkness, which is anti-Scriptural and illogical.

We base our faith on facts and reason, not emotions, feelings, and prophecies.

Padre Pio was in error about several other things as well. He believed the book by Maria Valorta *"The Poem of the Man God"* was good, but this book was on the index of forbidden books for some heretical statements within it.

Padre Pio was not perfect. He may have been misinformed and didn't have the divine spiritual help with these above things but he was made spiritually informed about other things as he said.

After throwing two bishops out of the confessional, Padre Pio was approached about the matter by his superior. Padre Pio responded: *"They may be bishops here on earth but the hierarchy in Heaven is not the same as that on earth."*

It is claimed that when someone asked Padre Pio about the 3rd Secret of Fatima he replied: *"Beware of all bishops."*

Padre Pio did in fact accept John XXIII and Paul VI at true popes and because of this fact many claim that Padre Pio would have rebuked sedevacantists. However, even the wonderworker himself, Saint Vincent Ferrer also believed Benedict XIII was the true pope and St. Catherine of Siena as with most others believed Benedict XIII was an antipope. If Benedict was in fact an antipope, St. Vincent Ferrer was wrong. If Benedict was in fact pope, then St. Catherine was wrong. Saints can be wrong, even super saints in touch with the supernatural as both St. Vincent and St. Catherine were.

However, 10 days before Padre Pio died, he wrote a letter to Paul VI saying, *"I pray that God may lead you with His Grace to follow the straight and painful way in defense of eternal truth, which does not change with the passing of years."* Yet the very next year, Paul VI in his general audience on July 2, 1969, *"If the world changes, should not religion also change? It is for this very reason that the Church has, especially after the 2nd Vatican Council, undertaken so many forms."*

The changes that took place were the very eternal truths Padre Pio spoke about were replaced with heresies and modernism, which is the synthesis of all heresies according to Pope St. Pius X.

Padre Pio never did the New Mass since he died a year before it was established. He said during Vatican II, *"For pity sakes, end it quickly."*

There is no doubt he would have been a sedevacantist if he were alive today from the Assisi Events to the World Youth Days with all kinds of sacrileges taking place in the Abominable New Mass, etc, etc.

For Padre Pio it all had not yet hit the fan. He didn't mislead anyone, for everybody was already misled. Hindsight is 20/20. Padre Pio did not have the new mass, Assisi Events, Ratzinger's outright denial of the Resurrection, etc. He also didn't have the Internet with all of the information we have to check this stuff out. Finally, he suffered so greatly from his wounds while many people didn't believe him. How should he have seen what we see now? He couldn't.

Interestingly enough, Pope Paul IV mentions in his Bull that is possible for all men to erroneously believe in a false pope, but he must still be rejected.

Bull *Cum ex Apostolatus Officio*, Feb. 15, 1559: "6. In addition, [by this Our Constitution, which is to remain valid in perpetuity

We enact, determine, decree and define:] that if ever at any time it shall appear that... the Roman Pontiff, prior to his promotion or his elevation as Cardinal or Roman Pontiff, has deviated from the Catholic Faith or fallen into some heresy... (ii) it shall not be possible for it to acquire validity (nor for it to be said that it has thus acquired validity) through the acceptance of the office, of consecration, of subsequent authority, nor through possession of administration, **nor through the putative enthronement of a Roman Pontiff, or Veneration, or obedience accorded to such by all**, nor through the lapse of any period of time in the foregoing situation;..."

5. The whole Church recognized John XXIII and Paul VI as true popes, and sedevacantism didn't exist until years later. What Fr. Noel Barbara dreamed up in the mid-70s was the sedevacantist theory. Nobody in the first decade after the Council ever claimed that Paul VI or John XXIII were not true popes.

This is completely untrue. Fr. Saenz Y Arriaga published a book on it in 1971 but held the position in the 60's. Fr. Noel Barbara was the first person to coin the phrase *"The New Montinian Church"* giving his good friend Fr. Saenz Y Arriaga, the title for his book.

The very first person to hold to sedevacantism was Vatican insider Dr. Elizabeth Gerstner who never recognized Roncalli in 1958. She knew the plan all along and predicted it by warning that the 1958 Conclave was already fixed.

Again, it should be emphasized that sedevacantism is a position, not a religion. The Vatican 2 Church is a completely new religion. They reject the position of sedevacantism, not only because the position rejects their *"popes"* but the position rejects the new religion with all it new doctrines, practices, and worship service.

6. Sedevacantists can't be sure that John XXIII through Benedict XVI have been obstinate against Church doctrine, therefore, they are still true popes. At worse they all are only material heretics.

This common objection has been used by all so-called traditional Catholics united to Rome. Part of this objection has already been answered on page 258.

True popes can most assuredly be in error in good faith as many have been. Such cases come from popes mistakenly speaking or writing something against Catholic doctrine which is defined after the incident.

For instance, Pope John XXII, on All Saints Day in 1331 AD, said in a sermon that souls do not attain the beatific vision until after the General Judgment.

Because the statement was very controversial, he retracted it on his deathbed.

However, the doctrine was not defined until after Pope John's death, making Pope John only a material heretic or a good-will Catholic in error.

His successor, Benedict XII, issued the Constitution *"Benedictus Deus"* in 1336 AD, asserting that the blessed souls of the dead *"see the face of the triune God immediately after death"*.

Interestingly enough, this case is used by anti-sedevacanters to demonstrate that popes can make serious doctrinal error without automatically losing his office reinforcing the original objection that we can't be sure of obstinacy. See Objection 30.

Of course, some of these same Vatican 2-ites can see how manifestly heretical this statement by John XXII was but fail to see how manifestly heretical the numerous statements that have come from John 23 through Benedict XVI which contradict previously defined and repeated doctrine unlike John XXII.

It is an absurd argument to use this case against sedevacantism.

But what about obstinacy?

Again, the original objection is stating that the last 5 claimants to the papacy are at best material heretics since it already implies that they are indeed against Church doctrine but not pertinacious or contumaciously so.

In other words, the last 5 claimants to the papacy were ignorant but in good faith.

In fact, with their PHD's of theology in hand, they were so incredibly stupid that when they decided to change the church with Vatican 2, they didn't realize that their new laws, doctrines, sacraments, and worship service were previously condemned by many popes?

You know better, I know better, our children know better, but they didn't know better!

Are you serious, anti-sedevacanters?

Really?

Was it a mere coincidence that Lucia warned (by Our Lady) that a very great chastisement (material and spiritual) was about to befall the world between 1957 and 1960?

Was it a mere coincidence that John XXIII refused to read the 3rd Secret of Fatima in 1960 as asked by Our Lady because, as she said, we would understand the message in that year?

Was it a mere coincidence that for years John XXIII and Benedict XVI were on record for suspicion of modernism when it was them that changed everything with Vatican 2 as Ratzinger said that the condemnations against modernism were obsolete?

Was it a mere coincidence that John XXIII and Paul VI (who were reported to have been initiated into the Masonic Brotherhood in Paris in the late 40's) incorporated the backbone of Masonry into Vatican 2 (which was previously and repeatedly condemned) by teaching that man has a right to practice his own (false) religion in public by way of speech or writing without hindrance?

Was it a mere coincidence that Rome's official (1994) catechism did not make one reference to the condemnations against modernism by Pope St. Pius X?

You really think we can't know for sure that they were obstinate?

This is not a real objection to sedevacantism but a mere excuse not to accept the truth.

Again, to recapitulate what was just stated, a material heretic is not a true heretic but an expression given to a Catholic in error through ignorance or erring in good faith. This argument is saying that the last 5 claimants to the papacy are ignorant of the historic Catholic Faith and all the major doctrines taught throughout history.

In the past, true popes have indeed been material heretics. This comes about when a pope holds to something contrary to doctrine that was defined after the fact.

Saints and Doctors of the Church have also been material heretics such St. John Chrysostom, St. Anselm, and St. Thomas Aquinas. All believed the Blessed Virgin Mary was a sinner, which is a heresy. However, the dogma was not defined till after they lived.

This argument does not hold up with the last 5 claimants to the papacy, since all were aware of previous teaching and knowingly rejected it.

John XXIII actually stated, *"I try to imagine what my predecessor would have done, and then I do just the opposite."* He rejected in toto Gregory XVI's *Mirari Vos* and *Singulari Nos*, and the *Quanta Cura* of Pius IX, to which was attached, as appendix, *The Syllabus of Errors.*

Since he was also a Mason, which would keep him from being a true pope, he could not possibly be a material heretic.

Paul VI, John Paul I, John Paul II, and Benedict also rejected the infallible document *Syllabus of Errors* of Pope Pius IX. All five rejected the first Mark of the Church from the historic Catholic understanding, which is an Article of Faith.

Paul VI was also a Mason. Therefore, he could not be a material heretic.

John Paul II held two doctorates and Benedict XVI holds one doctorate and both reject the Credo as it has always been understood.

This argument falls miserably short as a justification for their acts and teachings. But it doesn't matter since the Law tells us that we are to presume obstinacy.

7. Sedevacantism contradicts The First Vatican Council.

When asked how sedevacantism contradicts the passages of Vatican I, an immediate misrepresentation of sedevacantism and Vatican I are given. Straw-man arguments are common with anti-sedevacanters.

Vatican I, Dogmatic Constitution on the Church of Christ, Sess. 4, July 18, 1870: *"But, that the episcopacy itself might be one and undivided, and that the entire multitude of the faithful through priests closely connected with one another might be preserved in the unity of faith and communion, placing Peter over the other apostles He established in him the perpetual principle and visible foundation of both unities, upon whose strength the eternal temple might be erected, and the sublimity of the Church might rise in the firmness of this faith."*

Part 1 of Argument: Since sedevacantism holds that the papacy has stopped, the perpetual principle and visible foundation failed.

Sedevacantism does not hold that the papacy has stopped. The context is Peter is Head over the faithful as the faithful are in unity to him.

Does this mean there must always be a pope? No. The office is what Christ established. The office of the papacy is perpetual and visible when it is vacant. If it meant that there must always be one holding the office, then this Vatican I statement fails every time a pope dies. The papacy endures forever even if the Chair of Peter is vacant. Every time a pope dies, the Chair is vacant, but the papacy remains with the perpetual principle, as does the visible foundation. See Appendix I, p. 433, and read how the very theologians of Vatican I understood this teaching and how it corresponds to the sedevacant position.

Anti-sedevacantists falsely interpret this passage to mean that there must always be a pope, but if that were true then Vatican I failed with the death of Peter.

The perpetual principle means two things. The Chair of Peter was intended to be filled (not that it would be filled if Christ comes during an interregnum period) at some point after the death of the last pope, but no time limit was ever given. Also, the Office of Peter is perpetually over the Church regardless if it were filled. In other words, the teachings of past Popes remain the primary and head of the Church. Never does a past teaching become equal to or less than a mere bishop or some other person.

However, perpetual principle does not mean there must always be a pope actually in the Chair. Therefore, sedevacantism is not contrary to this passage of Vatican I.

Vatican I, Dogmatic Constitution on the Church of Christ, Sess. 4, Chap. 2:

Chapter 2.
On the permanence of the primacy of blessed Peter in the Roman pontiffs

1. "Moreover, what the Chief of pastors and the Great Pastor of sheep, the Lord Jesus, established in the blessed Apostle Peter for the perpetual salvation and perennial good of the Church, this by the same Author must endure always in the Church which was founded upon a rock and will endure firm until the end of time."

Part 2 of Argument: Sedevacantism does not believe the Chair of Peter will be successfully filled until the end of time.

Vatican I is not saying that the Chair of Peter must be successfully filled until the end of time. It is saying the **PRIMACY** of Peter and his successors must remain until the end of time. Does this mean there will always be a pope? Absolutely not!

Does this mean there will always be a pope in office until the end of time? Absolutely not! Christ could return during an interregnum period. Therefore, the papal office need not always be filled till the end of time.

Vatican 2 apologists' line of argumentation is faulty. If Christ came a year after Pope St. Marcellinus died, then Vatican I would have already have failed, since it was three and half years after St. Marcellinus before St. Marcellus was elected. Perpetual does not mean always having a pope in office.

2. "For no one can be in doubt, indeed it was known in every age that the holy and most blessed Peter, prince and head of the apostles, the pillar of faith and the foundation of the Catholic Church, received the keys of the kingdom from our lord Jesus Christ, the savior and redeemer of the human race, and that to this day and forever he lives and presides and exercises judgment in his successors the bishops of the Holy Roman See, which he founded and consecrated with his blood."

Part 3 of Argument: Sedevacantism cannot hold that Peter lives and resides forever if there is no forever.

Sedevacantists do not believe there is no forever. This passage means that as long as there is a pope in office, Peter exercises judgment in him, and this is how He lives forever. This passage doesn't even imply that there would always be a pope in office as it couldn't without failing each time a pope dies or voluntary leaves his office.

3. Therefore whoever succeeds to the chair of Peter obtains by the institution of Christ himself, the primacy of Peter over the whole Church. So what the truth has ordained stands firm, and blessed Peter perseveres in the rock-like strength he was granted, and does not abandon that guidance of the Church which he once received.

Part 4 of Argument: Sedevacantism can't hold that guidance and truth can be given to the whole Church since there may never be another pope.

This argument doesn't reflect the passage. Does this say there will always be a pope? No, it says that whoever succeeds the Chair of Peter has the same primacy as Peter did for the truth to remain.

4. For this reason it has always been necessary for every Church--that is to say the faithful throughout the world--to be in agreement with the Roman Church because of its more effective leadership. In consequence of being joined, as members to head, with that see, from which the rights of sacred communion flow to all, they will grow together into the structure of a single body.

> **Part 5 of Argument:** Sedevacantism can't have a single body, since there may never be another pope.

Every time a pope dies, the Church remains a single body. Even when the Church went three-and-a-half years without a pope, the Church remained. Does this passage mean there will always be a pope? No, it says that each individual church is to be in union with the church of the pope.

5. Sess. 4, Chap. 2, [Canon]: "Therefore, if anyone then says that it is not from the institution of Christ the Lord Himself, or by Divine right that the blessed Peter has perpetual successors in the primacy over the universal Church . . . let him be anathema. or that the Roman pontiff is not the successor of blessed Peter in this primacy: let him be anathema."

> **Part 6 of Argument:** Sedevacantism doesn't believe the Church has had perpetual successors.

There are two ways of looking at this Canon. Both ways are harmonic with sedevacantism.

One way of understanding this passage is that there will always be successors to the papacy, which we've had perpetual successors up to Pius XII and now are in the interregnum period. We are still waiting for the next pope to be elected. Since Vatican I does not give a time limit on an interregnum period, it cannot be argued that sedevacantism is going against Vatican I.

Some Vatican 2 apologists argue that he interregnum period ends with the death of the last cardinal. See Objection 9 how this is not true.

Another way of looking at this and perhaps the best way is there is perpetual successors IN THE PRIMACY because the Eastern Orthodox recognize that Peter has successors but not in the primacy. The pope is the successor of St. Peter in the primacy perpetually, meaning, every time there is a pope until the end of time, he is a successor in the same primacy with the same authority St. Peter had.

Now notice what follows, ***"or that the Roman pontiff is not the successor of blessed Peter in this primacy: let him be anathema."***

This counters the Protestants that don't believe that the Roman Pontiff is the successor of Blessed Peter in this primacy.

The first part counters the Eastern Orthodox that recognize that Peter has successors but not in the primacy. The second part counters the Protestants.

This explanation flows with the overall statement because the first part is countering the argument that Peter's successors have primacy, and the next part ***"or that the Roman pontiff"*** is countering the argument that popes are not Peter's successors.

None of the Vatican I statements say there must always be a pope or else every time a pope dies, Vatican I statements would fail.

This argument from Vatican I is a straw-man argument against sedevacantism, and it is used over and over.

Part 7 of Argument: Since sedevacantists say John XXIII through Benedict XVI are not the successors of blessed Peter, they have anathematized themselves.

This argument is placing *"Benedict, JPII, etc"* in place of the word *"Roman pontiff"* and therefore sedevacantists must be saying that whoever is presumed to be the Roman pontiff is not the successor because there must be a successor in the office until the end of time.

This is not what the statement is saying.

Sedevacantists believe the Roman pontiff is the successor of Peter but we don't believe John through Benedict are the Roman pontiffs, and article 1 is referring to the *"OFFICE"* which does hold the primacy until the end of time regardless if one is actually holding the office. Vatican I never states that there will always be a pope in the office. It couldn't say that or it fails every time a pope dies.

And just because someone is presumed to be pope doesn't mean he actually is pope. Only a Catholic can be pope. If one is a heretic, then his election cannot be valid regardless if everybody thinks it is.

The *"OFFICE"* will always hold the primacy and this is what Catholics say when trying to convert Protestants and Eastern Orthodox. When sedevacantists attempt to convert them, they always tell them that they must accept the papacy and believe that it holds the primacy over the whole church, knowing that the office is vacant. All sedevacantists believe Peter's successors hold the primacy and always will till the end of time.

This argument (part 7) is adding words to Vatican I to mean something other than the original intent. Vatican I means precisely what it states and nothing more.

Anti-sedevacanters use Vatican I to say that sedevacantists don't believe in perpetual successors. This is a lie. Now, if Vatican I says there must be a pope every 4 years, then sedevacantists are in trouble. This would only prove the Gates of Hell have prevailed.

Of course, when valid elections take place then there will be a pope in office perpetually. Heretics cannot vote. Heretics cannot be elected. Heretics cannot hold the office of papacy. This is the crisis today. There is another possibility which is covered in Objection 9.

8. The new law *Vacantis Apostolicae Sedis* of Pope Pius XII supersedes the law, Bull *Cum ex Apostolatus Officio* of Pope Paul IV. Along with Canon Law, the Church has all of these laws to keep the spotless Church airtight.

Part 1 of the Argument: Canon 2313Â§1 (in the 1917 Code) states that apostates and heretics incur a *latae sententiae* excommunication. That is not in dispute. Canon 2263 (also in the 1917 Code) declares that an excommunicated person "is forbidden to exercise ecclesiastical offices or duties." This is also not in dispute. However, the very next canon, 2264, then declares: An act of jurisdiction carried out by an excommunicated person, whether in the internal or the external forum, is illicit: and if a condemnatory or declaratory sentence has been pronounced, it is also invalid, without prejudice to canon 2262Â§3; otherwise it is valid.

Canon 2261Â§3 makes an exception to his invalidity when it is a case of an officially excommunicated priest giving absolution to someone in danger of death." But the key here is the Code made very clear that in order for an excommunication to invalidate the acts of an excommunicated person (that would include the Pope), the excommunication would have to have been pronounced, not simply an interpretation of law by some group within or without the Church. Since the law of the Church is very clear that an inferior cannot pronounce an official excommunication upon a superior, there would be no one on earth who could legally excommunicate the Pope. Only a future Pope or Council ratified by a Pope could do so. Thus, the heretical Pope would continue to act illicitly, but validly in all of his official acts and all would be bound to obey his official legislation.

The only exception to the above where there would be no need of a superior to declare officially an excommunication in order for a priest or bishop to lose all jurisdiction (except for danger of death), according to the 1917 Code, is found in canon 188Â§4. However, this canon speaks of "public defection," where the offender makes very clear that he is abandoning the Catholic Faith in no uncertain terms as when a priest leaves the Church and joins a Fundamentalist sect so that all of the world, Catholic and non-Catholic alike would know—and indeed he himself would say—he has resigned from his position and duties. This does not apply in the case of our last five popes.

The problem with this argument is it concludes that the jurisdiction of the priesthood equates the papacy. There is a major difference between the ordinary jurisdiction of the priesthood from the Sacrament of Holy Orders, which can never be lost even through heresy, and the jurisdiction of the Office of the Papacy, which can be lost through abandonment, heresy, schism, or apostasy.

This argument also fails to distinguish between ordinary and supplied jurisdictions.

Amazingly, Vatican 2 apologists would actually argue that these laws are to keep the spotless Church airtight. The Church doesn't need a law to keep the Church airtight. A pope cannot formally teach a heresy and no law is needed to prevent a pope from trying.

All these arguments demonstrate how Vatican 2 apologists have such a low regard for the papacy, that they'll argue that even a non-Catholic heretic can be pope and head of the Catholic Church!

Part 2 of the Argument: Part of the problem with *Cum Ex Apostolatus Officio* [CEAO] is, juridically speaking, there is no one to appeal to from the decision of the Pope. If someone was going to accuse the Pope of heresy, he could only appeal to the Pope himself. And, of course, we know that it is impossible for the Pope to teach error *ex cathedrae.* But, even if we are talking about the Pope's private teaching where he is not speaking in his official capacity, if the Pope does not agree with the accuser, the only thing that could happen in this case would be an appeal to a future Pope or Council ratified by the Pope. A case of this actually occurring never happened under this law as it was promulgated by Pope Paul IV. That would have been interesting. However, in God's providence, the law of the Church in this matter has been changed for the better by the authority of Pope Pius XII.

See Objection 23 to see how this argument is logically absurd.

Part 3 of the Argument: *CEAO* was not an infallible teaching. It concerned a matter of discipline, not doctrine. If you look at paragraph 8 of this same document, this becomes clear:

[The provisions of this Our Constitution, which is to remain valid in perpetuity are to take effect] notwithstanding any Constitutions, Apostolic Ordinations, privileges, indults or Apostolic Letters, whether they be to these same Bishops, Archbishops, Patriarchs, Primates and Cardinals or to any others, and whatsoever may be their import and form, and with whatsoever sub-clauses or decrees they may have been granted, even *"motu proprio"* and by certain knowledge, from the fullness of the Apostolic power or even consistorially or otherwise howsoever; and even if they have been repeatedly approved and renewed, have been included in the corpus of the Law or strengthened by any capital conclaves whatsoever (even by oath) or by Apostolic confirmation or by anysoever other endorsements or if they were legislated by ourselves. By this present document instead of by express mention, We specially and expressly derogate the provisions of all these by appropriate deletion and word-for-word substitution, so that these may otherwise remain in force.

The fact that Our Holy Father declared this law was to derogate all other laws to the contrary tells us that we are talking about matters of discipline. One Pope cannot change a teaching of the Church proclaimed with "the fullness of the Apostolic power," however, a Pope can change a disciplinary law issued by "the fullness of the Apostolic power" even if that law was "to remain valid in perpetuity" heretofore.

This argument misrepresents the difference between what is infallible and immutable. This is a common misunderstanding among Vatican 2 apologists.

Infallibility means without error. Immutability means unchangeable. By confusing the two, heretics use the excuse that since Church disciplines can change they are not infallible and therefore could be problematic is some way, even harmful.

In fact, Church disciplines are changeable but they are also infallible. They change for reasons other than being problematic.

See Objection 12.

CEAO was applying the Divine law that a heretic can't be elected to the papacy. Therefore, this aspect of the *CEAO* is infallible anyway.

Part 4 of the Argument: A bishop who appoints a certain priest as pastor of a parish knowing that the man is morally or psychologically unfit for the task acts illicitly, since the appointment violates canon law (cf. canon 521Â§2, 1983 Code; canon 453Â§2, 1917 Code). But the appointment is still *valid*. In other words, that priest is the rightful pastor of the parish so that, for instance, the marriages he witnesses there will be true marriages.

Pope Pius XII's Apostolic Constitution *Vacantis Apostolicae Sedis* (December 8, 1945), which declares: "34. None of the cardinals may in any way, or by pretext of any excommunication, suspension, or interdict whatsoever, ***or of any other ecclesiastical impediment***, be excluded in the active and passive election of the Supreme Pontiff. We hereby suspend such censures solely for the purposes of the said election; at other times they are to remain in vigor (AAS 38 [1946], p. 76)."

Active means they are allowed to vote, passive means they can be elected validly to the Papacy. The same language is used as was used by Pope Paul IV in *CEAO* 3. Here Pope Paul says of those who have been declared to be heretics that they:

... shall also automatically, without any exercise of law or application of fact, be thoroughly, entirely and perpetually deprived of:- their Orders and Cathedrals, even Metropolitan, Patriarchal and Primatial Churches, the honour of the Cardinalate and the office of any embassy whatsoever, not to mention both active and passive voting rights

This final argument fails to distinguish between different types of excommunication. Pope Pius XII and Pope Paul IV are actually implying that there is a difference but the Vatican 2 apologists don't want to see it. Popes Gregory X and Innocent IV also distinguish different penalties between the minor and major excommunications.

Heretics lose all jurisdiction of authority, therefore any cardinal who becomes a heretic ceases to be a Cardinal.

God himself has bound Himself to certain laws. For instance, He could not allow evil to enter Heaven. Heresy is evil, which is the absence of good. Heretics deprive themselves with membership with the Church and citizenship of Heaven. It is impossible to lift an excommunication from one who obstinately remains a heretic. A Pope does not have more authority than God and therefore cannot lift such an excommunication.

What Pope Pius XII means in *Vacantis Apostolicae Sedis* are those cardinals that were excommunicated for something other than heresy or apostasy. Those types of excommunications classified as minor as opposed to major, do not cause a loss of membership with the Church but rather barred one from the Sacraments of the Church. An example of a minor excommunication would include those that falsified relics (canon 2326).

A cardinal under a minor excommunication is still a cardinal since the law against him is an ecclesiastical law. Heresy is a major excommunication that falls under the Divine Law and needs no declaration. It is always automatic. See Objection 23.

Both types of excommunications are serious but one can be suspended for a time as Pope Pius XII did in *Vacantis Apostolicae Sedis.* The other cannot precisely because it falls under the Divine Law, which cannot be suspended.

Pope Benedict XIV also makes a distinction between minor and major excommunications in *Ex Quo Primum* (# 23), March 1, 1756: "***Moreover heretics and schismatics are subject to the censure of major excommunication by the law of Can. de Ligu. 23, quest. 5, and Can. Nulli, 5, dist. 19.***"

The teaching that heresy falls under the Divine Law as opposed to mere Church law is taught in those sections of major pre-Vatican II commentaries on the Code of Canon Law that deal with elections to the papal office and the qualities required in the person elected.

"***Heretics and schismatics are barred*** *from the Supreme Pontificate* ***by the divine law itself***... *They* ***must certainly be regarded as excluded*** *from occupying the throne of the Apostolic*

See, which is the infallible teacher of the truth of the faith and the center of ecclesiastical unity." (Maroto, *Institutiones I.C.* 2:784)

*"Appointment to the Office of the Primacy. 1. What is required **by divine law** for this appointment... Also **required for validity** is that the one elected be a member of the Church; hence, **heretics and apostates** (at least public ones) **are excluded**."* (Coronata, *Institutiones I.C.* 1:312)

*"All those who are not **impeded by divine law** or by an invalidating ecclesiastical law are validly eligible [to be elected pope]. Wherefore, a male who enjoys use of reason sufficient to accept election and exercise jurisdiction, and who is a true member of the Church can be validly elected, even though he be only a layman. Excluded as **incapable of valid election**, however, are all women, children who have not yet arrived at the age of discretion, those afflicted with habitual insanity, **heretics and schismatics**." (Wernz-Vidal,* Jus Can. *2:415)*

Again, when Pope Pius XII states that all cardinals, whatever ecclesiastical impediment they are under, can vote and be elected in a Papal conclave, he was speaking about cardinals under minor excommunications that have nothing to do with heresy.

Ecclesiastical impediment is just that. It can be lifted by the Ecclesiastical authority we call the pope.

Finally to demonstrate how silly the Part 4 argument truly is; take notice that Pius XII states: *"We hereby suspend such censures solely for the purposes of the said election; **at other times they are to remain in vigor**."* If the Part 4 argument were taken to the logical conclusion, Pius XII would be saying that the excommunication of such a cardinal is suspended **only for the time of the election; at other times it remains in vigor. This would mean that the said election of such a cardinal would immediately lose the papacy since the suspended excommunication would fall back into force after the election.** See Appendix II p. 435 for more.

9. If sedevacantism is true, there could never be a true pope in the future. The interregnum period ends with the death of the last Cardinal since without Cardinals no future election is possible. No sedevacantist has ever come up with a theory as to how God could now restore the papacy in such a way that all faithful Catholics could join in recognizing the new pope as certainly valid. Therefore, declaration of Vatican I on perpetual succession fails.

If all faithful Catholics must be able to recognize a new pope as certainly valid, then sedevacantism is just proven true. Over 10,000 faithful Catholics don't recognize the last 5 claimants. Who determines faithful Catholics anyway, when nearly the entire world that claims Catholicism reject the Faith as it has been handed down?

Vatican 1 Canon stated: "if anyone then says that it is not from the institution of Christ the Lord Himself, or by Divine right that the blessed Peter has perpetual successors in the primacy over the universal Church . . . let him be anathema."

Keep in mind that successors to the papacy is a Divine right.

It's true that Pope Pius XII legislation on papal elections requires the voting of the College of Cardinals, but this not a new legislation. It's been the law of the Church for hundreds of years.

Vatican I doesn't reject the possibility that the College of Cardinals could become extinct (theologians from Vatican I have testified to this truth), as it has now. Now the Church is under extraordinary conditions, and the normal laws don't necessarily apply. This principle applies to the other things in the Church as well. Ordinary conditions would apply to Baptism, but under extraordinary conditions, desire and contrition will suffice. The laws of God and Church don't necessarily apply to those in extraordinary conditions. Many more examples could be given.

However, since the law of the Church doesn't apply in extraordinary conditions, then cardinals would not be necessary to have a new pope if no cardinals existed. Therefore, it is still possible to have a valid election.

This is confirmed by several theologians.

"Even if St. Peter would have not determined anything, once he was dead, the Church had the power to substitute him and appoint a successor to him ... If by any calamity, war or plague, all Cardinals would be lacking, we cannot doubt that the Church could provide for herself a Holy Father...Hence such an election should be carried out by all the Church and not by any particular Church. And this is because that power is common and it concerns the whole Church. So it must be the duty of the whole Church." *(De Potestate Ecclesiae,* Vitoria)

".. . by exception and by supplementary manner this power (that of electing a pope), corresponds to the Church and to the Council, either by the absence of Cardinal Electors, or because they are doubtful, or the election itself is uncertain, as it happened at the time of the schism." (*De Comparatione Auctoritatis Papae et Concilii,* Cajetan, OP)

"When it would be necessary to proceed with the election, if it is impossible to follow the regulations of papal law, as was the case during the Great Western Schism, one can accept, without difficulty, that the power of election could be transferred to a General Council...Because natural law prescribes that, in such cases, the power of a superior is passed to the immediate inferior because this is absolutely necessary for the survival of the society and to avoid the tribulations of extreme need." *(De Ecclesia Christi,* Billot)

These statements must be accepted for all time because no Church law or the inability to follow the law under normal circumstances can prohibit a Divine right.

It is by Divine right that Peter has perpetual successors even if the laws of the Church under normal conditions can't be applied.

The rule that only the College of Cardinals elects the pope will always apply unless a future pope overturns it, or if it can't be applied.

The pope would elect new cardinals if they became extinct, but if they became extinct during an interregnum, then what?

Imagine if for some reason a pope suddenly died, and during the conclave, a Muslim terrorist bombed the Sistine Chapel and killed all the cardinals. Does this mean we can't have a future pope since only cardinals can elect one? No, because Church law would only apply when there are cardinals. If they became extinct, then by Divine law, the rest of the Church, be that of bishops, priests, lay, etc. could still elect a future pope since as the Dogma of Vatican 1 says, it is by Divine right that Peter has successors. This Divine law of God would supply the rule of an election of a pope by non-cardinals in extreme circumstances. To deny this is to deny the Dogma.

Some Vatican 2 apologists teach that it would be impossible for a terrorist to annihilate the cardinal elect. That such an event would make the Gates of Hell prevail. Where do they get this teaching? Low and behold, they base it on the law of Pius XII that only cardinals can elect a pope, thus they actually create a new doctrine and deny the dogma.

Pope Pius XII never intended for his law to be binding in the absolute sense under all conditions.

Anti-sedevacanters are looking for an argument against sedevacantism so that they don't have to defend the apostasies of their popes.

Cardinal Billot

We've also had true popes who were unlawfully elected such as Vigilius and St. Eugene. Therefore, a true pope need not necessarily be lawfully elected. As a matter of fact, if the current antipope Benedict XVI rejected his errors; he could be considered a true pope. It's that simple!

Lastly, if Christ were to come in this generation, then no explanation is needed. Everything is actually fitting into the prophecy of the great apostasy quite nicely therefore; no pope would necessarily be needed.

The argument would hold water only if all the bishops died off.

10. Church must be visible which it wouldn't be without a pope. Sedevacantists believe in a headless monster.

The Church is visibly headless each time a pope dies, but it always has Christ has Her Head. The Church remains visible nonetheless.

The Vatican 2 apologists apparently don't believe in the great apostasy, but the Bible knows it quite well and so does the Catholic Faith.

However, the same apologists believe that it is possible to have the monster of a Heretic/Apostate (Gates of Hell) as Head of the Church. This, the Bible and the Church know nothing of.

11. There are no bishops with ordinary jurisdiction therefore, no authority. Also, Matthew 18:17-18 cannot apply without a pope or bishops with supplied jurisdiction.

First of all, there is no dogma that says the Church must have ordinary jurisdiction to exist.

Supplied jurisdiction is still in effect and it is real authority. Bishops can consecrate, priests can administer the Sacraments, and the Church still functions. The Great Schism is a historic precedent for the conditions today. Back then, a true pope was unrecognizable, yet bishops continue to be consecrated and act. Supplied jurisdiction was all that the Church had during those times.

Matt 18:17-18, *"If he refuses to listen to them, tell it to the church; and if he refuses to listen even to the church, let him be to you as a Gentile and a tax collector. Truly, I say to you, whatever you bind on earth shall be bound in heaven, and whatever you loose on earth shall be loosed in heaven."*

Vatican 2 apologists like to use this verse to show how the pope is infallible yet the pope is not necessarily infallible when this verse is applied.

We can apply this verse in the real case of bishops from a particular country that disagree with something about a doctrine. If they ask the pope to solve it, his answer would not necessarily be infallible. Only if he solves the issue for the whole church would infallibility count.

Vatican 2 apologists like to create false arguments using Scripture as they do in this case.

In the Gospel of Matthew, Jesus was speaking to all the Apostles, not just Peter. The context was about sinning against one another, not necessarily about Divine or Church doctrine. The binding and loosing refers to the decision on how the problem was solved and that decision acts like one out of a court of law. If one refuses to accept such a decision, Christ is giving the power to the highest authorities in the Church to anathematize the individual.

It is true that a decision could ultimately come down to one person, and this decision cannot be rejected, but it does not follow that the decision is infallible.

The binding and loosing in Matt. 16 is quite different in that Christ was speaking specifically to Peter out of the group of Apostles immediately after Jesus said that he was going to give Peter the keys to the Kingdom of Heaven.

Be that as it may, Christ or His Church never said Matthew 18 would or could apply till the end of time. As a matter of fact, it could not apply many times in history as in Japan when the Church survived centuries without priests. England went years without bishops during the 15th and 16th centuries. During the French Revolution and the 20 years following, it could not apply. The Arian heresy decimated the Church during the fourth century and it couldn't apply all over the place. If it could happen in those places and for such a long time, there is no reason to believe that it couldn't during the great apostasy at the end of time.

12. If they are doubtful, we must give them the benefit of the doubt. It is possible they are insane, therefore not true heretics.

This argument doesn't apply because there is no doubt with sedevacantists.

The *"if"* are those who are ignorant of the Faith, or the events that have taken place since 1958, or those who are afraid and just use this excuse to keep from accepting the position of sedevacantism.

However, is the argument legit if such a case where true? Not according to St. Robert Bellarmine.

Rev. Francis X Doyle, S.J. explains: *"The Church is a visible society with a visible Ruler. If there can be any doubt about who that visible Ruler is, he is not visible, and hence, where there is any doubt about whether a person has been legitimately elected Pope, that doubt must be removed before he can become the visible head of Christ's Church. Blessed Bellarmine, S.J., says: 'A doubtful Pope must be considered as not Pope'; and Suarez, S.J., says: 'At the time of the Council of Constance there were three men claiming to be Pope.... Hence, it could have been that not one of them was the true Pope, and in that case, there was no Pope at all...." The Defense of the Catholic Church,* 1927, Fr. Francis X. Doyle, S.J.

In light of this teaching, it makes sense since a doubtful pope would lead to doubtful cardinals, which in turn would lead to more doubtful popes through doubtful elections.

"Not a few canonists teach that, outside of death and abdication, the pontifical dignity ***can also be lost by falling into certain insanity****, which is legally equivalent to death, as well as*

through manifest and notorious heresy. In the latter case, a pope would automatically fall from his power, and this indeed without the issuance of any sentence, for the first See (i.e., the See of Peter) is judged by no one ... The reason is that, by falling into heresy, the pope ceases to be a member of the Church. He who is not a member of a society, obviously, cannot be its head." *Introductio in Codicem* [1946] - Udalricus Beste

This dispels the myth that a pope could be insane.

13. Look at the chaos of sedevacantism. There are so many types all rendering each other as non-Catholics. There is no unity and yet the Church is one faith. The chaos of not knowing what is valid or not is also present.

The problem with this argument is it can be turned on the Vatican 2 church. Look at the chaos of the Vatican 2 church. It is much more chaotic then the sedevacantist position.

Besides, it only makes sense that sedevacantists are divided, but not in doctrine. When you strike the shepherd, the sheep will scatter if given enough time. However, the sheep would not scatter if a true pope were in place, which ironically means the argument against sedevacantists actually helps to show their position to be correct. The Church is still one since there are Catholic sedevacantists and heretical sedevacantists.

It is argued that if we admit we had antipopes for the past 50 years we would be unable to tell what is valid and what is not and there would be chaos.

The problem is that we are there for those who are sincere about the truth. It's totally chaotic now in the Vatican 2 church admitting they are popes. Sedevacantists are very aware what is valid and what is not which makes this argument used bunk.

14. All laws and disciplines of the Vatican 2 Church are not infallible, therefore sedevacantists cannot use this argument against the Church.

One of the foundations that demonstrates the truth of sedevacantism is the infallible doctrine that laws and disciplines are infallible. Vatican 2 has shown otherwise in many of its practices with female servers being the most apparent. Since the Catholic Church is indefectible, She cannot contradict Herself.

Examples of the teaching of infallible disciplines from 4 popes and 7 theologians:

The Popes

Pope Pius VI, *Auctorem Fidei*, 78 (1794): "The prescription of the synod about the order of transacting business in the conferences, in which, after it prefaced 'in every article that which pertains to faith and to essence of religion must be distinguished from that which is proper to discipline,' it adds, 'in this itself (discipline) there is to be distinguished what is necessary or useful to retain the faithful in spirit, from that which is useless or too burdensome for the liberty of the sons of the new Covenant to endure, but more so, from that which is dangerous or harmful, namely, leading to superstition and materialism'; in so far as by the generality of the words it includes and submits to a prescribed examination even the discipline established and approved by the Church, **as if the Church which is ruled by the Spirit of God could have established discipline which is not only useless and burdensome for Christian liberty to endure, but which is even dangerous and harmful and leading to superstition and materialism, - false, rash, scandalous, dangerous, offensive to pious ears, injurious to the Church and to the Spirit of God by whom it is guided, at least erroneous.**" (*Denzinger* 1578; DS 2678)

Pope Gregory XVI, *Mirari Vos*, 9 (1832): "Furthermore, **the discipline sanctioned by the Church must never be rejected or branded as contrary to certain principles of the natural law. It must never be called crippled, or imperfect or subject to civil**

authority. In this discipline the administration of sacred rites, standards of morality, and the reckoning of the Church and her ministers are embraced."

Pope Gregory XVI, *Quo Graviora*, 4-5 (1833): "...[the evil "reformers"] state categorically that there are **many things in the discipline of the Church** in the present day, in its government, and in the form of its external worship which are not suited to the character of our time. **These things, they say, should be changed, as they are harmful for the growth and prosperity of the Catholic religion, before the teaching of faith and morals suffers any harm from it.** Therefore, showing a zeal for religion and showing themselves as an example of piety, they force reforms, conceive of changes, and pretend to renew the Church. **While these men were shamefully straying in their thoughts, they proposed to fall upon the errors condemned by the Church in proposition 78 of the constitution *Auctorem fidei* (published by Our predecessor, Pius VI on August 28, 1794).** They also attacked the pure doctrine which they say they want to keep safe and sound; either they do not understand the situation or craftily pretend not to understand it. While they contend that the entire exterior form of the Church can be changed indiscriminately, do they not subject to change even those items of discipline which have their basis in divine law and which are linked with the doctrine of faith in a close bond? Does not the law of the believer thus produce the law of the doer? Moreover, **do they not try to make the Church human by taking away from the infallible and divine authority, by which divine will it is governed? And does it not produce the same effect to think that the present discipline of the Church rests on failures, obscurities, and other inconveniences of this kind? And to feign that this discipline contains many things which are not useless but which are against the safety of the Catholic religion?** Why is it that private individuals appropriate for themselves the right which is proper only for the pope?"

Pope St. Pius X, *Pascendi Dominici Gregis*, Sept 13, 1907: "Venerable Brethren, the principles from which these doctrines spring have been solemnly condemned by Our predecessor, Pius VI, in his Apostolic Constititution *Auctorem fidei*."

Pope Pius XII, *Mystici Corporis*, 66 (1943): "**Certainly the loving Mother is spotless** in the Sacraments, by which she gives birth to and nourishes her children; in the faith which she has always preserved inviolate; **in her sacred laws imposed on all**; in the evangelical counsels which she recommends; in those heavenly gifts and extraordinary graces through which, with inexhaustible fecundity, she generates hosts of martyrs, virgins and confessors."

The Theologians

Monsignor G. Van Noort, S.T.D. *Dogmatic Theology* 2:91 (1958): "The Church's infallibility extends to....ecclesiastical laws passed for the universal Church for the direction of Christian worship and Christian living....But the Church is infallible in issuing a doctrinal decree as intimated above - and to such an extent that it can never sanction a universal law which would be at odds with faith or morality or would be by its very nature conducive to the injury of souls.... If the Church should make a mistake in the manner alleged when it legislated for the general discipline, it would no longer either be a loyal guardian of revealed doctrine or a trustworthy teacher of the Christian way of life. It would not be a guardian of revealed doctrine, for the imposition of a vicious law would be, for all practical purposes, tantamount to an erroneous definition of doctrine; everyone would naturally conclude that what the Church commanded squared with sound doctrine. It would not be a teacher of the Christian way of life, for by its laws it would induce corruption into the practice of religious life."

P. Hermann, *Institutiones Theologiae Dogmaticae* (4th ed., Rome: Della Pace, 1908), vol. 1, p. 258: "The Church is infallible in her general discipline. By the term general discipline is understood the laws and practices which belong to the external ordering of the whole Church. Such things would be those which concern either external worship, such as liturgy and rubrics, or the administration of the sacraments. . . . "If she [the Church] were able to prescribe or command or tolerate in her discipline something against faith and morals, or something which tended to the detriment of the Church or to the harm of the faithful, she would turn away from her divine mission, which would be impossible."

A Dorsch, *Institutiones Theologiae Fundamentalis.* Innsbruck: Rauch 1928. 2:409: 'The Church is also rightfully held to be infallible in her disciplinary decrees....By disciplinary decrees are understood all those things which pertain to the ruling of the Church, insofar as it is distinguished from the magisterium. Referred to here, then, are ecclesiastical laws which the Church laid down for the Universal Church in order to regulate divine worship or to direct the Christian life."

R.M. Schultes *De Ecclesia Catholica.* Paris: Lethielleux 1931. 314-7: "*The infallibility of the Church in Enacting Disciplinary Laws.* Disciplinary laws are defined as 'ecclesiastical laws laid down to direct Christian life and worship'..... The question of whether the Church is infallible in establishing a disciplinary law concerns the substance of universal disciplinary laws - that is, whether such laws can be contrary to a teaching of faith or morals, and so work to the spiritual harm of the faithful....*Thesis. The Church, in establishing universal laws, is infallible as regards their substance.* The Church is infallible in matters of faith and morals. Through disciplinary laws, the Church teaches about matters of faith and morals, not doctrinally or theoretically, put practically and effectively. A disciplinary law therefore involves a doctrinal judgment.... The reason, therefore, and foundation for the Church's infallibility in her general discipline is the intimate connection between truths of faith or morals and disciplinary laws. The principal matter of disciplinary laws is as follows: a) worship...."

Valentino Zubizarreta *Theologia Dogmatico-Scholastica.* 4th ed. Vitoria: El Carmen 1948. 1:486: " *Corollary II.* In establishing disciplinary laws for the universal Church, the Church is likewise infallible, in such a way that she would never legislate something which would contradict true faith or good morals. Church discipline is defined as 'that legislation or collection of laws which direct men how to worship God rightly and how to live a good Christian life.'.... *Proof of the Corollary.* It has been shown above that the Church enjoys infallibility in those things which concern faith and morals, or which are necessarily required for their preservation. Disciplinary laws, prescribed for the universal Church in order to worship God and rightly promote a good Christian life, are implicitly revealed in matters of morals, and are necessary to preserve faith and good morals. Therefore, the Corollary is proved."

Serapius Iragui, *Manuale Theologiae Dogmaticae.* Madrid: Ediciones Stadium 1959. 1:436, 447: "Outside those truths revealed in themselves, the object of the magisterium's infallibility includes other truths which, while not revealed, are nevertheless necessary to integrally preserve the deposit of the faith, correctly explain it, and effectively define it.... D) *Disciplinary Decrees.* These decrees are universal ecclesiastical laws which govern man's Christian life and divine worship. Even though the faculty of establishing laws pertains to the power of jurisdiction, nevertheless the power of the magisterium is considered in these laws under another special aspect, insofar as there must be nothing in these laws opposed to the natural or positive law. In this respect, we say that the judgment of the Church is infallible.... 1º) This is required by the nature and purpose of infallibility, for the infallible Church must lead her subjects to sanctification through a correct exposition of doctrine. Indeed, if the Church in her universally binding decrees would impose false doctrine, by that very fact men would be turned away from salvation, and the very nature of the true Church would be placed in peril. All this, however, is repugnant to the prerogative of infallibility with which Christ endowed His Church. Therefore, when the Church establishes disciplinary laws, she must be infallible."

Joachim Salaverri, *Sacrae Theologiae Summa.* 5th ed. Madrid: BAC 1962. 1:722,723: "3) Regarding disciplinary decrees in general which are by their purpose [*finaliter*] connected with things which God has revealed. A. The purpose of the infallible Magisterium requires infallibility for decrees of this kind.... Specifically, that the Church claims infallibility for herself in liturgical decrees is established by the law of the Councils of Constance and Trent solemnly enacted regarding Eucharistic Communion under one species. This can also be abundantly proved from other decrees, by which the Council of Trent solemnly confirmed the rites and ceremonies used in the administration of the sacraments and the celebration of the Mass."

Disciplines do change unlike doctrines, which don't. What Vatican 2 apologists don't understand is this is immutability. They think infallibility also means immutability but it doesn't.

Rome actually approved the theologian Herman in 1908 when he stated, *"Disciplines are infallible."* The document of Gregory XVI says that there is nothing even *"crippled"* in disciplines. This means INFALLIBILITY.

Perfect can be understood in several ways. Perfect can mean, without spot or blemish, which is what Pope Gregory means. It can mean, complete or thorough. It can also mean, lacking nothing. It can mean, completely suited such as: That is the perfect car to deliver pizzas in.

When the Church changed the fasting rule before Communion at least three times, was the first decision infallible and perfect? If so, why did it need to be changed from midnight, to three hours, to one?

Answer: It was infallible and perfect on at least two levels. It was pure, without spot or blemish, and it was suitable. It changed because it ceased to be either suitable or something else, but it was always without spot or blemish just as Pope Gregory said and meant. Laws and practices may not be "lacking nothing" and in this sense they would not be infallible and perfect.

Part 1 of the Argument: If nothing is wrong with an approved discipline without spot or blemish, it needs no further improvement because it is complete, perfect, and lacking nothing, otherwise something is wrong with it. Changing it wouldn't be necessary. Webster's defines the word perfect: 1. excellent or complete beyond improvement. 2. without flaws or blemish. 3. accurate in every detail. 4. thorough, utter. 5. Some commentators object to the use of comparative terms such as most, more, and rather with perfect on the grounds that perfect describes an absolute condition that cannot exist in degrees.

On the contrary, all the definitions do not mean the same thing. That is why the dictionary gave DIFFERENT definitions. To demonstrate the truth about the Church and the changing of disciplines and how they are perfect:

When kids were in the first and second grade, their mom and dad told them to go to bed at 8:30pm. This is a discipline. When they were in the 6th and 7th grade, the discipline changed to 9:30pm. When they were in high school, it changed again to 10pm and later.

So there are changes in the disciplines but none of these disciplines had flaws. They were all without spot or blemish, yet they changed. Why? Because the mom and dad thought it would be more suitable to change them as they got older.

The Church changes disciplines because She thinks they are more suitable, not because there is anything wrong with them in of themselves.

Another example, if one had the perfect daisy and the perfect rose, many would say the rose is more beautiful. This does not mean the daisy had some flaw in it just because it was not as pretty as the rose. Both are perfect, in the fact that there is no spot or blemish. However, one may be "lacking" something. The daisy lacked beauty in comparison to something else, but that does not mean that it was not a perfect daisy.

Church laws and practices are the same. They all are perfect. Fasting from midnight is perfect. Fasting just 3 hours is perfect. There are no flaws, spots, or blemishes in any of these disciplines. One may be more suitable but that doesn't mean that one is any less than perfect in the sense that that it had some flaw.

The disciplines or practices, of female servers, lectors, acolytes, (Eucharistic Ministers) etc., are evil. It is severely flawed. The Church said so. Therefore, this discipline can never be practiced. All disciplines of the True Church are perfect. This is how we can tell whether we are in the True Church.

Whether or not the law or practice changes, has nothing to do with it. The rose and daisy analogy was to show examples such as the East and West both having their own particular liturgies. The East is the daisy and the West is the Rose, or vice versa. Both liturgies are perfect but one may be more beautiful.

Even the fast from Midnight may be the Rose while the 3hr fast is the daisy. Both are perfect, pure, without spot, but one may very well be better. That doesn't mean the other is imperfect in the sense that there is something wrong with it.

> **Part 2 of Argument:** There is nothing wrong with having females serving and altar girls, lectors, acolytes. The previous condemnation was against the practice before it was approved because it was about disobedience not the practice itself.

This is absolutely false. The practice was condemned precisely because it an objective evil. Again, notice that the pope calls it an evil practice.

Pope Benedict XIV, *Encyclical Allatae Sunt*; promulgated on July 26, 1755: **"Pope Gelasius** in his ninth letter to the bishops of Lucania **condemned the evil practice which had been introduced of women serving the priest at the celebration of Mass**. Since this abuse had spread to the Greeks, **Innocent IV strictly forbade it in**

his letter to the bishop of Tusculum: 'Women should not dare to serve at the altar; they should be altogether refused this ministry.' **We too have forbidden this practice in the same words in Our oft-repeated constitution ..."**

Pope Gelasius called the practice evil which was introduced in his time. He stated, "We have heard with sorrow of the great contempt [mépris] with which the sacred mysteries have been treated. It has reached the point where women have been encouraged to serve at the altar, and to carry out roles that are not suited to their sex, having been assigned exclusively to those of masculine gender."

If something is not suited because of one's sex then it is part of the natural law. Never has women been allowed to do so for 2000 years precisely because altar girls are contrary to the Divine law and the Catholic Faith.

The Vatican 2 Ape Church gives permission because they don't think that girl altar servers are evil, just like women lector(esses). Never mind what St. Paul said about women should not speak in the churches of the holy ones. (I Corinthians 14:34) He wasn't referring to the priesthood but about SPEAKING. The Vatican 2 Church takes St. Paul out of context or just thinks St. Paul was speaking culturally and therefore it's okay now in our modern age. Girls servers and women lector(esses) were only permitted in Ape Church after Vatican 2.

Is this all some coincidence? No, even lay people realize that this is wrong. They don't need to know about theology to realize that something has gone seriously wrong with their church.

Since the Church is indefectible, it is impossible to have these practices since the same Church condemned them as evil.

15. The harmful law and discipline doctrine applies only when they are universal. Females serving the altar was not a universal practice, therefore it does not apply. Altar girls are harmful but were not imposed on the whole

church. Pope Pius XII in *Mystici Corporis*, 66 (1943) states: "Certainly the loving Mother is spotless in the Sacraments, by which she gives birth to and nourishes her children; in the faith which she has always preserved inviolate; in her sacred laws imposed on all; in the evangelical counsels which she recommends; in those heavenly gifts and extraordinary graces through which, with inexhaustible fecundity, she generates hosts of martyrs, virgins and confessors." Therefore, the church could issue harmful disciplines to part of the church as it has with altar girls.

Pope Pius XII may have stated, *"laws imposed on all"* but that doesn't imply that it could issue a harmful law to part of the Church. As a matter of fact, since Pius XII refers to the Church as "loving Mother" who is *"spotless"* then the implication would be that the loving spotless Mother must be spotless in all her disciplines. The position of this argument is saying that the Church who is the loving spotless Mother, is only loving to the whole church at once but not parts of it, or is only spotless to the whole church at once but not parts of it.

Then you have other papal pronouncements and they don't speak at all about the disciplines of the Church are spotless only when they are universal. Such as: Pope Pius VI, *Auctorem Fidei*, 78 (1794) and Pope Gregory XVI, *Mirari Vos*, 9 (1832).

Finally, altar girls have been universally permitted to the taste of the local bishop or priest which means that it has universally imposed the possibility of having a harmful discipline to every church that has such a cleric. That particular church would then have a harmful discipline and it could be rightly said that it was imposed by Rome as a universal discipline because it gives every modernist cleric the right to do so.

Be that as it may, the Church is a loving spotless Mother, which means that she loves each and everyone and not just the body as a whole. Altar girls could have never been even permitted by the true Church.

16. The *Novus Ordo Missae* is not a new rite but a new form of old rite.

Vatican 2 apologists like to use this argument because they know full well that a new rite would constitute a false pope based of the Council of Trent. What constitutes a new rite is a question they can't answer without subverting their own argument.

The Council of Trent, in Session 7, Canon 13 on the sacraments, the Council infallibly declared: *"If anyone e says that the received and approved rites customarily used in the Catholic Church for the solemn administration of the Sacraments can be changed into other new rites by any pastor in the Church whosoever, let him be anathema"*

Part 1 of Argument: First, if the pope were not allowed to change the rubrics of the Mass, then the Latin Mass that was created in the 5th century by Pope Gelasius or the seventh century by Pope Gregory, and confirmed by Pius V, would be the first candidate for the offense of "changing the rite," since the previous rite used in the 1-3 centuries was different than what was adopted later. Rest assured, if Pope Gelasius could change the rubrics of the Mass, then so can Paul VI.

Someone might argue that Gelasius and Gregory were permitted to change the rite because the Council of Trent did not come along until about a 1000 years later, but this argument is fallacious because, if Gelasius and Gregory changed the rite, then the Council of Trent, if Canon 13 applied to popes, would have never said that the rite could not be change, otherwise the council would have indicted Gelasius and Gregory.

This argument immediately confuses the subject. Changing a rite and changing into other new rites are two different things. Trent forbade changing the mass into a new rite not necessarily changing something in the rite itself. However, the argument that Gelasius and Gregory could have changed a mass into a new rite before Trent is not fallacious. Trent's pronouncements on forbidding something from happening in the future would not be retroactive as suggested. There is no reason to believe that they would be.

> **Part 2 of Argument:** The definition of a new rite is the Church's to define, not the sedevacantists. Evidently, the Church understands a new rite other than what occurred in 1968 when Paul VI gave us the *Novus Ordo*, and that is because the *Novus Ordo* contains the same consecration formula as the previous mass. A new rite would be a mass that changed the consecration formula, or did away with it altogether.

The consecration formula did change which is why there is controversy over the validity of the mass. See section Abomination of Desolation. This argument has just proven the sedevacantist position. But where does the Church say that a new rite must be one with a different formula? After all, there are different Eastern rites with the very same consecration formula as the Latin rite. Vatican 2 apologists like to invent doctrines that don't exist. The problem with saying that changing the consecration formulas makes a new rite is contrary to what the pope actually said.

Pope St. Pius V said in *"De Defectibus"* Chapter 5, Part 1: *"The words of Consecration, which are the form of this Sacrament, are these: For this is My Body. and: for this is the Chalice of My Blood, of the New and Eternal Testament: the mystery of faith, which shall be shed for you and for many unto the remission of sins. Now if one were to remove, or change anything in the form of the consecration of the body and blood, and in that very change of words the [new] wording would fail to mean the same thing, he would not consecrate the sacrament."*

Notice that St. Pius V did not say that one could not remove, or change anything in the form but one could not remove, or change anything, which would give it a different meaning. This is a very crucial distinction, because some forms have variants. Therefore, one could change the formula without changing the rite.

Part 3 of Argument: The language of Session 7, Canon 13, does not say "the pastor of THE CHURCH," but "any PASTORS (plural) of the CHURCHES" (plural). Hence, the universal church is not in view, otherwise "pastors" and "churches" would be in the singular.

What a second, Trent says, *"by any pastor of the church whosoever" not "any pastor(s) of the church(s)."* However, let's presume this statement is correct. The pope is a pastor of the particular church in Rome and not just the pastor of the whole church. Therefore, the pope would still be included even if what it stated is true. The universal church does not have to be in view since there are many different rites within the Church. The Latin Rite of the Mass is not a universal rite. This argument has nothing to do with it.

Part 4 of Argument: The original Latin of Canon 13 says *quemcumque ecclesiarum pastorem* which means whichever pastor of the churches. Because churches is in the plural, Trent is first referring to the churches of the world under a particular bishop. Moreover, the fact that the pope has allowed various rites in the world (e.g., Latin rite, Byzantine rite, Melchite rite, etc) shows that he alone has the authority to allow or disallow them, and that the particular bishop of that church does not have the authority. It is granted, however, that the pope cannot change or eliminate the consecration formula of the Mass, for if he did, it would be a new rite. If Canon 13 is applicable to the pope, it is only applicable in that sense, but it is not Canon 13 that is the main obstacle to this limitation, but Session 13 and Session 22 on the Mass and Eucharist.

Again, the Canons are not retroactive. Allowing or disallowing other rites is not what the canon is speaking about but rather changing them into new rites.

Part 5 of Argument: The council's purpose was not to tie the hands of future popes in doing what the popes thought best for the dissemination of the Mass among the populace.

The pope was tying the hands of future popes. Anytime, a pope defines a dogma or declares erroneous beliefs, he ties the hands of every future pope from changing the dogma or from allowing heresies to be held. This he did with the Mass.

Part 6 of Argument: The pope is the supreme authority, has the right to decide what is best for his people. The Council of Trent would have never said something to the effect: "We bind all future popes to the stipulation that they cannot change the rubrics or words of the Mass for any reason," but that's what the council would have had to say to prohibit future popes from doing so, but it would never have done so, and did not do so in Canon 13.

This is a fallacious argument. Trent said, *"into other new rites by any pastor in the Church whosoever, let him be anathema."* Trent is not saying that rubrics or words of the rite cannot be changed but that the rites cannot be made INTO OTHER NEW RITES. And if this happens, that pastor whoever he is, even the pope, will have anathematized himself.

The language is so clear that it takes someone like Vatican 2 apologists to actually twist the very words of Trent so that they can have the New Rite / Protestant Mass (cake) without any condemnation (and eat it too)

Why argue the Mass of Paul VI is not a new rite if the canon does not refer to future popes which allows future popes to give us new rites, after all, that is the argument first used? But look at what they are saying, one can change every single aspect of the mass but as long as the consecration formula remains we still have the same rite. Where does the Church say this? According to Pope Pius V, the Consecration can be changed provided nothing in it changes the meaning and you still can have the same rite. So where does the Church say that only the changing of the consecration formula makes a new rite? And why argue this point, if they first admitted that the canon was not referring to future popes? Vatican 2 apologists are just digging themselves into a deep grave.

It's about new rites not merely changing something in a rite. Changing something in a rite does not necessarily give us a new rite. The *Novus Ordo* is not just some little alteration of the Ancient Mass but it is entirely a new rite and we know this since the Ancient Rite was never abolished, therefore we have another new rite altogether. It would be entirely dishonest to say the *Novus Ordo* is essentially the same rite as the Ancient rite.

> **Part 7 of Argument:** The pope can be included by logical extension (although the language of Canon 13 applies mainly to pastors of the Churches in the plural). But the only entity that has the authority to define what a new rite is the Catholic Church, not any other sedevacantist. As such, Paul VI, Pope John Paul I, Pope John Paul II and Pope Benedict XVI have all agreed that the *Novus Ordo* is not a new rite under the definition of Session 7, Canon 13 of Trent. Because of that, (if you read about the development of the *Novus Ordo* wording) Paul VI was very careful to keep the traditional wording of the consecration formula, thus it is not a new rite.

The very words of Our Lord where changed into something else. Vatican 2 apologists wants their *"popes"* to have limitless authority, but this not reality. Supreme authority is not limitless.

It would not prove the point because we know that Trent's pronouncements are not worthless and yet we know the words *"any pastor whosoever"* could very well include the pope and therefore binding on future popes.

According to Vatican 2 apologists, a future pope could interpret Trent's canons on justification to mean that man is saved by faith alone but not by a faith that is alone as many Protestants hold. And according to them, we would have to just accept this interpretation. But we know, the anathemas attached to the canons and how they would apply to a pope if he did such a thing. But not to Vatican 2 apologists, their popes have limitless authority and there are no automatic anathemas for their popes.

Also, the pope's authority is not limitless when he interprets. If it did, this means that he can interpret to mean anything he wants. So how is it that the pope cannot interpret justification to mean that man is saved by faith alone but he can interpret that a *"new"* rite is not new and that two distinct rites are really the same rite? How is the pope limited in one canon and not the other? Just as a side not, John Paul II did affirm that man is justified by faith alone in the Joint Declaration with Lutherans. The fact is the pope cannot interpret any canon to mean something completely contrary to the plain wording.

Vatican 2 apologists want everybody to check their minds at the front door and stop thinking and just accept their antipopes and their heresies, and apostasies.

17. New mass is not harmful since Christ is present.

This argument assumes Christ is present. In my book "The Key to the Apocalypse" I prove that Christ is not present in the new mass.

However, assuming that Christ is present, Benedict XVI says that he believes the new mass is harmful.

"The drastic manner in which Pope Paul VI reformed the Mass in 1969 provoked extremely serious damage to the Church...*I am convince that the ecclesial crisis in which we find ourselves today depends in great part upon the collapse of the liturgy, which at times is actually being conceived of etsi Deus non daretur: as though in the liturgy it did not matter anymore whether God exists and whether He speaks and listens to us."* (Joseph Cardinal Ratzinger, *La Mia Vita*, San Paolo Editor, 1997)

This means even Benedict is holding to a heresy that the Church could issue a harmful mass.

Be that as it may, some Satanic Black Masses are valid since real priests using the correct words and intention who worship Lucifer, need the valid Hosts to desecrate, etc. Such masses are very harmful rendering argument 17 ridiculous.

18. Eucharistic Miracles involving "popes" prove they're true popes.

The following argument is used as a defense that John Paul II was a true pope. The substance of the answer given can be used for all such so-called miracles.

Since 30th June1985, when the statue of Our Lady belonging to Julia Kim, a humble Korean housewife, began to shed tears, tens of thousands of pilgrims have flocked to the small city of Naju in South Korea to visit the shrine of Our Lady, after hearing about the miraculous signs and happenings that occurred there. Many have personally seen the supernatural signs such as the shedding of tears and tears of blood as well as a fragrant of oil oozing from the statue of Our Lady. Many more have witnessed the Stigmata on Julia and the Eucharistic Miracles that repeatedly happened when the Sacred Host turned into flesh and blood on her tongue (One particular case was that of John Paul II on Oct. 31st, 1995.) Physical healing has also occurred on numerous occasions when Julia was praying and when people washed themselves with water from the miraculous spring on the mountain near Naju.

> If John Paul II weren't the pope, why would God allow this miracle? The only argument is that it was a fraud. But, there is no way she could change that host to blood as soon as he stuck it in her mouth. If someone said she is possessed and the devil did it, God still wouldn't allow it.

Okay, first question: If John Paul II wasn't pope why allow the miracle?

Assuming it was not a fraud and a true miracle, John Paul II is a valid bishop (if not Catholic) and assuming the words of Consecration in Korean was correct for validity, God might allow a miracle for the purpose of those who are good-willed even if incorrect to confirm their love and faith in Christ (not the errors, of course) who is truly Present.

Since there is a valid mass (if not Catholic) God is still truly Present, just like all non-Catholic liturgies that are valid, such as the Eastern Orthodox, etc. Since God is truly Present, He would want good-willed men to love and adore Him and a miracle would make men love and adore Him more.

Of course, this is all assuming that it was not a fraud.

There have been Eucharistic and other miracles in the Orthodox Churches, too, such as blood and oil spewing out of a crucifix in an Orthodox Church in Michigan. The Virgin Mary appeared many times over several years in Zeitoun, Egypt over a non-Catholic Coptic Church. Millions saw her. She cured a girl with breast cancer there. Many miracles are attributed to Our Lady of Zeitoun.

Why did God allow all these miracles in Orthodox Churches? Should we all become members of some non-Catholic Orthodox Church?

The answer for all this is: *"For he makes his sun rise on the evil and on the good, and sends rain on the just and on the unjust."* (Matt. 5)

It doesn't matter if it were a true miracle or not. However, the miracle appears to be a fraud anyway. Why would the Host turn into Blood in her mouth and not before giving Communion?

The whole point of Bread being the accident of Christ's Body and Blood is precisely because we are not to eat flesh and blood in those properties. This is why Christ said in John 63 about the spirit giving life and the flesh is of no avail. We can't eat flesh and blood in those properties. That would be too disgusting. So Christ gives Himself in the form of Bread and Wine.

One can never be sure that what you saw in Julia Kim was a trick or not. It was stated, *"there is no way she could change that host to blood as soon as he stuck it in her mouth."*

One could if the host was the trick devise that changed. In other words, it wasn't bread, but something that looked like it. A chemical reaction took place when it met with the saliva on her tongue. That is a real possibility and you can't say that it is not. Just look at the amazing tricks done by the world's greatest illusionists. Most of those are devises. We're not seeing what we think we are seeing.

Finally, it was said, *"If someone said she is possessed and the devil did it, God still wouldn't allow it."*

How do we know? God allowed the Egyptian magicians use demonic power to mimic God's real miracles through Moses. One may say that God wouldn't do that with his Eucharist. But it may not be a true Eucharist. The words of Consecration may have been faulty, the Church is the false church, and if all this were true then God very well could have allowed it as He said He would do with the coming of antichrist.

"Therefore God sends upon them a strong delusion, to make them believe what is false" (II Thess. 11).

So one can't say God wouldn't allow it. Not only would He allow it but promised that He would and there would be no better time than with John Paul II who was *"an"* if not *"the"* antichrist.

All possibilities have been covered. The argument of Eucharistic miracles against sedevacantism is without foundation. If one were to base this argument on this point, then there is no reason to condemn Eastern Orthodoxy and refuse to acknowledge them also as part of the true Church, which would in turn make several official Church teachings false, which would then make the Catholic Church a false Church. Yes, this heresy is taught by the Vatican 2 church.

19. Why would God allow such a thing as sedevacantism?

The answer is punishment for the sins of man.

Sister Maria das Dores (Lucia de Santos), the oldest seer, once told Father Augustin Fuentes on December 26, 1957, *"Father, the Blessed Virgin is very sad because no one heeds her message; neither the good nor the bad. The good continue on with their life of virtue and apostolate, but they do not unite their lives to the message of Fatima. Sinners keep following the road of evil because they do not see the terrible chastisement about to befall them. Believe me, Father, God is going to punish the world and very soon. The chastisement of heaven is imminent. In less than two years, 1960 will be here and the chastisement of heaven will come and it will be very great. Tell souls to fear not only the material punishment that will befall us if we do not pray and do penance but most of all the souls who will go to hell."*

Controversy has surrounded this interview with Fr. Augustin Fuentes. Two years later, an anonymous note came from the episcopal curia of Coimbra denouncing the interview as fraudulent. Sr. Lucy was then silenced. Fr. Joaquin Alonso, who wrote over 5,000 documents on Fatima at the request of the bishop of Fatima, wrote in 1975 that the interview with Fr Augustine Fuentes was authentic.

20. John XXIII through Benedict XVI have not been heretics at all as their teachings are ambiguous at best.

Some teachings are ambiguous, but not all. The teachings of Vatican 2 are their teachings. All of them hold to Vatican 2, which contains substantial unambiguous heretical teachings.

John Paul II rejects the historic teaching of the Credo on Christ's descent into hell along with other heresies. Benedict XVI rejects the historic teaching of the Credo on the Resurrection of the Body along with many other heresies.

Heresies are just one part of the problem. Acts of apostasy, and establishing evil laws and disciplines also demonstrate that these men are not true popes.

However, this argument is still a damning condemnation against the Vatican 2 Church because God doesn't allow AMBIQUITY to be taught by the Church.

How do we know? Because Pope Pius XI said so in *Mortalium Animos*: "The teaching authority of the Church in the divine wisdom was constituted on earth in order that the revealed doctrines might remain forever intact and might be brought with EASE and SECURITY to the knowledge of men."

Pope Pius VI also tells us that ambiguity is how heretics hide their heresies when condemning the Synod of Pistoia, Bull *"Auctorem fidei,"* August 28, 1794: "[The Ancient Doctors] knew the capacity of innovators in the art of deception. In order not to shock the ears of Catholics, they sought to hide the subtleties of their tortuous maneuvers by the use of seemingly innocuous words such as would allow them to insinuate error into souls in the most gentle manner. Once the truth had been compromised, they could, by means of slight changes or additions in phraseology, distort the confession of the faith which is necessary for our salvation, and lead the faithful by subtle errors to their eternal damnation. This manner of dissimulating and lying is vicious, regardless of the circumstances under which it is used. For very good reasons it can never be tolerated in a synod of which the principal glory consists above all in teaching the truth with clarity and excluding all danger of error.

"Moreover, if all this is sinful, it cannot be excused in the way that one sees it being done, under the erroneous pretext that the seemingly shocking affirmations in one place are further developed along orthodox lines in other places, and even in yet other places corrected; as if allowing for the possibility of either affirming or denying the statement, or of leaving it up the personal inclinations of the individual – such has always been the fraudulent and daring method used by innovators to establish error. It allows for both the possibility of promoting error and of excusing it.

"It is as if the innovators pretended that they always intended to present the alternative passages, especially to those of simple faith who eventually come to know only some part of the conclusions of such discussions which are published in the common language for everyone's use. Or again, as if the same faithful had the ability on examining such documents to judge such matters for themselves without getting confused and avoiding all risk of error. It is a most reprehensible technique for the insinuation of doctrinal errors and one condemned long ago by our predecessor Saint Celestine who found it used in the writings of Nestorius, Bishop of Constantinople, and which he exposed in order to condemn it with the greatest possible severity. Once these texts were examined carefully, the impostor was exposed and confounded, for he expressed himself in a plethora of words, mixing true things with others that were obscure; mixing at times one with the other in such a way that he was also able to confess those things which were denied while at the same time possessing a basis for denying those very sentences which he confessed."

"In order to expose such snares, something which becomes necessary with a certain frequency in every century, no other method is required than the following: whenever it becomes necessary to expose statements which disguise some suspected error or danger under the veil of ambiguity, one must denounce the perverse meaning under which the error opposed to catholic truth is camouflaged."

21. How could God expect us to know they are antipopes? It is too difficult to understand.

It is too difficult to understand without a good understanding of Catholicism. God expects us to know the truth insofar as we can. He most certainly would want us to know of the great apostasy and how to avoid it. He most certainly would want us to know if antipopes are fooling the Church with heresy. This is why we have the Holy Scriptures telling us about the great apostasy and antichrist.

God expects us to know what we ought under the usual conditions.

This argument does not change the fact that Rome has lost the faith with antipopes claiming the Chair of Peter.

Protestants could also use this invalid argument against Catholicism, but it would not change the fact that Catholicism remains the one and only true Church of Christ outside of which no one at all is saved.

22. What authority do you have to judge them? No one can judge the Holy See. It is unfair to judge them without a trial.

Part 1 of Argument: Given the maxim *Prima Sedes a nemine iudicatur*---- "no one may judge the First See"----- how is any isolated member of the Church to determine on his own that the conditions for formal heresy have been met? That no one may judge the Pope-----that is, his *personal sin* of heresy as opposed to the heretical import of his words----- is a fundamental truth of our religion, as well as a dictate of reason. This is because by the will of the Church's Divine Founder there is no office on earth above the papal office.

That being the case, how would isolated members of the Church know for certain that a Pope who uttered a heresy had not lost his mind, made some awful mistake in his choice of words, been subjected to some compulsion such as a threat on his life, or had somehow persuaded himself that his erroneous opinion was not contrary to the Faith?

Absent a procedure to investigate the papal statement and the surrounding circumstances, including direct questioning of the Pope himself with an opportunity to retract, it would be impossible to judge the matter fully and fairly.

Indeed, even Martin Luther was summoned to defend his views and then given sixty days to retract his 41 distinct heresies before finally suffering the sentence of excommunication.

Who exactly would afford the Pope this due process? Or are we to believe that the holder of the papal office is entitled to less justice than the likes of Martin Luther? Ultimately, only an authorized court or pope can decide if a pope was "ipso facto" a heretic before his election.

This argument locks one up in heresy and schism since it is arguing that a Catholic can't tell if one is a heretic and therefore can't judge him as one. Yet, the Catholic Church has taught differently.

St. Robert Bellarmine, *De Romano Pontifice, II, 30*:

"... for men are not bound, or able to read hearts; but ***when they see that someone is a heretic by his external works, they judge him to be a heretic pure and simple, and condemn him as a heretic."***

It is as simple as that. This is the same document St. Bellarmine was referring to a pope losing his office automatically.

Ipso facto means automatic. That means nobody is needed to decide. You must only be able to recognize it.

Pope Paul IV, *Bull Cum ex Apostolatus Officio*: *"(i) the promotion or elevation, even if it shall have been uncontested and by the unanimous assent of all the Cardinals, shall be null, void and worthless; (iii) it shall not be held as partially legitimate in any way... (vi) those thus promoted or elevated shall be deprived automatically, and* ***WITHOUT THE NEED FOR ANY FURTHER DECLARATION****, of all dignity, position, honor, title, authority, office and power..."*

Also, all the teachings provided in Objection 1, couldn't apply and would be totally meaningless.

As for Martin Luther, he was a formal heretic long before he was declared a heretic and thus excommunicated. His case actually proves sedevacantism.

Luther declared after learning of Pope Leo X warning to retract, *"As for me, the die is cast: I despise alike the favor and fury of Rome; I do not wish to be reconciled with her, or ever to hold any communion with her. Let her condemn and burn my books; I, in turn, unless I can find no fire, will condemn and publicly burn the whole pontifical law, that swamp of heresies."* (*The Catholic Encyclopedia*, "Luther," Robert Appleton Company, 1910, pp. 445-446)

Martin Luther already admits to separating himself from Rome. He excommunicated himself and this can be seen by his own words.

Luther was already known as the heretic by Rome from the great Cardinal Cajetan.

Are we to believe that Luther *"had somehow persuaded himself that his erroneous opinion was not contrary to the Faith"* and therefore was still Catholic?

This argument leads into Argument 25.

Pope St. Nicholas, epistle (8), *Proposueramus quidem*, 865: "... *"Neither by Augustus, nor by all the clergy, nor by religious, nor by the people will the judge be judged...* ***'The first seat will not be judged by anyone.'***"

Part 2 of Argument: No one can judge the Holy See.

Those who use this argument would accuse St. Robert Bellarmine of rejecting Pope St. Nicholas.

Since heretics cannot occupy the Holy See then no one is judging the Holy See. What is being judged is a usurper to the Holy See, a false pope or antipope.

What Pope St. Nicholas was referring to particularly were trials held to accuse a true Pope of a crime.

23. It's only the private judgment of sedevacantists concerning John XXIII through Benedict XVI, their elections, Vatican 2, etc. as they use their private interpretation of papal teachings, Scripture, and Canon law against them.

Everybody must use his private judgment. It is inescapable. However, private judgment should be based on facts and logic.

There are many antipopes in the world today. Imagine if one of their followers said, it is only a private judgment that says my pope is not true.

This would be silly.

Catholics are not puppets on a string. We are demanded to use our minds to think and make decisions. All decisions ultimately are private ones.

As Christians, it is our responsibility to judge. We all have to make judgments of some kind, whether right from wrong, truth from error, good from evil, and safe from danger. We must particularly be able to judge what is and who is or is not Christian.

Beware of evildoers...beware of bad company...etc. These require making judgments.

Christ states in Matt 7:1-5, *"Judge not, that you be not judged. [2] For with the judgment you pronounce you will be judged, and the measure you give will be the measure you get. [3] Why do you see the speck that is in your brother's eye, but do not notice the log that is in your own eye? [4] Or how can you say to your brother, 'Let me take the speck out of your eye,' when there is the log in your own eye? [5] You hypocrite, first take the log out of your own eye, and then you will see clearly to take the speck out of your brother's eye."*

Here, Christ is using hyperbole in verse 1. In other words, you will be judged in the same manner that you judge. We are going to face God's judgment. Period. He will judge and determine our reward or punishment. We cannot judge men's souls, determining where one should go. Only God can judge men on that level. We can judge men whether one is living in sin, so that we are able admonish such a person. This is an act of mercy. What Christ is saying is not to judge men as if we are without faults. Our judgments determine our judgment upon ourselves. Within the same context, Christ actually indicates that you may judge once you get yourself in the right place.

Jesus also states in Matt 7:15-20, *"Beware of false prophets, who come to you in sheep's clothing but inwardly are ravenous wolves. You will know them by their fruits...the bad tree bears evil fruit...Thus you will know them by their fruits."*

Unless, you can make judgments on men, this verse is meaningless.

You must be able to judge men to know when to beware of them.

In John 7:24, Christ says, *"Do not judge by appearances, but judge with right judgment."*

Christ was speaking about judging hypocritically in Matt 7:1 as the context shows, but here He was speaking about judging rashly.

We have to judge everything to make decisions on how to act with one another. Love requires judgment. Not to judge at all is uncharitable.

If a man is evil, he is bad willed. You can tell if a man is evil as the Bible says to judge by the fruits if the tree is good or bad.

This is Divine Revelation and it does imply that one can judge the will of man by judging him by his fruits. However, contempt is something else. We're not to have contempt with an evil man. Christ says to love them, not have contempt with them. These are two different matters.

We can't escape making judgments on men, yet we seem to have gotten it in our heads that we are not to judge men or that we do not have the authority.

However, there is a protocol to how we should treat those who refuse to follow Christ.

There is an axiom that goes like: Hate the sin, but love the sinner.

This translates to: Tolerate the sinner and treat him equally. Don't ever speak offensively or treat them as outcasts.

This, however, is not Christian at all. The following Scripture verses clearly demonstrate this.

Matt. 10:14: *"And if any one will not receive you or listen to your words, shake off the dust from your feet as you leave that house or town."*

Mark 6:11, and Luke 9:5: *"And if any place will not receive you and they refuse to hear you, when you leave, shake off the dust that is on your feet for a testimony against them."*

Matt. 18:17: *"If he refuses to listen to them, tell it to the church; and if he refuses to listen even to the church, let him be to you as a Gentile and a tax collector."*

I Cor. 16:22: *"If any one has no love for the Lord, let him be accursed. Our Lord, come!"*

Gal.1: 8-9: *"But even if we, or an angel from heaven, should preach to you a gospel contrary to that which we preached to you, let him be accursed. [9] As we have said before, so now I say again, If any one is preaching to you a gospel contrary to that which you received, let him be accursed."*

2 Pet. 2:14: *"They have eyes full of adultery, insatiable for sin. They entice unsteady souls. They have hearts trained in greed. Accursed children!"*

Gal. 3:1-3: *"O foolish (stupid) Galatians! Who has bewitched you, before whose eyes Jesus Christ was publicly portrayed as crucified? Are you so foolish? Having begun with the Spirit, are you now ending with the flesh?"*

Matt. 3:7: *"But when he saw many of the Pharisees and Sad'ducees coming for baptism, he said to them, "You brood of vipers! Who warned you to flee from the wrath to come?"*

Matt. 12:34: *"You brood of vipers! how can you speak good, when you are evil? For out of the abundance of the heart the mouth speaks."*

Matt. 23:33: *"You serpents, you brood of vipers, how are you to escape being sentenced to hell?"*

Luke 3:7: *"He said therefore to the multitudes that came out to be baptized by him, "You brood of vipers! Who warned you to flee from the wrath to come?"*

Matt. 23:27: *"Woe to you, scribes and Pharisees, hypocrites! for you are like whitewashed tombs, which outwardly appear beautiful, but within they are full of dead men's bones and all uncleanness."*

Acts. 23:3: *"Then Paul said to him, "God shall strike you, you whitewashed wall! Are you sitting to judge me according to the law, and yet contrary to the law you order me to be struck?"*

How are we to treat others according to Jesus? The same way He and his followers did.

Once a man rejects Christ and sets himself apart from the laws of God, after being warned beforehand, that man no longer has a right to be treated equally.

To give such a person that right is contrary to Christ.

When judgment concerns whether the claimant to the papacy is a true pope, the first thing that needs to be assessed is whether he is a Catholic.

The Catholic Encyclopedia, "Papal Elections," 1914, Vol. 11, p. 456: *"Of course, the election of a heretic, schismatic, or female [as Pope] would be null and void."*

The bull of Pope Paul IV would be meaningless if private judgment was out of the picture since he presumes that private judgment is how one makes the judgment to begin with.

How would the bull apply if all the cardinals and the whole Church recognized a heretic as pope? This is what the Pope implied could happen. What good is the statement in the Catholic Encyclopedia if the Catholic could not use his right judgment by rightly refusing to acknowledge such an election?

Argument 23 is patently absurd and makes a mockery out of Christ and the teaching of the entire history of Christianity.

24. Vatican 2 is not infallible and therefore, it is possible for the Church to error through this council. Vatican 2 was meant as a merely pastoral council with nothing more than a bunch of opinions that can be resisted. Unless the Pope defines a dogma on faith and morals as Pope, we as Catholics may resist or call into question all those other teachings. Even so, Vatican 2 is not heretical nor does it contradict previous teaching. There is no need to become a sedevacantist.

There are several parts to this objection but let's start with a question: What would it take for you to become a sedevacantist?

This is the question no Vatican 2 or *Novus Ordo* church member wants to answer.

The reason is three-fold.

First, nobody wants to believe that Christ left the Church without a pope for such a long time. It is such a difficult position to hold in society. The consequences are devastating to say the least. They know that by saying nothing may imply they would follow an antipope if it could be proven so and yet they realize how deadly this position would be. Fear is the bottom line.

Secondly, they know by saying they will convert if you can prove the claimant of the papacy a manifest heretic would put them on the spot of honoring their word. The fear of being put on the spot and to accept the awful position is not worth taking the chance of answering this way.

Thirdly, is the belief that the pope does not need to be Catholic. If this were the case, God would prevent the heretic pope from teaching formal heresy. Therefore, there is no convincing them of becoming a sedevacantist, because the position presents to them the problem of Christ's promise to always be with the Church, which, for these people, means always having a pope. See Objection 1.

Due to charges laid against the *Novus Ordo* pope by traditionalists, a book called *"More Catholic than the Pope"* mocks traditionalists right from the title. It tries to demonstrate how silly it is to think a lay Catholic could be more knowledgeable about Catholic theology than the Pope himself.

One funny tidbit that can be found in the book rejects the traditionalist's claim that Vatican 2 was merely a pastoral council, yet that very phrase came from Joseph Ratzinger aka Pope Benedict XVI. It would seem the writers of the book know more than their own pope, as they mock the traditionalists for quoting Ratzinger.

Joseph Ratzinger (Benedict XVI). Address to the Chilean bishops, July 13, 1988 he stated, *"the truth is that this particular Council defined no dogma at all, and deliberately chose to remain on a modest level, as a merely pastoral council..."*

Interestingly, these same *Novus Ordo* apologists claim the pope doesn't even need to be Catholic. According to this absurd argument, the title of the book could actually be true!

A heretic pope is an oxymoron.

Objection 1 revisited:

Pope Leo XIII stated in Satis Cognitum (#15), June 29, 1896, ***"Bishops Separated from Peter and his Successors Lose All Jurisdiction***: *"From this it must be clearly understood that* ***Bishops are deprived of the right and power of ruling, if they deliberately secede from Peter and his successors****; because, by this secession, they are separated from the foundation on which the whole edifice must rest.* ***They are therefore outside the edifice itself; and for this very reason they are separated from the fold,*** *whose leader is the Chief Pastor; they are exiled from that Kingdom, the keys of which were given by Christ to Peter alone...* ***No one, therefore, unless in communion with Peter can share in his authority, since it is absurd to imagine that he who is outside can command in the Church****."*

Think about this for a moment... This means all true popes must be in communion with Peter and his successors, and if they are not in communion with Peter and his successors, then they cannot share in his authority, **since it is absurd to imagine that he who is outside can command in the Church**.

Pope Pius XII never intended that a heretical or schismatic bishop could be elected pope **and remain a heretic or schismatic, because it is absurd to imagine that he who is outside the Church could command the whole Church.**

However, there is another argument for sedevacantism and it based on Matt. 16:18. If the Church did something that it dogmatically said it couldn't do then the gates of hell would prevail.

The *Novus Ordo* church has done two things that the Catholic Church has dogmatically stated that the Church cannot do.

First, the Second Vatican Council (Vatican 2) has taught heresy and blasphemy which would be impossible as will be demonstrated in a moment.

Second, the *Novus Ordo* church has given us many harmful disciplines, which the Church (5 popes) dogmatically said it couldn't do.

Because of these two things, the *Novus Ordo* church is either, not the true Catholic Church and an antipope is reigning or Christ is a liar and the gates of hell prevailed.

In a 1973 movie called *The Conflict*, a modernist priest asks a traditional priest, *"how do we begin to define heresy today?"* The traditionalist gives the answer for the modernist by stating, *"yesterday's orthodoxy is today's heresy."*

Perhaps, this is why Modernist Rome has not tried to defend itself against the sedevacantists. Throughout history, Catholic Rome always condemned heretics and schismatics with an explanation of theology. This has not been the case with sedevacantism, which claims at least 10,000 Catholics.

How can Rome condemn Catholics for holding fast to the Faith? It can't and so it ignores them with hopes they will disappear.

With this in mind, one major reason will be given why Catholics must be sedevacantists to remain Catholic to answer the last part of the objection.

The First Vatican Council (Vatican 1) stated:

[The object of faith]. Further, by divine and Catholic faith, all those things must be believed which are contained in the written word of God and in tradition, and those which are proposed by the Church, either in a solemn pronouncement or in her ordinary and universal teaching power, to be believed as divinely revealed. (Dogmatic Constitution concerning the Catholic Faith, Ch. 3, FIRST VATICAN COUNCIL, Pope Pius IX) (Denz. 1792)

Notice, that all teachings from the supreme and ordinary (not just extraordinary) Magisterial must be believed.

Pope Pius IX stated: *"And, we cannot pass over in silence the boldness of those who "not enduring sound doctrine" [II Tim. 4:3], contend that "without sin and with no loss of Catholic profession, one can withhold assent and obedience to those judgments and decrees of the Apostolic See, whose object is declared to relate to the general good of the Church and its right and discipline, provided it does not touch dogmas of faith or morals." There is no one who does not see and understand clearly and openly how opposed this is to the Catholic dogma of the plenary power divinely bestowed on the Roman Pontiff by Christ the Lord Himself of feeding, ruling, and governing the universal Church."* (Pope Pius IX *Quanta Cura* Dec 8, 1864)

"You will firmly abide by the true decision of the Holy Roman Church and to this Holy See, which does not permit errors." (Lateran Council V, Bull *'Cum postquam'* by Pope Leo X)

Pope Leo XIII, *Satis Cognitum* (# 9), June 29, 1896: *"The practice of the Church has always been the same, as is shown by the unanimous teaching of the Fathers,* ***who were wont to hold as outside Catholic communion, and alien to the Church, whoever would recede in the least degree from any point of doctrine proposed by her authoritative Magisterium."***

This statement confirms Vatican 1 that all teachings must be believed because Pope Leo says *"any point of doctrine"* which would include all doctrines of the Magisterium and not just dogmatized doctrines of the extraordinary Magisterium.

Pope Leo XIII, *Satis Cognitum* (# 9), June 29, 1896: *"...But he who dissents even in one point from divinely revealed truth absolutely rejects all faith, since he thereby refuses to honor God as the supreme truth and the formal motive of faith."*

This is a bold statement, because to reject *"one point"* of divinely revealed truth, which is, as Vatican 1 says, all teachings universal and ordinary and extraordinary magisterial teachings, is to reject *"all faith."* In other words, to reject one point of doctrine is to literally become apostate.

To answer the other part of the objection, it was stated, "Unless the pope defines a dogma on faith and morals as pope, we as Catholics may resist or call into question all those other teachings."

Is this not what all non-sedevacantist traditionalists say and believe?

Well, according to the infallible teaching of the Church, this is a lie.

Not only do Vatican 1 and Pope Leo XIII, but also Pope Pius IX in his *Syllabus of Errors* and *Quanta Cura* condemns this proposition by implication those who recognize Ratzinger as pope but rejects Vatican II and other teachings and practices.

From the Infallible/*Ex Cathedra Syllabus of Errors* of Pope Pius IX number 22: *"The obligation by which Catholic teachers and authors are strictly bound is confined to those things only which are proposed to universal belief as dogmas of faith by the infallible judgment of the Church."* -- Letter to the Archbishop of Munich, *"Tuas libenter,"* Dec. 21, 1863. CONDEMNED

and *Quanta Cura* of the same Pope:

"Nor can we pass over in silence the audacity of those who, not enduring sound doctrine, contend that "without sin and without any sacrifice of the Catholic profession assent and obedience may be refused to those judgments and decrees of the Apostolic See, whose object is declared to concern the Church's general good and her rights and discipline, so only it does not touch the dogmata of faith and morals." But no one can be found not clearly and distinctly to see and understand how grievously this is opposed to the Catholic dogma of the full power given from God by Christ our Lord Himself to the Roman Pontiff of feeding, ruling and guiding the Universal Church."

Again, this whole objection argument stems from several statements but mainly from *"Cardinal"* Joseph Ratzinger (Benedict XVI). Address to the Chilean bishops, July 13, 1988 he stated, *"the truth is that this particular Council defined no dogma at all, and deliberately chose to remain on a modest level, as a merely pastoral council..."*

Does this mean it is truly so? Does it mean Vatican 2 was meant to be nothing more than opinions put together by the world's bishops, which would have no real bearing on the faithful? Can it be resisted (rejected)?

The answer to these questions must be a resounding NO!

"Cardinal" Joseph Ratzinger (Benedict XVI), The Ratzinger Report, 1985, p. 28: *"It is likewise impossible to decide in favor of Trent and Vatican I, but against Vatican II. Whoever denies Vatican II denies the authority that upholds the other two councils and thereby detaches them from their foundation. And this applies to the so-called 'traditionalism', also in its extreme forms."*

On Jan. 12, 1966 General Audience, Paul VI said that *"... the Council gave its teaching the authority of the Supreme Ordinary Magisterium..."*

If the Council meant to give its teachings the authority of the Supreme Ordinary Magisterium, does that mean it would be merely pastoral, sub-magisterial, giving mere opinions leaving open dissent or suspended assent from its faithful?

Let's go a step further.

Paul VI in *Ecclesiam Suam* (# 30), Aug. 6, 1964 stated: *"It is precisely because the Second Vatican Council has the task of dealing once more with the doctrine de Ecclesia (of the Church) and of defining it, that it has been called the continuation and complement of the First Vatican Council."*

Paul VI, *"Papal"* Brief declaring Council Closed, Dec. 8, 1965: *"At last all which regards the holy Ecumenical Council has, with the help of God, been accomplished and all the constitutions, decrees, declarations, and votes have been approved by the deliberation of the synod and promulgated by us. Therefore, we decided to close for all intents and purposes, with our apostolic authority, this same Ecumenical Council called by our predecessor, Pope John XXIII, which opened October 11, 1962, and which was continued by us after his death. We decide moreover that all that has been established synodally is to be religiously observed by all the faithful, for the glory of God and the dignity of the Church... We have approved and established these things, decreeing that the present letters are and remain stable and valid, and are to have legal effectiveness, so that they be disseminated and obtain full and complete effect, and so that they may be fully convalidated by those whom they concern or may concern now and in the future; and so that, as it be judged and described,* ***all efforts contrary to these things by whoever or whatever authority, knowingly or in ignorance, be invalid and worthless from now on.*** *Given at Rome, at St. Peter's, under the [seal of the] ring of the fisherman, December 8... the year 1965, the third year of our Pontificate."*

So one might ask: But Paul VI said in his General Audience on Jan. 12, 1966, that Vatican II ***"had avoided proclaiming in an extraordinary manner dogmas affected by the mark of infallibility."***

This does not mean that it was somehow sub-magisterial giving mere opinions, which one could resist or reject. For Paul VI and Ratzinger have affirmed that it is the Supreme Universal and Ordinary Magisterium, which according to Vatican 1 is also to be believed as divinely revealed. Never could a Council which gave its teaching the authority of the Supreme Ordinary Magisterium be evil or harmful leading men astray and to hell.

Since it is impossible for the Church to contradict itself in solemn declarations with dogmatic teachings, Vatican 2 is not a Catholic Council nor did it come from the Catholic Church. It must be rejected for the simple observation that it teaches heresy and even blasphemy.

The next logical conclusion is John XXIII who called the council, or Paul VI who closed the council could not be true popes since true popes could not give and approve a non-Catholic council teaching heresies and blasphemies. All *"popes"* afterwards who approve of the council and promoted it could also not be true popes for as Pope Leo X said the Church does not even permit errors much less teach them.

Now that the teaching of the Catholic Church has been establish, Vatican 2 will now be shown to be a non-Catholic robber council; that it is heretical and contradicts previous teaching and all subsequent *"popes"* are imposters.

Since Vatican 2 claims to be a Catholic Ecumenical Council with the teaching authority of the supreme universal and ordinary Magisterium, only one substantial heresy is needed to demonstrate this claim to be false thus rendering Vatican 2 a non-Catholic robber council.

However, three principle and substantial heresies will be dealt with, which are clear and unambiguous. They clearly teach contrary to the historic Catholic Faith, as it will be demonstrated by comparing them to historic Catholic teaching. As a matter of fact, these heresies are so substantially contrary to the Catholic Church, they could rightly be called apostate.

The mark of holiness means that all teachings and practices are holy. The Vatican II church has teachings previously condemned with practices previously condemned as unholy. The mark of apostolicity means it comes from the Apostles, which means the particular teachings and practices that came from Vatican II did not come from the Apostles.

The three principle and substantial heresies of Vatican 2...

The First Principle Heresy is:

The true Church of Christ is not only the Catholic Church, therefore it is not one and universal.

The dogma is the Church is one in faith.

Contrary to Protestantism's understanding of the Church, the Catholic understanding was taught by Pope Leo XIII.

"4 He, who founded it, willed that it should be one. But when we consider what was actually done we find that Jesus Christ did not, in point of fact, institute a Church to embrace several communities similar in nature, but in themselves distinct, and lacking those bonds which render the Church unique and indivisible after that manner in which in the symbol of our faith we profess: 'I believe in one Church.' 'The Church in respect of its unity belongs to the category of things indivisible by nature, though heretics try to divide it into many parts...We say, therefore, that the Catholic Church is unique in its essence, in its doctrine, in its origin, and in its excellence...Furthermore, the eminence of the Church arises from its unity, as the principle of its constitution - a unity surpassing all else, and having nothing like unto it or equal to it'...

9 it is clear that God absolutely willed that there should be unity in His Church, and as it is evident what kind of unity He willed, and by means of what principle He ordained that this unity should be maintained...

15 The Divine founder decreed that the Church should be one in faith, in government, and in communion...

16 the Divine Founder of the Church willed that it should be preserved [in unity]." (*Satis Cognitum*)

Pope Pius XII repeatedly taught that *"the Mystical Body of Christ and the Roman Catholic Church are one and the same thing."* (*Mystici Corporis,* 1943, *Humani Generis,* 1950)

The new teaching of Rome from Vatican 2

***Lumen Gentium* (Dogmatic Constitution on the Church)**

Chapter 1. The Mystery of the Church

This is the one Church of Christ which in the Creed is professed as one, holy, catholic and apostolic, (12) which our Saviour, after His Resurrection, commissioned Peter to shepherd, (74) and him and the other apostles to extend and direct with authority, (75) which He erected for all ages as "the pillar and mainstay of the truth". (76) This Church constituted and organized in the world as a society, subsists in the Catholic Church, which is governed by the successor of Peter and by the Bishops in communion with him, (13*) although many elements of sanctification and of truth are found outside of its visible structure. These elements, as gifts belonging to the Church of Christ, are forces impelling toward catholic unity.*

Vatican 2 has subtly rejected the historic Catholic teaching and redefined the meaning of the Church the Christ.

In an interview with the German newspaper, *Frankfurter Allgemeine,* Ratzinger, aka Benedict XVI, stated:

"When the Council Fathers replace the word 'is,' used by Pius XII, with the word *'subsistit,'* they did so for a very precise reason. The concept expressed by *'is'* (to be) is far broader than that expressed by *'to subsist.' 'To subsist'* is a very precise way of being, that is, to be as a subject, which exists in itself. **Thus the Council Fathers meant to say: *the being of the Church as such extends much further than the Roman Catholic Church,*** but within the latter it acquires, in an incomparable way, the character of a true and proper subject."

Vatican 2 theologians confirm this meaning taught by Ratzinger.

Avery Cardinal Dulles, a member of the International Theological Commission: "**The Church of Christ is not exclusively identical to the Roman Catholic Church**. It does indeed subsist in Roman Catholicism but it is also present in varying modes and degrees in other Christian communities." *(Toward the Church of the Third Millennium: Verso la Chiesa del Terzo Millennio,* Brescia: Queriniana, 1979)

Fr. Edward Schillebeeckx, one of the main drafters of Vatican II documents, stated: "It is difficult to say that the Catholic Church is still one, Catholic, apostolic, when one says that the others (other Christian communities) are equally one, Catholic and apostolic, albeit to a lesser degree. —· at Vatican Council II, the Roman Catholic Church officially abandoned its monopoly over the Christian religion."

Walter J. Burghardt, S.J., "First, all of us who are baptized (Protestant, Catholic, Orthodox) — all of us belong in a very real way to the Church of Christ."

Fr. Gregory Baum, "Concretely and actually the Church of Christ may be realized less, equally, or even more in a Church separated from Rome than in a Church in communion with Rome. This conclusion is inescapable on the basis of the understanding of Church that emerges from the teaching of Vatican Council II." (Quotes taken from Joseph Maurer's *Open Letter to Catholic Family News*)

To say that it subsists in the Catholic Church is to also say that it subsists elsewhere such as in non-Catholic churches.

When the Faithful say in the Nicene/Constantinopian Creed: I believe in One, Holy, Catholic, and Apostolic Church, we mean the whole Church of Christ, the Catholic Church, which is united, separated from the world, universal, and from the Apostles. The Councils of Nicea and Constantinople expounded the Apostle's

Creed I believe "the Holy Catholic Church." These are articles of Faith and must be believed as the Church has always taught.

The four marks: One, Holy, Catholic, and Apostolic describe the Catholic Church.

However, Vatican 2 is saying the four marks are describing the Church of Christ, which, according to LG, only subsists in the Catholic Church. This is precisely the same thing Protestants believe that also recite the same creed.

Vatican 2 expounds on the principle that the Church of Christ only subsists in the Catholic Church:

***Lumen Gentium* Chapter 2.**

The people of God

15. *"For several reasons the Church recognizes that it is joined to those who, though baptized and so honored with the Christian name, do not profess the faith in its entirety or do not preserve communion under the successor of St. Peter."*

These statements for Vatican 2 are completely contrary to the historic Catholic Faith, which has always taught:

Pope Pius IX, *Amantissimus* (# 3), April 8, 1862: *"There are other, almost countless, proofs drawn from the most trustworthy witnesses which clearly and openly testify with great faith, exactitude, respect and obedience that all who want to belong to the true and only Church of Christ must honor and obey this Apostolic See and the Roman Pontiff."*

Pope Pius VI, *Charitas* (# 32), April 13, 1791: *"Finally, in one word, stay close to Us. For no one can be in the Church of Christ without being in unity with its visible head and founded on the See of Peter."*

Notice that the Church of Christ is the Catholic Church.

Pope Leo XIII, *Satis Cognitum* (# 13), June 29, 1896: *"Therefore if a man does not want to be, or to be called, a heretic, let him not strive to please this or that man... but let him hasten before all things to be in communion with the Roman See."*

Notice again, not to be in communion with the Roman See is to be called heretic.

What follows from these dogmatic proclamations found in *Lumen Gentium* chapters 1 and 2? According to the Vatican 2 document *Unitatis Redintegratio* the true Church of Christ is not one or united nor is it catholic or universal.

This means Vatican 2 is now denying the Articles of Faith by refusing to believe the Catholic Church is the whole true Church of Christ.

***Unitatis Redintegratio* (Decree on Ecumenism)**

Chapter 1. Catholic principles of ecumenism

1. "Yet almost all, though in different ways, long for the one visible Church of God, that truly universal Church whose mission is to convert the whole world to the gospel, so that the world may be saved, to the glory of God."

4. "Nevertheless, the divisions among Christians prevent the Church from realizing in practice the fullness of Catholicity proper to her, in those of her sons and daughters who, though attached to her by baptism, are yet separated from full communion with her. Furthermore, the Church herself finds it more difficult to express in actual life her full Catholicity in all its bearings."

The Catholic Church does not long for one visible Church of God for it alone is the one visible Church of God. The Catholic Church is does not long for that truly universal Church for it alone is the true universal church. It also is not and cannot be prevented from realizing in practice the fullness of Catholicity proper to her. What the Catholic Church longs for is for all heretical and schismatic churches to renounce their heresies and join the one true Catholic Church.

All heretics and schismatics believe themselves to be authentic Christians. Non-Catholics claiming to be Christians are not true Christians at all. Vatican 2 denies that heretics and schismatics are heretics and schismatics and now calls them separated brothers and sisters. Try to find the word heretic or schismatic anywhere in Vatican 2.

The Catholic Church teaches that heretics are the gates of Hell. See Objection 2.

Since Vatican 2 now says these heretical and schismatic churches are Christian and are separated bodies within the Church of Christ, the logical conclusion is they also possess the life of grace and the means of salvation and even build up, give life to and help the true Church of Christ to grow.

The document continues:

3. "Moreover some, and even most, of the significant elements and endowments which together go to build up and give life to the Church itself, can exist outside the visible boundaries of the Catholic Church: the written word of God; the life of grace; faith, hope and charity, with the other interior gifts of the Holy Spirit, and visible elements too."

This is directly contrary to the solemn *ex cathedra* dogmatic teaching of Pope Boniface VIII in the Bull *Unam Sanctam.*

Pope Boniface VIII, *Unam Sanctam*, Nov. 18, 1302: *"With Faith urging us we are forced to believe and to hold the one, holy, Catholic Church and that, apostolic, and we firmly believe and simply confess this Church outside of which there is no salvation nor remission of sin, the Spouse in the Canticle proclaiming: 'One is my dove, my perfect one."*

Vatican II has rejected the dogma by asserting that one can possess the life of grace, which means the remission of sins outside the Catholic Church.

Again, *UR 3. "It follows that these separated churches and communities as such, though we believe them to be deficient in some respects, have by no means been deprived of significance and importance in the mystery of salvation. For the Spirit of Christ has not refrained from using them as means of salvation whose efficacy comes from that fullness of grace and truth which has been entrusted to the Catholic Church."*

This means these other churches are good enough for salvation according to Vatican II, but the Catholic Church has taught differently.

Pope Leo XIII, *Satis Cognitum* (# 9), June 29, 1896: *"The Church alone offers to the human race that religion – that state of absolute perfection – which He wished, as it were, to be incorporated in it. And it alone supplies those means of salvation which accord with the ordinary counsels of Providence."*

Pope Pius X, *Editae saepe* (# 29), May 26, 1910: *"The Church alone possesses together with her magisterium the power of governing and sanctifying human society. Through her ministers and servants (each in his own station and office), she confers on mankind suitable and necessary means of salvation."*

Pope Eugene IV, Council of Florence, "*Cantate Domino*," 1441, *ex cathedra*: *"The Holy Roman Church firmly believes, professes and preaches that all those who are outside the Catholic Church, not only pagans but also Jews or heretics and schismatics, cannot share in eternal life and will go into the everlasting fire which was prepared for the devil and his angels, unless they are joined to the Church before the end of their lives ..."*

Pope Clement VI, *Super quibusdam*, Sept. 20, 1351: *"We ask: In the first place, whether you and the Church of the Armenians which is obedient to you, believe that all those who in baptism have received the same Catholic faith, and afterwards have withdrawn and will withdraw in the future from the communion of this same Roman Church, which one alone is Catholic, are schismatic and heretical, if they remain obstinately separated from the faith of this Roman Church."*

Pope Leo XIII, *Satis Cognitum* (# 9), June 29, 1896: *"The practice of the Church has always been the same, as is shown by the unanimous teaching of the Fathers, who were wont to hold as outside Catholic communion, and alien to the Church, whoever would recede in the least degree from any point of doctrine proposed by her authoritative magisterium."*

According to Vatican 2, since these non-Catholic heretical and schismatic churches are part of the Church of Christ, *"are a means of salvation", "live the life of grace", "build up", "give life"* and *"help grow"* the true Church, then it must follow that we treat each other equally. (Wasn't equality one on the foundations of the French Revolution?)

Unitatis Redintegratio Chapter 2. The practice of ecumenism

9. "We must get to know the outlook of our separated fellow Christians... Most valuable for this purpose are meetings of the two sides – especially for discussion of theological problems – where each side can treat with the other on an equal footing, provided that those who take part in them under the guidance of their authorities are truly competent."

This contradicts Pope Pius XI in *Mortalium Animos* (# 7), Jan. 6, 1928, speaking of heretics: *"Meanwhile they affirm that they would willingly treat with the Church of Rome, but on equal terms, that is as equals with an equal."*

Unitatis Redintegratio Chapter 3. Churches and ecclesial communities separated from the Roman apostolic see

13-15. "We now turn our attention to the two chief types of division as they affect the seamless robe of Christ. The first division occurred in the east, when the dogmatic formulas of the councils of Ephesus and Chalcedon were challenged, and later when ecclesiastical communion between the eastern patriarchates and the Roman See was dissolved... Everyone knows with what great love the Christians of the east celebrate the sacred liturgy... Hence, through the celebration of the Holy Eucharist in each of these Churches, the Church of God is built up and grows, and through concelebration their communion with one another is made manifest."

Benedict XVI, *Joint Declaration with Schismatic Patriarch Bartholomew*, Nov. 30, 2006: "This fraternal encounter which brings us together, Pope Benedict XVI of Rome and Ecumenical Patriarch Bartholomew I, is God's work, and in a certain sense his gift. We give thanks to the Author of all that is good, who allows us once again, in prayer and in dialogue, to express the joy we feel as brothers and to renew our commitment to move towards full communion. This commitment comes from the Lord's will and ***from our responsibility as Pastors in the Church of Christ***... As far as relations between the Church of Rome and the Church of Constantinople are concerned, we cannot fail to recall the solemn ecclesial act effacing the memory of the ancient anathemas which for centuries had a negative effect on our Churches." (www.zenit.org, *Zenit news report*, Nov. 30, 2006)

Common Declaration of Benedict XVI with Orthodox "H.B." Chrysostomos II, June 16, 2007: "We, Benedict XVI, Pope and Bishop of Rome, and Chrysostomos II, Archbishop of Nea Justiniana and All Cyprus... we assure our faithful of our fervent prayers as ***Pastors in the Church***... "

Benedict XVI, *letter to schismatic "Orthodox" Romanian Patriarchate*, published August 2, 2007: "In conveying my closeness in prayer at this time of grief, I also wish to express my earnest good wishes for you and your brother Bishops as ***you guide the Church*** in this time of transition."

Ratzinger was echoing Paul VI who addressed in a telegram to the newly elected Patriarch of Constantinople: "At the moment when you assume a heavy ***charge in the service of the Church of Christ...*** (*L'Osservatore Romano,* July 27, 1972, p. 12)

Obviously, the popes of Vatican 2 teach that *"subsists"* consists of determining that non-Catholics and other religions are at least partially in the Church. Benedict XVI and Paul VI referred to non-Catholic Patriarchs as *"Pastors in the Church of Christ"* and referred to their schismatic churches as being part of the Church of Christ. For the popes of Vatican 2, the Church is not one in faith.

The Second Principle Heresy is:

The rejection of Christ is not a rejection of the one true God.

Lumen Gentium **(Dogmatic Constitution on the Church)**

Lumen Gentium Chapter 2. The people of God

16. "But the plan of salvation also embraces those who acknowledge the Creator, and among these the Muslims are first; they profess to hold the faith of Abraham and along with us they worship the one merciful God who will judge mankind on the last day."

This statement is saying by implication that the rejection of Christ is not a rejection of the one true God.

Pope St. Damasus I, Council of Rome, Can. 15: *"If anyone does not say that he (Jesus Christ)...will come to judge the living and the dead, he is a heretic."*

Nostra aetate **(Declaration on the church's relation to non-Christian religions)**

3. "The Church also looks upon Muslims with respect. They worship the one God living and subsistent, merciful and mighty, creator of heaven and earth, who has spoken to humanity and to whose decrees, even the hidden ones, they seek to submit themselves whole-heartedly, just as Abraham, to whom the Islamic faith readily relates itself, submitted to God...Hence they have regard for the moral life and worship God in prayer, almsgiving and fasting."

These are the most ridiculous statements of all because there is no way one can defend them logically. It doesn't matter what the claim Muslims hold to profess, but what they actually profess. They reject Christ and the Trinity and therefore do not *"actually"* hold to the faith of Abraham. They reject the same God we worship.

St. John in chapter 8 writes about Jesus condemning those who claim to hold the faith of Abraham. Jesus says their father is the devil because they do not believe the truth of the Gospel. The Muslims reject the Gospels which means they are in the same boat as the Jews whom Christ condemns.

As a matter of fact, this statement of Vatican 2 is the doctrine of antichrist. St. John says anyone who denies that Jesus is the Christ is the antichrist and there are many of them. Muslims deny Jesus as God and Messiah, which means they are all antichrists and now Vatican II is supporting this position. This means Vatican II is the council of the antichrist and this heresy is one of if not the single worse heresy of all.

Here is what three popes had to say:

Pope Eugene IV, Council of Basel, Session 19, Sept. 7, 1434: *"Moreover, we trust that with God's help another benefit will accrue to the Christian commonwealth; because from this union, once it is established, there is hope that very many from the abominable sect of Mahomet will be converted to the Catholic faith."*

Pope Clement V, Council of Vienne, 1311-1312: *"It is an insult to the holy name and a disgrace to the Christian faith that in certain parts of the world subject to Christian princes where Saracens (i.e., The followers of Islam, also called Muslims) live, sometimes apart, sometimes intermingled with Christians, the Saracen priests, commonly called Zabazala, in their temples or mosques, in which the Saracens meet to adore the infidel Mahomet, loudly invoke and extol his name each day at certain hours from a high place... This brings disrepute on our faith and gives great scandal to the faithful. These practices cannot be tolerated without displeasing the divine majesty. We therefore, with the sacred council's approval, strictly forbid such practices henceforth in Christian lands. We enjoin on Catholic princes, one and all. They are to forbid expressly the public invocation of the sacrilegious name of Mahomet... Those who presume to act otherwise are to be so chastised by the princes for their irreverence, that others may be deterred from such boldness."*

Pope Benedict XIV, *Quod Provinciale,* Aug. 1, 1754: *"The Provincial Council of your province of Albania... decreed most solemnly in its third canon, among other matters, as you know, that Turkish or Mohammedan names should not be given either to children or adults in baptism... This should not be hard for any one of you, venerable brothers, for none of the schismatics and heretics has been rash enough to take a Mohammedan name, and unless your justice abounds more than theirs, you shall not enter the kingdom of God."*

Vatican 2 officially rejects all of these papal statements and now says men can reject Christ as God and at the same time believing and worshiping the one true God.

This is outrageous blasphemy!

Pope St. Gregory VII is often brought up in defense of Vatican 2 because he wrote to a Muslim King stating, *"This affection we and you owe to each other in a more peculiar way than to people of other races because we worship and confess the same God though in diverse forms and daily praise and adore Him as the creator and ruler of this world."* Was Pope St. Gregory a heretic, too? Was the Church that canonized him not the Catholic Church?

Those that use this argument never really think about it. The problem with this defense is that Pope Gregory didn't know exactly what the Muslims believed since the Koran wasn't in a language that the pope could read. The Koran rejects and blasphemes the Holy Trinity. How can a Muslim believe and do such a thing and yet, still worship Him in love and adoration?

The Third Principle Heresy is:

Man has the right to be wrong.

***Dignitatis Humanae* (Declaration of religious freedom)**

2. "This Vatican synod declares that the human person has a right to religious freedom. Such freedom consists in this, that all should have such immunity from coercion by individuals, or by groups, or by any human power, that no one should be force to act against his conscience in religious matters, nor prevented from acting according to his conscience, whether in private or in public, within due limits."

2. "Therefore this right to non-interference persists even in those who do not carry out their obligations of seeking the truth and standing by it; and the exercise of this right should not be curtailed, as long as due public order is preserved."

This heresy is the result of all the rest and is the synthesis of all the others. It declared man has a 'right' to be wrong. It clearly contradicts the infallible *Syllabus of Errors.*

Pope Pius IX, *Syllabus of Errors*, Dec. 8, 1864, # 77: "In this age of ours it is no longer expedient that the Catholic religion should be the only religion of the state, to the exclusion of all other cults whatsoever." – Condemned.

78: *"Hence in certain regions of Catholic name, it has been laudably sanctioned by law that men immigrating there be allowed to have public exercises of any form of worship of their own." – Condemned.*

55: *"The Church is to be separated from the state, and the state from the Church." – Condemned.*

In defense of this teaching, *Novus Ordo* apologists use two strategies: The first is: "There is no real contradiction. Vatican 2 is not saying that people should have the *"right to error"* but the right to worship God."

The second is: *"Vatican 2 was not saying men have the moral right, but the civil right, especially now when there are no longer Catholic states."*

However, both arguments severely miss the point.

Sure we all have a right to worship God, but Vatican 2 is saying everybody has a *"right"* to worship any god they want to or falsely worship the true God in the public arena. Therefore, it is saying men have a 'right' to error, making it a contradiction.

It does not matter if the government is non-Catholic or pagan. It would be inexcusable to say Satanism is a *"right."*

The *Syllabus of Errors* is infallible which means it cannot be altered in light of some condition such as false governments, and he *Syllabus* was not using some conditions or limits as a condition for it to apply only to Christian states.

The *Novus Ordo* apologists will emphasize the documents wording that people cannot be coerced to follow or reject a particular religion because it is contrary to man's nature as being free.

However, the emphasis is not just that people cannot be coerced into a religion, but that erroneous actions cannot be prevented in public. Vatican 2 completely contradicts the historic Catholic teaching on this point. Again, DH 2 states: *"in religious matters, nor prevented from acting according to his conscience, whether in private or in public... the exercise of this right should not be curtailed..."*

Then we have *Dignitatis Humanae # 4: "In addition, religious communities are entitled to teach and give witness to their faith publicly in speech and writing without hindrance."*

This clearly contradicts: Pope Gregory XVI, *Mirari Vos* (# 15), Aug. 15, 1832: *"Here We must include that harmful and never sufficiently denounced freedom to publish any writings whatever and disseminate them to the people, which some dare to demand and promote with so great a clamor. We are horrified to see what monstrous doctrines and prodigious errors are disseminated far and wide in countless books, pamphlets, and other writings which, though small in weight, are very great in malice."*

Pope Leo XIII, *Libertas* (# 42), June 20, 1888: *"From what has been said it follows that it is quite unlawful to demand, to defend, or to grant unconditional freedom of thought, of speech, or writing, or of worship, as if these were so many rights given by nature of man."*

Pope Leo XIII, *Immortale Dei* (# 34), Nov. 1, 1885: *"Thus, Gregory XVI in his encyclical letter Mirari Vos, dated August 15, 1832, inveighed with weighty words against the sophisms which even at his time were being publicly inculcated – namely, that no preference should be shown for any particular form of worship; that it is right for individuals to form their own personal judgments about religion; that each man's conscience is his sole and all-sufficing guide; and that it is lawful for every man to publish his own views, whatever they may be, and even to conspire against the state."*

Pope Pius IX, *Quanta Cura* (#'s 3-6), Dec. 8, 1864, *"From which totally false idea of social government they do not fear to foster that erroneous opinion, most fatal in its effects on the Catholic Church and the salvation of souls, called by Our predecessor, Gregory XVI, an insanity, namely, that 'liberty of conscience and worship is each man's personal right, which ought to be legally proclaimed and asserted in every rightly constituted society; and that a right resides in the citizens to an absolute liberty, which should be restrained by no authority whether ecclesiastical or civil, whereby they may be able openly and publicly to manifest and declare any of their ideas whatever, either by word of mouth, by the press, or in any other way. but while they rashly affirm this, they do not understand and note that they are preaching liberty of perdition... therefore, by our apostolic authority, we reprobate, proscribe, and condemn all the singular and evil opinions and doctrines specially mentioned in this letter, and will and command that they be thoroughly held by all the children of the catholic church as reprobated, proscribed and condemned."*

It is true that people should not be coerced but this is not the problem. Since the Catholic Church has solemnly declared that only the Catholic Church is keeping to true worship, then worshiping God in some other way, or worshiping false gods, and freely speaking and writing about it is not only error but serious error that will lead people to hell. Vatican 2 is advocating that man has a right to these errors.

John Paul I most clearly saw it when he stated, *"the Church had always taught that only the truth had rights, but now the Council made it clear that error also has rights."* (Time Magazine)

John Paul I voted at Vatican 2 knowing full well what Vatican 2 meant.

Finally, this heresy is blatantly contrary to the Papal Bull against Martin Luther.

33. That heretics be burned is against the will of the Spirit. CONDEMNED as error of Martin Luther in Bull Exsurge Domine **June 15, 1520 by Pope Leo X**

According to Vatican 2, it is contrary to the Spirit to burn heretics, since man has a "right" to his own religion, and the state could not burn him for simply being a heretic.

Vatican 2 agrees with the apostate Martin Luther and rejects Pope Leo X.

This heresy of Vatican 2 alone clearly demonstrates the rejection of official and infallible teachings of the Catholic Church and must be rejected as anti-catholic as with all her *"popes."*

The articles of the Apostles' Creed, which Vatican 2 redefined against the historic Catholic understanding is a condemned error of modernists.

Pope St. Pius X: ***62. The principal articles of the Apostles' Creed did not have the same meaning for the Christians of the earliest times as they have for the Christians of our time. CONDEMNED*** **as an error of the Modernists, by Pope St. Pius X in** ***Lamentabili,*** **July 3, 1907**

Vatican 2 new understanding of the sacred dogmas of the Creed also falls under the condemnation of Vatican 1, which stated:

Vatican 1, Session 3, April 24, 1870 Chapter 4 *"On Faith and Reason" For the doctrine of the faith which God has revealed is put forward not as some philosophical discovery capable of being perfected by human intelligence, but as a divine deposit committed to the spouse of Christ to be faithfully protected and infallibly promulgated. Hence, too, that meaning of the sacred dogmas is ever to be maintained which has once been declared by holy mother church, and there must never be any abandonment of this sense under the pretext or in the name of a more profound understanding. May understanding, knowledge and wisdom increase as ages and centuries roll along, and greatly and vigorously flourish, in each and all, in the individual and the whole church: but this only in its own proper kind, that is to say, in the same doctrine, the same sense, and the same understanding."*

The demonstrations of these heresies of Vatican II reflect the modernism of the modernist John XXIII and Paul VI who said in his general audience on July 2, 1969, *"If the world changes, should not religion also change? It is for this very reason that the Church has, especially after the 2nd Vatican Council, undertaken so many forms."*

Yet Pope St. Pius X stated: *53. The organic constitution of the Church is not immutable; but Christian society, just as human society, is subject to perpetual evolution. CONDEMNED* as an error of the Modernists, by Pope St. Pius X in *Lamentabili*, July 3, 1907

The purpose of Vatican 2 was to change the organic constitution of the Church to fit modern society.

All of the Vatican 2 popes refused to take the oath against modernism, which states:

The *Oath Against the Errors of Modernism* by Pope St. Pius X, Sept. 1, 1910:

"I....firmly embrace and accept all and everything that has been defined, affirmed, and declared by the unerring magisterium of the Church. ...I reject the heretical invention of the evolution of dogmas, passing from one meaning to another... I disapprove the error of those who affirm that the faith proposed by the Church can be in conflict with history, and that Catholic dogmas, in the sense in which they are now understood, cannot be reconciled with the more authentic origins of the Catholic religion"

What does this tell you?

The new 1992 Catechism of the Catholic Church does not reference any of St. Pius X writings that solemnly condemn modernism. The greatest pope in the last 500 years and his greatest achievement is completely rejected by the new modernist religion of Rome.

Pope St. Pius X said modernism was the synthesis of all heresies, which would mean that modernists are the synthesis of all heretics.

Again, if you believe Benedict XVI is the pope...

You must believe the Church rejected her history by now acknowledging that man's 'right' to be wrong, that non-Catholic churches are a means of salvation and heretics and schismatics help the true Church grow, that those, like Muslims, who reject Christ as God still worship the same God as Catholics despite the fact that Christ Himself said the contrary, and that the Catholic Church is joined to those who reject her.

You cannot even say anything is wrong with the *"Protestant" Novus Ordo* mass and yet, the very mock pope Ratzinger said in his autobiography that something was wrong with it.

You must either become a Modernist/New Ager, which is now called Catholic by the world or be a true Catholic who's only possible position is sedevacantism.

There is no other choice.

Rome has completely apostatized, just as many saints, fathers, and popes prophesied.

If you see the truth as it has just been presented and the bottom line comes down to the terrible prospect that Christ has indeed left the Church without a pope for 50 years keeping you from accepting the position of sedevacantism, think about the alternative. Would Christ leave us with a Church with 5 modernist satanic popes who reject the Catholic Faith leading the entire Church to hell for the past 50 years with its Protestant *Novus Ordo* mass and blasphemous heresies?

Are you going to ignore all of it and say it's impossible? Pretend it's not so and call sedevacantists whackos? Continue down the path of ignorance, which can no longer be considered invincible?

In other words, be a man of bad will?

Will you accept the position of sedevacantism but continue to go to mass in union with apostate Rome, which is not really sedevacantism at all?

Again, what would it take for you to become a sedevacantist?

Examples of practices of the Vatican II church and how they are condemned:

The Vatican II church practices:

Altar girls, female lectors, and female acolytes as in ministers of the Eucharist

Condemned by:

Pope Benedict XIV, *Encyclical,* July 26, 1755 *Allatae Sunt:*

Women Assisting at Mass

Pope Gelasius in his ninth letter (chap. 26) to the bishops of Lucania condemned the evil practice which had been introduced of women serving the priest at the celebration of Mass. Since this abuse had spread to the Greeks, Innocent IV strictly forbade it in his letter to the bishop of Tusculum: "Women should not dare to serve at the altar; they should be altogether refused this ministry." We too have forbidden this practice in the same words in Our oft-repeated constitution *Etsi Pastoralis*, sect. 6, no. 21.

Pope Gelasius stated, "We have heard with sorrow of the great contempt [*mépris*] with which the sacred mysteries have been treated. It has reached the point where women have been encouraged to serve at the altar, and to carry out roles that are not suited to their sex, having been assigned exclusively to those of masculine gender."

And

St. Paul and the Holy Spirit in the First Letter to the Corinthians 14:33-36 and the First Letter to Timothy 2:8-15.

And

Never practiced for the entire history of the Church until Rome allowed it 1970. Why? It is contrary to both the Divine and Church laws.

25. There needs to be a declaration of excommunication to recognize them as excommunicated. Only a future pope can make that declaration.

A reoccurring argument that keeps popping up is: *"We don't have the authority to judge whether a "pope" is a true pope. Only a future pope can make that judgment."*

This argument has a three-fold problem.

First, it is an illogical argument.

Secondly, there is no Church doctrine that says such a thing precisely because it is illogical.

If the current pope is an antipope and his teachings are heretical or has harmful practices, then one must hold to the heresies or bad practices until the next pope says otherwise. This would mean the system of the papacy would be flawed since you would HAVE to be in error until some future moment. You have no real ground for your beliefs. It is only an illusion.

Let's say the current pope is an antipope. Some of his official teachings from Vatican 2 are heretical and some of the laws and disciplines, including sacraments, that have been issued since the 1960's are evil, harmful, and even invalid. The Catholic Church has already declared that She cannot issue problematic sacraments. If the people believe the current pope is a true pope, they would be bound to accept the evil, harmful and invalid sacraments, and would have to follow those evil and harmful laws, etc. If they believe or suspect that something is wrong, but hold fast to the belief that they can do nothing until a future pope fixes things, they would be obligated to follow the antipope.

Let's say the next pope (Pope X) declares the last five claimants to the papacy antipopes. He condemns Vatican 2, the new mass, and declares the new rite of orders invalid. This means many, if not all, of the teachings for the past fifty years would be declared invalid. All priests and bishops ordained in the new rite for the past forty years would be considered invalid and would have to be reordained or consecrated. All the past annulments and remarriages would be declared invalid. So on and so forth. Many people will think something is wrong with Pope X, but will say only a future pope can decide on his fate, and so they wait. Pope X reigns for twenty years and dies.

Pope Y gets elected and says Pope X was a heretic for rejecting Vatican 2, and the mass, sacraments, etc. and therefore excommunicates Pope X and declares all his teachings for the past twenty years worthless or wrong. Everything goes back to way things were before Pope X. Pope Y reigns for twenty years and dies.

Pope Z gets elected and says Pope Y was one of the heretics that came out of Vatican 2 and therefore he was an antipope, and Pope X was a true pope. The Church would have to flip-flop again and reject the whole Vatican 2 way of things again. This means the last ninety years had been nothing but a complete mess with no end in sight. The process could be endless, and you would never know for sure what you should believe.

One's faith would only be as good as the so-called pope that reigns at that time. A Catholic could never be sure if a true pope is reigning or not. It would be impossible to defend a Church teaching, because there would be no ground for the current papacy. This means the system of the papacy would be flawed since one would HAVE to be in error until some future moment. It would all be just an illusion. Being Catholic would be reduced down to an absurdity. One might argue that this scenario would never happen. Nevertheless, this principle behind their argument is present, and so the absurdity remains.

Christ built His Church on a rock. The position that only a future pope can decide about whether a current pope is valid is not a position with a rock foundation. It has no foundation. It's illogical, and contrary to Scripture. Our faith should be placed in Christ and His promise. While the papacy is an important part of the Faith, it is to be understood correctly in light of Tradition, the Fathers of the Church, and the laws and teachings of the Church.

Thirdly, the only-a-future-pope-can-decide argument is impractical, especially for the current situation.

If one had some doubt about whether the last five claimants have been true popes and are waiting because they believe that they're in no position to judge, they might be waiting for a very long time. It's been fifty years and it hasn't happened yet. See Objection 12. Only the cardinals that were handpicked by the last four claimants will do the electing. They all believe in the same heresies, laws, etc. as the last four claimants and only they will be elected to the papacy. In other words, the modernist conciliar popes have rigged the system to keep the same type of heretics and apostates in office. In fact, no orthodox cardinal exists. The new religion of Rome has been completely established. Therefore, all hope is gone for those waiting for a future pope from this new religion to fix things back. You don't fix a new religion back to an old one, anyway. That's the concept of Protestantism.

Also, you can have no doubt about whether a pope is true or not. He doesn't get the benefit of the doubt for precisely the reason provided in Objection 12. Also, a doubtful pope would lead the faithful to doubt everything he does as pope. What good would that do?

Based on the current situation with the Catholic Church, it would appear that we are in the time of the Great Apostasy foretold in Holy Scripture.

Those who are determined to hold to the personal and non-existent dogma that only-a-future-pope-can-decide argument HAVE LOCKED themselves in the Great Apostasy because they refuse to see the obvious. They must accept evil practices and blasphemous heresies until they die or until the Second Coming, whichever comes first, because they can't break free from the confines of their own minds and hearts fixated on a lie.

For the position 'that only future pope to decide' to be held in this day and age is that you must follow the current laws, which means only the cardinals that were handpicked by the last 4 claimants will do the electing. They all believe in the same heresies (maybe more) of the last 4 claimants and only they will be elected.

They have rigged the system to keep the same type of heretics and apostates in office. In fact, no orthodox cardinal exists and so you have a clear sign that their new religion has been completed. It is totally a new religious sect.

The only way out is to abandon the illogical and impractical position and realize that a heretic can't be pope since one can't be the head of the Church of which he is not a member. A true pope loses his office automatically without any further declaration. This is the universal position of the popes and saints. Therefore, one must be able to judge for himself.

Everybody must use his private judgment. It's inescapable. However, private judgment should be based on facts and logic. If you couldn't make private judgments on who claims to be pope, you would have been obligated to follow several antipopes in history, such as Anacletus II. He was an antipope and most of the cardinals recognized him. Benedict X was an antipope and reigned for nine months. It would have taken Catholics to use their private judgment to reject them. See Objection 23.

Christ built His Church on a rock and the unanimous consent of the fathers on Matt 16:18 is that the rock is Peter and his faith. The Office of the Papacy can only be occupied by one like

Peter, a man with the Faith whom you must be able to recognize. It's that simple.

The Popes are the Gates of the Church according to Pope Leo XIII. The Gates of Hell are heresies and heretics according to Popes Vigilius and Leo IX. Therefore, the Gates of the Church can't also be the Gates of Hell or else Christ's promise is broken and the Church of Christ becomes Hell.

Not knowing, not recognizing, or not believing that a contradiction is a contradiction and living in it would be Hell for sure.

Christ's Church doesn't contradict itself. It's not an illusion. It's not illogical. It's not impractical. It's perfect, indefectible, and infallible because it's built by Christ on a rock!

Notre Dame's theologian Fr. Richard McBrien rejects the existence of the devil. Does this mean he is still a Catholic and member of the Catholic Church until he is declared a heretic? According to argument 25, this is precisely the case.

Those who are determined to hold to this argument HAVE LOCKED themselves in the great apostasy and refuse to see the obvious. They must accept evil practices and blasphemous heresies until they die or the Second Coming and lose their souls in the end, because they can't get out with their illogical position.

26. The Church cannot exist such a long time without a pope.

This is only an opinion and erroneous since the Church has now existed over 50 years without a pope.

The longest interregnum before was three and half years between the death of Marcellinus in 304 and the election of Marcellus I in 308. The Church remained visible despite the fact there was no pope for such a long time. However, when there are antipopes and only a few Catholics can recognize just who is the true pope, the condition can be far worse than when there are long interregnums.

Fr O'Reilly was an eminent theologian who wrote this particular piece after Vatican 1 and was not censored but was praised. This is what he wrote about the Great Western Schism and how it might apply in the future:

> *"We may here stop to inquire what is to be said of the position, at that time, of the three claimants, and their rights with regard to the Papacy. In the first place, there was all through, from the death of Gregory XI in 1378, a Pope – with the exception, of course, of the intervals between deaths and elections to fill up the vacancies thereby created. There was, I say, at every given time a Pope, really invested with the dignity of the Vicar of Christ and Head of the Church, whatever opinions might exist among many as to his genuineness;* ***not that an interregnum covering the whole period would have been impossible or inconsistent with the promises of Christ, for this is by no means manifest****, but that, as a matter of fact, there was not such an interregnum."* (Fr. Edmund James O'Reilly, *The Relations of the Church to Society – Theological Essays, 1882)*

Though Fr. O'Reilly was not a Pope or a Doctor of the Church, the following should demonstrate that he was one of the most eminent theologians of the 19th Century:

> *"Cardinal Cullen, then Bishop of Armagh, chose him [Fr. O'Reilly] as his theologian at the Synod of Thurles in 1850. Dr. Brown, bishop of Shrewsbury, chose him as his theologian at the Synod of Shrewsbury. Dr. Furlong, bishop of Ferns and his former colleague as professor of theology at Maynooth, chose him as his theologian at the Synod of Maynooth. He was named professor of theology at the Catholic University in Dublin on its foundation. The General of the Society of Jesus, Fr. Beckx, proposed to appoint him professor of theology at the Roman College in Rome... At a conference held regarding the philosophical and*

theological studies in the Society of Jesus, he was chosen to represent all the English-speaking 'provinces' of the Society – that is, Ireland, England, Maryland, and other divisions of the United States. In short, Father O' Reilly was widely recognized as one of the most erudite and important theologians of his time."

In fact, on page 287 of his book, Fr. O'Reilly gives this prophetic warning:

"The great schism of the West suggests to me a reflection which I take the liberty of expressing here. If this schism had not occurred, the hypothesis of such a thing happening would appear to many chimerical [absurd]. They would say it could not be; God would not permit the Church to come into so unhappy a situation. Heresies might spring up and spread and last painfully long, through the fault and to the perdition of their authors and abettors, to the great distress too of the faithful, increased by actual persecution in many places where the heretics were dominant. But that the true Church should remain between thirty and forty years without a thoroughly ascertained Head, and representative of Christ on earth, this would not be. Yet it has been; and we have no guarantee that it will not be again, though we may fervently hope otherwise. What I would infer is, that we must not be too ready to pronounce on what God may permit. We know with absolute certainty that He will fulfill His promises... We may also trust that He will do a great deal more than what He has bound Himself by his promises. We may look forward with cheering probability to exemption for the future from some of the trouble and misfortunes that have befallen in the past. But we, or our successors in the future generations of Christians, shall perhaps see stranger evils than have yet been experienced, even before the immediate approach of that great winding up of all things on earth that will precede the day of judgment. I am not setting up for a prophet, nor pretending to see unhappy wonders, of which I have no knowledge whatever. All I mean to convey

is that contingencies regarding the Church, not excluded by the Divine promises, cannot be regarded as practically impossible, just because they would be terrible and distressing in a very high degree."

This is teaching is confirmed by Rev. M. P. Hill, S.J.: *"If during the entire schism (nearly 40 years) there had been no Pope at all—that would not prove that the office and authority of Peter was not transmitted to the next Pope duly elected."* (*The Catholic's Ready Answer* [1915], Rev. M. P. Hill, S.J)

However, Fr O'Reilly at Vatican I told the faithful how Vatican I should be interpreted and he clearly says that we could go 40 plus years without a pope. He was praised in Rome for saying it. Thus, sedevacantists have the correct interpretation of Vatican I and everything is else is heresy or plain silly.

TRY TO FOLLOW THIS LOGIC....

A doubtful pope cannot be a true pope. See Objection 12.

In light of this teaching, it makes sense since a doubtful pope would lead to doubtful cardinals, which in turn would lead to more doubtful popes through doubtful elections.

Now, can the church be without a pope for 50 years?

It has before!

DURING THE GREAT SCHISM WHICH LASTED FROM 1378 TILL 1429....51 YEARS!

During that time, it was impossible for the church to tell who the true pope was, therefore, making all of them at best doubtful which makes all of them null and void!

In my book "Papal Anomalies and their Implications" I cover this event in detail and prove that the Church can go 50 years without a pope since it has done so before practically speaking.

27. Sedevacantism is not the best solution to the problem. St. Robert Bellarmine taught that Catholics may resist the pope.

Instead of dealing with the problem head on and in truth because it would give the (appearance of chaos), some Vatican 2 apologists think by staying in the Church of heretics (which they believe is the visible church) they will win over the heretics to the point of claiming back what they want which is the Catholic Church.

This democratic style of acting is what got them into trouble to begin with. This is Masonry at its best and was adopted in full at the Second Vatican Council. It is how America operates and is part of the New World Order. It is not Catholic at all. Catholicism remains faithful to the faithful and operates from the top down.

Part 1 of Argument: St. Robert Bellarmine taught resistance.

One of the quotes from St. Robert Bellarmine used to say one could resist papal teachings comes from his writing known as *De Romano Pontifice.*

> *"Just as it is licit to resist the Pontiff who attacks the body, so also is it licit to resist him who attacks souls or destroys the civil order or above all, tries to destroy the Church. I say that it is licit to resist him by not doing what he orders and by impeding the execution of his will. It is not licit, however, to judge him, to punish him, or to depose him, for these are acts proper to a superior. (De Romano Pontifice. II.29)*

This group of so-called Traditional Catholics also uses a statement by the late great theologian Suarez. Incidentally, the statement came 100 years before *Auctorem Fidei.* This document by Pope Pius VI solemnly declared that which Suarez suggests is completely impossible therefore his statement cannot be used to begin with, not to mention the fact that it also falls under the same category as Suarez's statement.

The problem with using the above St. Robert Bellarmine quote for the *"Resistance"* is it is taken completely out of context.

St. Robert Bellarmine is responding to 9 arguments used to defend the positions that the pope is subject to civil authorities and ecumenical councils.

> *"Argument 7. Any person is permitted to kill the pope if he is unjustly attacked by him. Therefore, even more so is it permitted for kings or a council to depose the pope if he disturbs the state, or if he tries to kill souls by his bad example."*

St. Bellarmine (in the context from the previous quote) answers: *"I respond by denying the second part of the argument. For to resist an attacker and defend one's self, no authority is needed, nor is it necessary that he who is attacked be the judge and superior of him who attacks. Authority is required, however, to judge and punish...Just as it is licit to resist the Pontiff who attacks the body, so also is it licit to resist him who attacks souls or destroys the civil order or above all, tries to destroy the Church. I say that it is licit to resist him by not doing what he orders and by impeding the execution of his will. It is not licit, however, to judge him, to punish him, or to depose him, for these are acts proper to a superior." (De Romano Pontifice. II.29)*

Again, look at the argument. Is St. Bellarmine saying one can resist the pope on teachings or disciplines or laws he lays out for the Church?

Absolutely not!

St. Bellarmine is referring to legitimate actions one may take if a pope were to act against the civil and political order or attacks souls. Civil authorities cannot legitimately depose such a pope but can resist him. That's all.

A pope could attempt to destroy the church *"if he tries to kill souls by his bad example"* but this quote has nothing whatsoever to do with resisting disciplines, practices (such as in the liturgy), and doctrines. Never did the saint and doctor ever speak to such things.

St. Bellarmine couldn't possibly be referring to doctrines, disciplines, or laws because in the following chapter in the very same writing St. Bellarmine states as a matter-of-factly that a pope can become a heretic and if he does then he would automatically lose his office. This means that a pope cannot destroy the church by giving us false doctrines, disciplines, etc because he would not be pope if held to false teachings that would destroy the church.

Again in full context (emphasis mine), St. Robert Bellarmine in *De Romano Pontifice* 30: *"The fourth opinion is that of Cajetan, for whom (de auctor. papae et con., cap. 20 et 21) the manifestly heretical Pope is not "ipso facto" deposed, but can and must be deposed by the Church. To my judgment, this opinion cannot be defended. For, in the first place, it is proven with arguments from authority and from reason that the manifest heretic is "ipso facto" deposed. The argument from authority is based on St. Paul (Titus, c. 3), who orders that the heretic be avoided after two warnings, that is, after showing himself to be manifestly obstinate - which means before any excommunication or judicial sentence. And this is what St. Jerome writes, adding that the other sinners are excluded from the Church by sentence of excommunication, but the heretics exile themselves and separate themselves by their own act from the body of Christ. Now, a Pope who remains Pope cannot be avoided, for how could we be required to avoid our own head? How can we separate ourselves from a member united to us?*

This principle is most certain. The non-Christian cannot in any way be Pope, as Cajetan himself admits (ib. c. 26). The reason for this is that he cannot be head of what he is not a member; now he who is not a Christian is not a member of the Church, and a manifest heretic is not a Christian, as is clearly taught by St. Cyprian (lib. 4, epist. 2), St. Athanasius (Scr. 2 cont. Arian.), St. Augustine (lib. de great. Christ. cap. 20), St. Jerome (contra Lucifer.) and others; therefore the manifest heretic cannot be Pope.

To this Cajetan responds (in Apol. pro tract. praedicto cap. 25 et in ipso tract. cap. 22) that the heretic is not a Christian "simpliciter" [i.e. without qualification, or absolutely], but is one "secundum quid" [i.e. in a qualified or relative sense]. For, granted that two things constitute the Christian - the faith and the [baptismal] character - the heretic, having lost the faith, is still in some way united to the Church and is capable of jurisdiction; therefore, he is also Pope, but ought to be removed, since he is disposed, with ultimate disposition, to cease to be Pope: as the man who is still not dead but is "in extremis" [at the point of death].

Against this: in the first place, if the heretic remained, "in actu" [actually], united to the Church in virtue of the character, he would never be able to be cut or separated from her "in actu", for the character is indelible. But there is no one who denies that some people may be separated "in actu" from the Church. Therefore, the character does not make the heretic be "in actu" in the Church, but is only a sign that he was in the Church and that he must return to her. Analogously, when a sheep wanders lost in the mountains, the mark impressed on it does not make it be in the fold, but indicates from which fold it had fled and to which fold it ought to be brought back. This truth has a confirmation in St. Thomas who says (Summ. Theol. III, q. 8, a. 3) that those who do not have the faith are not united "in actu" to Christ, but only potentially - and St. Thomas here refers to the internal union, and not to the external which is produced by the confession of faith and visible signs. Therefore, as the character is something internal, and not external, according to St. Thomas the character alone does not unite a man, "in actu," to Christ.

Further against the argument of Cajetan: either faith is a disposition necessary "simpliciter" for someone to be Pope, or it is only necessary for someone to be a good Pope ["ad bene esse," to exist well, to be good, as opposed to simply existing]. In the first hypothesis, in case this disposition be eliminated by the contrary disposition, which is heresy, the Pope immediately ceases to be Pope: for the form cannot maintain itself without the necessary dispositions. In the second hypothesis, the Pope cannot be deposed by reason of heresy, for otherwise he would also have to be deposed for ignorance, immorality, and other similar causes, which impede the knowledge, the morality, and the other dispositions necessary for him to be a good Pope ("ad bene esse papae"). In addition to this, Cajetan recognises (tract. praed., ca. 26) that the Pope cannot be deposed for the lack of dispositions necessary, not "simpliciter", but only "ad bene esse.

To this, Cajetan responds that faith is a disposition necessary "simpliciter", but partial, and not total; and that, therefore, even if his faith disappears he can still continue being Pope, by reason of the other part of the disposition, the character, which still endures.

Against this argument: either the total disposition, constituted by the character and by faith, is necessary "simpliciter," or it is not, the partial disposition then being sufficient. In the first hypothesis, the faith disappearing there no longer remains the disposition "simpliciter" necessary, for the disposition "simpliciter" necessary was the total, and the total no longer exists. In the second hypothesis, the faith is only necessary "ad bene esse", and therefore its absence does not justify the deposition of the Pope. In addition to this, what finds itself in the ultimate disposition to death, immediately thereafter ceases to exist, without the intervention of any other external force, as is obvious; therefore, also the Pope heretic ceases to be Pope by himself, without any deposition.

Finally, the Holy Fathers teach unanimously not only that heretics are outside of the Church, but also that they are "ipso facto" deprived of all ecclesiastical jurisdiction and dignity. St. Cyprian (lib. 2, epist. 6) says: 'We affirm that absolutely no heretic or schismatic has any power or right'; and he also teaches (lib. 2, epist. 1) that the heretics who return to the Church must be received as laymen, even though they have been formerly priests or bishops in the Church. St. Optatus (lib. 1 cont. Parmen.) teaches that heretics and schismatics cannot have the keys of the kingdom of heaven, nor bind nor loose. St. Ambrose (lib. 1 de poenit., ca. 2), St. Augustine (in Enchir., cap 65), St. Jerome (lib. cont. Lucifer.) teach the same.

Pope St. Celestine I (epist. ad Jo. Antioch., which appears in Conc. Ephes., tom. I, cap. 19) wrote: 'It is evident that he [who has been excommunicated by Nestorius] has remained and remains in communion with us, and that we do not consider destituted [i.e. deprived of office, by judgment of Nestorius], anyone who has been excommunicated or deprived of his charge, either episcopal or clerical, by Bishop Nestorius or by the others who followed him, after they commenced preaching heresy. For he who had already shown himself as deserving to be excommunicated, could not excommunicate anyone by his sentence.'

And in a letter to the clergy of Constantinople, Pope St. Celestine I says: 'The authority of Our Apostolic See has determined that the bishop, cleric, or simple Christian who had been deposed or excommunicated by Nestorius or his followers, after the latter began to preach heresy shall not be considered deposed or excommunicated. For he who had defected from the faith with such preachings, cannot depose or remove anyone whatsoever.'

St. Nicholas I (epist. ad Michael) repeats and confirms the same. Finally, St. Thomas also teaches (S. Theol., II-II, q. 39, a. 3) that schismatics immediately lose all jurisdiction, and that anything they try to do on the basis of any jurisdiction will be null.

There is no basis for that which some respond to this: that these Fathers based themselves on ancient law, while nowadays, by decree of the Council of Constance, they alone lose their jurisdiction who are excommunicated by name or who assault clerics. This argument, I say, has no value at all, for those Fathers, in affirming that heretics lose jurisdiction, did not cite any human law, which furthermore perhaps did not exist in relation to the matter, but argued on the basis of the very nature of heresy. The Council of Constance only deals with the excommunicated, that is, those who have lost jurisdiction by sentence of the Church, while heretics already before being excommunicated are outside the Church and deprived of all jurisdiction. For they have already been condemned by their own sentence, as the Apostle teaches (Tit. 3:10-11), that is, they have been cut off from the body of the Church without excommunication, as St. Jerome affirms.

Besides that, the second affirmation of Cajetan, that the Pope heretic can be truly and authoritatively deposed by the Church, is no less false than the first. For if the Church deposes the Pope against his will it is certainly above the Pope; however, Cajetan himself defends, in the same treatise, the contrary of this. Cajetan responds that the Church, in deposing the Pope, does not have authority over the Pope, but only over the link that unites the person to the pontificate. In the same way that the Church in uniting the pontificate to such a person, is not, because of this, above the Pontiff, so also the Church can separate the pontificate from such a person in case of heresy, without saying that it is above the Pope.

But contrary to this it must be observed in the first place that, from the fact that the Pope deposes bishops, it is deduced that the Pope is above all the bishops, though the Pope on deposing a bishop does not destroy the episcopal jurisdiction, but only separates it from that person. In the second place, to depose anyone from the pontificate against the will of the deposed, is without doubt punishing him; however, to punish is proper to a superior or to a judge. In the third place, given that according to Cajetan and the other Thomists, in reality the whole and the parts taken as a whole are the same thing, he who has authority over the parts taken as a whole, being able to separate them one from another, has also authority over the whole itself which is constituted by those parts.

The example of the electors, who have the power to designate a certain person for the pontificate, without however having power over the Pope, given by Cajetan, is also destitute of value. For when something is being made, the action is exercised over the matter of the future thing, and not over the composite, which does not yet exist, but when a thing is destroyed, the action is exercised over the composite, as becomes patent on consideration of the things of nature. Therefore, on creating the Pontiff, the Cardinals do not exercise their authority over the Pontiff for he does not yet exist, but over the matter, that is, over the person who by the election becomes disposed to receive the pontificate from God. But if they deposed the Pontiff, they would necessarily exercise authority over the composite, that is, over the person endowed with the pontifical power, that is, over the Pontiff.

Therefore, the true opinion is the fifth, according to which the Pope who is manifestly a heretic ceases by himself to be Pope and head, in the same way as he ceases to be a Christian and a member of the body of the Church; and for this reason he can be judged and punished by the Church. This is the opinion of all the ancient Fathers, who teach that manifest heretics immediately lose all jurisdiction, and outstandingly that of St. Cyprian (lib. 4, epist. 2) who speaks as follows of Novatian, who was Pope [i.e. antipope] in the schism which occurred during the pontificate of St. Cornelius: 'He would not be able to retain the episcopate [i.e. of Rome], and, if he was made bishop before, he separated himself from the body of those who were, like him, bishops, and from the unity of the Church.'

According to what St. Cyprian affirms in this passage, even had Novatian been the true and legitimate Pope, he would have automatically fallen from the pontificate, if he separated himself from the Church.

This is the opinion of great recent doctors, as John Driedo (lib. 4 de Script. et dogmat. Eccles., cap. 2, par. 2, sent. 2), who teaches that only they separate themselves from the Church who are expelled, like the excommunicated, and those who depart by themselves from her or oppose her, as heretics and schismatics. And in his seventh affirmation, he maintains that in those who turn away from the Church, there remains absolutely no spiritual power over those who are in the Church. Melchior Cano says the same (lib. 4 de loc., cap. 2), teaching that heretics are neither parts nor members of the Church, and that it cannot even be conceived that anyone could be head and Pope, without being member and part (cap. ult. ad argument. 12). And he teaches in the same place, in plain words, that occult heretics are still of the Church, they are parts and members, and that therefore the Pope who is an occult heretic is still Pope. This is also the opinion of the other authors whom we cite in book I De Ecclesia.

The foundation of this argument is that the manifest heretic is not in any way a member of the Church, that is, neither spiritually nor corporally, which signifies that he is not such by internal union nor by external union. For even bad Catholics [i.e. who are not heretics] are united and are members, spiritually by faith, corporally by confession of faith and by participation in the visible sacraments; the occult heretics are united and are members although only by external union; on the contrary, the good catechumens belong to the Church only by an internal union, not by the external; but manifest heretics do not pertain in any manner, as we have already proved."

St. Robert Bellarmine never said or implied that one could resist the pope when he taught something for the whole church or resist him in some law, discipline or practice. However, since the Church has solemnly declared that She cannot give us some harmful law or discipline or proclaim a false doctrine, then one could not be in a state of resistance since there would be no need of it. To be in a state of resistance is to reject the solemn proclamations of the Church itself necessarily putting one outside the faith anyway.

Part 2 of Argument: Resistance is necessary because the Catholic Church gave us novel teachings and practices that are and have been harmful to the faithful.

The Catholic Church has solemnly declared that it cannot give us evil or harmful practices or laws. This is one of the ground principles of sedevacantism. See Objection 14.

28. Pope Honorius was declared a heretic and yet is on the official list of true popes.

Pope Honorius I was elected pope Oct. 27, 625. Later, in a reply to Sergius I, patriarch of Constantinople, he approved the heresy of monothelitism, which said Christ had only one will.

Honorius, *"Scripta fraternitatis vestrae"* to Sergius, Patriarch of Constantinople in the year 634, stated: "Hence, we confess one will of our Lord Jesus Christ."

In his *"Scripta dilectissimi filii"* to Sergius, Patriarch of Constantinople in the year 634, Honorius taught one operation in Christ.

When explaining Honorius one operation teaching, Pope John IV says Honorius was implying that Christ did not have two contrary wills. Both wills of Christ are united thus forming one operation.

Pope John IV in *"Dominus qui dixit"* to Constantius the Emperor, 641: *"...So,* ***my aforementioned predecessor [Honorius] said*** *concerning the mystery of the incarnation of Christ, that there were not in Him, as in us sinners, contrary wills of mind and flesh;* ***and certain ones converting this to their own meaning, suspected that he taught one will of His divinity and humanity which is altogether contrary to the truth.****"*

Pope St. Martin I condemned monothelitism at the Lataran Council in 649: Canon 10. *If anyone does not properly and truly confess according to the holy Fathers two wills of one and the same Christ our God...let him be condemned.*

Canon 11. *If anyone does not properly and truly confess according to the holy Fathers two operations of one and the same Christ our God uninterruptedly united, divine and human, from this that through each of His natures He naturally is the same operator of our salvation, let him be condemned.*

Pope St. Agatho at the Third Council of Constantinople in 680 condemned Pope Honorius as a heretic (an instrument of Satan) but St. Agatho died before it was ratified.

Pope St. Leo II at the 13th session of the Council finally condemns and excommunicates Honorius. *"Also Honorius, who was shown to be incapable of enlightening this Apostolic Church by the doctrine of Apostolic Tradition, in that he allowed its immaculate faith to be blemished by a sacrilegious betrayal."*

Notice, that Pope St. Leo condemns him not for heresy but for allowing it.

The Seventh Ecumenical Council, Nicea II, decreed, *"We affirm that in Christ there be two wills and two operations according to the reality of each nature, as also taught by the Sixth Synod held at Constantinople, casting out Sergius, Honorius, Cyrus, Pyrrhus, Macarius, and all those who agree with them".*

Popes from the 5th to the 11th Century took an oath in a form prescribed by Gregory II, which included the phrase *"smites with eternal anathema the originators of the new heresy, Sergius,... together with Honorius, because he assisted in the base assertion of heresies." (Liber diurnus, ii, 9)*

Again...

Pope St. Agatho anathematized Honorius at the Third Council of Constantinople, but died before deliberations. Pope St. Leo II confirmed St. Agatho and ratified it in 682.

Third Council of Constantinople, Exposition of Faith, 680-681: *"... the contriver of evil did not rest, finding an accomplice in the serpent and through him bringing upon human nature the poised dart of death, so now too he has found instruments suited to his own purpose – namely, Theodore... Sergius, Pyrrhus, Paul and Peter... and further Honorius, who was pope of elder Rome, Cyrus... and Macarius... - and has not been idle in raising through them obstacles of error against the full body of the Church, sowing with novel speech among the orthodox people the heresy of a single will and a single principle of action..."*

The Church then recognized that a pope could become a heretic, and indeed Honorius did become one at least materially.

If he were a formal heretic, then his anathema would have meant that Honorius could have been considered a non-pope at the time of his heresy since a pope cannot be a heretic and pope at the same time.

It has been argued that Honorius was unjustly excommunicated since the dogma had not yet been defined or that he could not be present to recant, which would mean he was only a material heretic or a Catholic in error, therefore making his excommunication null.

The fact is Pope St. Agatho believed Honorius was a true heretic, which means he also believed a true pope could become a true heretic. This is sometimes called contrary to Scripture by some apologists but not to Pope St. Agatho. It is uncertain what Leo believed but he did anathematize him for at least allowing heresy.

Whatever the truth is about Honorius, he is at least a doubtful pope after his heresy, which means he might be considered an antipope from then on. Whatever, the case may be, his condemnation at Constantinople did not say that Honorius remained Pope until he died.

Be that as it may, Honorius had issued no dogmatic decrees, and only *"reigned"* for three and a half years after his letter. It really is not a matter that needed to be settled and it still has not been.

The objection says he was a heretic and a pope.

Based on the information given, he was a true pope but not as a heretic at the same time. If he actually became a formal heretic, he would have immediately lost his pontificate. If only a material heretic, then he remained a pope until the end of his life.

St. Francis De Sales (17th century), Doctor of the Church, *The Catholic Controversy*, pp. 305- 306: ***"Thus we do not say that the Pope cannot err in his private opinions, as did John XXII; or be altogether a heretic, as perhaps Honorius was. Now when he [the Pope] is explicitly a heretic, he falls ipso facto from his dignity and out of the Church..."***

Notice that St. Francis de Sales is not sure if Honorius was a true heretic, but continues that when the Pope is explicitly a heretic, he loses his office automatically.

As we've seen in Objection 1, all the popes and saints that said something about the papacy and heretics all agree that such a man would not be Pope despite the fact that all were aware of Honorius.

This means that this objection is blatantly false. It proves nothing but the sede vacant position.

29. Pope Liberius signed the Arian Creed as he condemned the great St Athanasius. He proves that a Pope can apostatize and remain the Pope.

The Catholic Church has spoken extensively on this case.

St. Athanasius said: *"Liberius, having been exiled, gave in after two years, and, in fear of the death with which he was threatened, signed...If he did not endure the tribulation to the end yet he remained in his exile for two years knowing the conspiracy against me." (Catholic Encyclopedia on Liberius)*

St. Jerome said that Liberius *"conquered by the tedium of exile and subscribing to heretical wickedness entered Rome in triumph". (Chronicle) He also speaks about Liberius yielding to the Arians in the preface to the "Liber Precum."*

Speaking on the condemnation of St. Athanasius, St. Hilary, writing at Constantinople in 360 AD, addresses Constantius thus: *"I know not whether it was with greater impiety that you exiled him than that you restored him" [Contra Const., II].*

Pope St. Anastasius I, epistle *Dat mihi plurimum*, about 400 AD: *"For at this time when Constantius of holy memory held the world as victor, the heretical African faction was not able by any deception to introduce its baseness because, as we believe, our God provided that the holy and untarnished faith be not contaminated through any vicious blasphemy of slanderous men... For this faith those who were then esteemed as holy bishops gladly endured exile, that is Dionysius, thus a servant of God, prepared by divine instruction, or those following his example of holy recollection, Liberius bishop of the Roman Church, Eusebius also of Vercelli, Hilary of the Gauls, to say nothing of many, on whose decision the choice could rest to be fastened to the cross rather than blaspheme God Christ, which the Arian heresy compelled, or call the Son of God, God Christ, a creature of the Lord."*

St. Robert Bellarmine writes: *"In addition, unless we are to admit that Liberius defected for a time from constancy in defending the Faith, we are compelled to exclude Felix II, who held the pontificate while Liberius was alive, from the number of Popes: but the Catholic Church venerates this very Felix as Pope and martyr .... Then two years later came the lapse of Liberius, of which we have spoken above. Then indeed the Roman clergy, stripping Liberius of his pontifical dignity, went over to Felix, whom they knew to be a Catholic. From that time, Felix began to be the true Pontiff. For although Liberius was not a heretic, nevertheless he was considered one, on account of the peace he made with the Arians, and by that presumption the pontificate could rightly be taken from him: for men are not bound or able to read hearts; but when they see that someone is a heretic by his external works, they judge him to be a heretic pure and simple, and condemn him as a heretic." (On the Roman Pontiff)*

Pope Pius VI, *Charitas* (# 14), April 13, 1791: *"Perhaps in appreciation of these actions, the bishop of Lidda, Jean Joseph Gobel, was elected Archbishop of Paris, while the archbishop was still living.* ***He is following the example of Ischyras, who was proclaimed bishop of Alexandria at the Council of Tyre as payment for his sinful service in accusing St. Athanasius and ejecting him from his See."***

Pope Pius IX, *Quartus Supra* (# 16), January 6, 1873, On False Accusations: *"And previously the Arians falsely accused Liberius, also Our predecessor, to the Emperor Constantine, because* ***Liberius refused to condemn St. Athanasius, Bishop of Alexandria, and refused to support their heresy."***

Pope Benedict XV, *Principi Apostolorum Petro* (# 3), Oct. 5, 1920: *"Indeed, lest they should prove faithless from their duty, some went fearlessly into exile, as did Liberius and Silverius and Martinus."*

When Pope Liberius (reigned 352-366) was banished to Beroea by Emperor Constantius II in 355, Felix II was elected pope.

Liberius was restored but the government recognized Felix as did by many supporters, including clergy. Felix is recognized in the official list of popes. He became known a courageous defender of the Nicene faith and laid his life down for it.

Pope Liberius went down in history as a traitor to orthodoxy and a persecutor of the faithful because he had been falsely accused of excommunicated Athanasius and accepted the ambiguous First Creed of Sirmium, which omitted the Nicene's *"consubstantial with the Father."*

It is said that later, after the death of the Emperor, he recanted everything and attempted to make amends for his wrongdoing. However, we know it is because he didn't actually do anything wrong but only appears that way.

The Catholic Encyclopedia calls Pope Felix II as (more properly Antipope).

For the sake of the argument, let's say Liberius did sign the creed. He would have lost his papacy for his weakness in pleasing man rather than God thus making Felix a true pope and making Liberius an antipope after his signature to the false creed. If Liberius were under real duress when signing the false creed, he would have been a true pope making Felix a real antipope the whole time. Felix could not be considered malicious or a non-Catholic for the mistake since Liberius would have at least been a doubtful pope.

A doubtful pope is as bad as an antipope or no pope at all since there would always be a doubt to his acts. There cannot be a doubtful pope for there cannot be any doubt about any authoritative papal act.

30. John XXII (1316-1334) was explicitly a heretic and yet remained the Pope.

John XXII was the second Avignon Pope before the Great Schism. He was a great reformer and preacher. On All Saints Day in 1331 AD, he said in a sermon that souls do not attain the beatific vision until after the General Judgment. Because the statement was very controversial, he retracted it on his deathbed.

However, the doctrine was not defined until after the death of Pope John, making Pope John only a material heretic or a good-will Catholic in error.

His successor, Benedict XII, issued the Constitution *"Benedictus Deus"* in 1336 AD. This asserted that the blessed souls of the dead *"see the face of the triune God immediately after death".*

This argument that Pope John was a heretic comes from a false condemnation from one of John's enemies, Cardinal Orsini. The reason for this was Pope John had condemned as heretical the teaching of a Franciscan group known as *"The Spirituals"* in the circle of William of Ockham at the court of the emperor King Louis of Bavaria who also held the teaching of this heretical group.

The Catholic Encyclopedia explains what happened.

The Catholic Encyclopedia, "John XXII," Vol. 8, 1910, p. 433: *"The Spirituals, always in close alliance with Louis of Bavaria, profited by these events to accuse the pope of heresy, being supported by Cardinal Napoleon Orsini. In union with the latter, King Louis wrote to the cardinals, urging them to call a general council and condemn the pope.... Pope John wrote to King Phillip IV on the matter (November, 1333), and emphasized the fact that, as long as the Holy See had not given a decision, the theologians enjoyed perfect freedom in this matter. In December, 1333, the theologians at Paris, after a consultation on the question, decided in favor of the doctrine that the souls of the blessed departed saw*

God immediately after death or after their complete purification; at the same time they pointed out that the pope had given no decision on this question but only advanced his personal opinion, and now petitioned the pope to confirm their decision. John appointed a commission at Avignon to study the writings of the Fathers, and to discuss further the disputed question. In a consistory held on 3 January, 1334, the pope explicitly declared that he had never meant to teach anything contrary to Holy Scripture or the rule of faith and in fact had not intended to give any decision whatever. Before his death he withdrew his former opinion, and declared his belief that souls separated from their bodies enjoyed in heaven the Beatific Vision."

It is interesting that Vatican 2 apologists would use this argument that John's teaching was manifestly heretical but fail to see how manifestly heretical the numerous statements that come from John XXIII through Benedict XVI, some of which were formal teaching (Vatican 2) unlike Pope John XXII which was merely a sermon.

What this objection does is once again prove sedevacantism while denouncing Vatican 2 apologists as hypocrites.

31. Council of Constance condemned that a heretical pope ceases to lose office.

Errors of John Hus, Condemned by the Council of Constance: *"20. If the Pope is wicked and especially if he is foreknown (as a reprobate), then as Judas, the Apostle, he is of the devil, a thief, and a son of perdition, and he is not the head of the holy militant Church, since he is not a member of it."* ***Condemned***

Some Vatican 2 apologist use this argument to say that what sedevacantists say is the same as what John Hus was condemned for saying.

This is a total misunderstanding of the Council of Constance. As a matter of fact, if this were true then you have all those

Doctors and Saints as shown in Objection 1 in the same boat as John Hus.

Popes can be wicked as many were. John Hus was saying the Pope cannot be wicked and this is what he was condemned for.

Takes notice of the teaching of Pope Pius XII in his *Mystici Corporis Christi* (23), June 29, 1943: *"For not every sin, however grave it may be, is such as of its own nature to sever a man from the Body of the Church, as does schism or heresy or apostasy."*

Merely wicked popes are still members of the Church, but heretics, schismatics, and apostates are not. The Pope must be Catholic even if a bad one.

32. The Church can't function properly.

Depends what is meant by properly. On certain levels, it functions just fine. It is true that it does not function as she would like. As seen on Objection 11, the great apostasy puts a serious obstacle in the way. However, this is to be expected.

Even if the Church doesn't function at all but merely exists until Christ's return, then the bare minimum that is required is present.

There is no promise that the Church would even function must less function properly. All those statements concerning anything that would be included for a perfectly healthy Church in her governmental form would only apply under ordinary conditions.

Church law and Divine law are two separate issues. Divine law requires the Church to exist and this can be done provided one person holds the faith.

Insofar as the Church functioning at the present, it does so as needed to maintain healthy Catholicism among its members.

Remember the Church existed in Japan for centuries without priests.

> **33. The proposition of sedevacantism is sheer madness. Those who hold such a position are like those who reject the holocaust, heliocentrism, a billion-year-old earth, and think the US government was behind the bombing of the Merrill building in Oklahoma and the 9/11 terrorist attack on the Trade Center and Pentagon. It's a conspiracy theory only. Sedevacantists are spiritually prideful.**

Sedevacantists are accused of being spiritually prideful but in fact, it is all those who accept John XXIII through Benedict as they reject the historic Catholic Faith that are the prideful ones.

The Church has spoken. Christ, Doctors and Saints, Popes, and Holy Scripture have warned of the very things that sedevacantists hold.

If as much evidence is brought forth that the holocaust didn't happen as reported, or that geocentrism is true, or the earth is relatively young, or the US was indeed involved in the Oklahoma bombing and the 9/11 terrorist attack, then they would not be mere conspiracy theories but real conspiracies.

The Vatican 2 Church is the greatest conspiracy in the history of the world. All the evidence is clearly present but denied by literally billions of people.

We are in the great apostasy foretold by many.

This objection can be turned on those who would make it. It is sheer madness to believe Rome is Catholic with Popes reigning gloriously over the last 50 years.

Truth is objective and those who refused to acknowledge it are either ignorant, prejudice, or evil. All the arguments have been laid out.

To disagree with the conclusion of any of the presented arguments against the 33 objections laid against sedevacantism, one must be able to show that a false premise or a logical fallacy was used in the arguments.

Otherwise, to reject the Catholic position of sedevacantism and remain united to Modernist Masonic Rome of today, is to admit that sedevacantists have proved their position as true, but is too ignorant, prejudice, or evil to accept it.

It may be very difficult to acknowledge, but that doesn't mean it's not true. Sedevacantists are not afraid of being labeled as mad, whacko, and conspiracy theorists, because they know the truth is on their side.

Is it worth ending up in hell because something is too difficult to believe or the fear of the world thinking of you as mad?

If one rejects the possibility of sedevacantism based on illogical propositions, then every heresy that comes down the pike becomes justified as a truth.

Lastly, all 33 objections are those used by professional Vatican 2 apologists. Their job is to defend the Vatican 2 Church at all costs.

Truth is not what these apologists care about. To acknowledge Catholic truth in totality would be for them unemployment and the loss of a paycheck.

Vatican 2 apologists are like magicians or illusionists. They are masters in the art of deception. This is why they twist every argument, skew the issues, creating straw-men arguments and when all else fails use *ad hominum* remarks and call sedevacantists whacko, out of touch with society, and just plain mad.

This last objection is just another deception to keep the innocent Catholic aloof.

Take notice that Vatican 2 apologists do not use saints, popes, and theologians to defend their position for the rare exception of taking St. Robert Bellarmine out of context on resistance as the Calvinists do with St. Augustine on grace and election, or just the private interpretation of Holy Scripture as do the rest of the Protestants on what constitutes the Church.

They often accuse sedevacantists of using mere private interpretation but as it was demonstrated in answering the 33 objections, this is a lie or another deception. Popes, saints, and theologians are all on the side of sedevacantists.

You will not find any Church father, pope or theologian that says a pope can be a formal heretic, or that the Church can issue an evil practice. This is found only with Vatican 2 apologists.

You will not find the particulars of the Vatican 2 Church in the historic Catholic Church. PERIOD! This is why they condemn traditional Catholics as they only seem to quote John XXIII, Paul VI, John Paul II, and Benedict XVI. The constant onslaught of so-called Catholic radio and TV is nothing more than a promotion of the new religion of Vatican 2 with the lie that theirs is the religion that was found on a rock.

Vatican 2 apologists are like the lawyers defending known murderers and rapists to win a court case. In this case, they defend the spiritual murderers of the Vatican 2 popes.

The fact is there is no option left if one truly wants to be a Catholic. To accept John XXIII through Benedict XVI as popes is to deny the Catholic religion.

To believe the Chair of Peter is currently filled is to reject what constitutes heresy and all the anathemas thereof. It is to reject the very duty of being a Catholic and doing what Christ orders: Beware of false teachers.

True popes cannot be false teachers but antipopes can be as those that have come out of Vatican 2. They have proven sedevacantism is true with their rejection of Catholic Doctrines.

To continue down the road following Modernist Masonic Rome means such individuals want the Catholic name but not the Catholic Faith.

This is madness!

The Blast that wiped out Nagasaki on Oct. 9, 1945

In remembering how America under the orders of 33rd degree Freemason and President Harry S. Truman, bombed the two most Catholic cities of Japan in 1945, should remind us of the great miracle which occurred at Hiroshima after the first explosion.

The Blast that wiped out Hiroshima on Oct. 6, 1945

Eight Jesuits living eight blocks from the center of the blast emerged alive and well. Everyone and everything within a mile-radius of the blast was annihilated.

Father Hubert Schiffer, a German-born missionary, described it as a blinding white light unlike anything he had ever seen before... and afterwards, there was only silence and it remained completely silent. (1) When Father Hubert was asked on American TV how they all survived the nuclear blast, he gave them the answer, "In that house, we were living the message of Fatima."(2)

—AP WIREPHOTO

RECALLING HIROSHIMA

Maj. Robert Lewis (l), who piloted the plane that dropped an atomic bomb over Hiroshima, talks with a survivor of that first nuclear bombing, the Rev. Hubert Schiffer, a German Jesuit priest, who was eight blocks from ground zero. Yesterday, 12th anniversary of the bombing, they met in New York.

It was the story of Fatima that has inspired millions to become a greater and more devoted Catholics. It entails the great miracle of the sun with a completely soaked countryside dried up in 10 minutes witnessed by 75,000 people, including the people themselves who's washed out clothing were pressed and dried during the event, the radical devotion of those three children seers who endured great penances, the incorruptible body of the youngest seer, Jacinta Marto, and, of course, the mystery of the three secrets especially the Third Secret.

There are several books and movies about Fatima and even whole apostolates founded, dedicated and devoted to the story of Fatima. What else could be said about Fatima and the Third Secret that has not already been said? It would seem the topic has been exhausted. However, there is one more very important point about Fatima and the Third Secret, which has been missed by everybody...Our Lady's hidden message.

To find this hidden message, one must ask several questions which apparently have never been asked before based on the following information:

Sister Maria das Dores (Lucia de Santos), the oldest seer, once told Father Augustin Fuentes on December 26, 1957, "Father, the **Blessed Virgin is very sad** because no one heeds her message; neither the good nor the bad. The good continue on with their life of virtue and apostolate, but they do not unite their lives to the message of Fatima. Sinners keep following the road of evil because they do not see the terrible chastisement about to befall them. Believe me, Father, **God is going to punish the world and very soon. The chastisement of heaven is imminent. In less than two years, 1960 will be here and the chastisement of heaven will come and it will be very great.** Tell souls to fear not only the material punishment that will befall us if we **do not** pray and do penance **but most of all the souls who will go to hell."** (3)

She clearly forewarned of a very great chastisement and it would occur within the next two years.

So what was it? What very great chastisement befell the world between the years 1958 and 1960?

Was Sister Lucia a false prophet?

Sister Lucia at approximately 40 years of age

Lucia from Our Lady clearly prophesied the Spanish Civil War under Pope Pius XI and World War II under Pope Pius XII which the world experience just 13 years earlier.

Are we not to suppose that a greater chastisement will befall the world?

The Third Secret, written down by Sister Lucia in 1939, was given to the popes down though the years and was supposed to be revealed by the pope in 1960 or after Sister Lucia's death, which ever happened first, because the world would better understand its contents in that time period. (4)

We know the Third Secret was not revealed in and by 1960. I say by 1960 since Sister Lucia was apparently not dead yet, which brings us to ask the questions:

Why did Our Lady say in 1960 or Lucia's death whichever comes first?

Did Our Lady know that Lucia would die around the year 1960?

If not, why bring up her death at all if 1960 was the time the world would understand the Secret?

All this is very interesting because pictures of the Lucia before 1960, without a doubt, show a different person than the Lucia after that year. One would have to conclude that cover-up was at hand. Did she die and it was kept hidden from public knowledge as an imposter played her role?

The daughter of a Masonic assassin claimed that her father killed Lucia in 1958. (5)

A young and happy Sister Lucia

Be that as it may, some other important questions need to be asked:

Since Our Lady foreknew the chastisements of the wars in the 1930's and 1940's, how is it she didn't foresee her Third Secret not being revealed in 1960?

Why did Our Lady say the pope of 1960 was to reveal the Secret if She knew that the pope of 1960 would not do so?

If She did foresee that it wouldn't be revealed, why did She say that it would be best understood in 1960?

Thus from these questions, we will be able to see a hidden message within Sister Lucia's prophecy to Fr. Augustin Fuentes and what Our Lady said about the reading of the Third Secret in 1960.

Before we look at what is this hidden message, we need to hear what was said about the Third Secret from a key figure of the Church... Fr. Malachi Martin.

Father Malachi Martin

Malachi Martin sees sinister workings in the Church.

The late Fr. Malachi Martin, doctor, exorcist, linguist, and advisor to several "popes", and made secret cardinal and bishop by Pope Pius XII, read the Third Secret in 1960 along with Cardinal Bea and John XXIII.

According Fr. Malachi Malachi, John XXIII did not believe in Fatima and therefore refused to read the Secret because it was not in line with what John XXIII had in mind for the future of the Church. (6) In 1962, at the Second Vatican Council, John XXIII referred to the three seers of Fatima as "Prophets of Doom."(7) This is interesting since John XXIII called Fatima, "the center of all Christian hopes."(8) Yet, he refused to read the Third Secret in 1960.

Fr Malachi Martin gave clues to the Third Secret saying the Secret was far worse than even a nuclear war. It would fill confessionals and Churches and it did not involve the chastisements as the earlier wars. (9)

Before Fr. Malachi Martin died, he actually revealed the Third Secret to close friends and began a tell-all book on the New Vatican. With great sadness, he came to hold the sede vacant position after visiting Rome and being told by John Paul II that his faith was not the same. (10)

Father Malachi left the Jesuit order and ceased to be a member of the clergy (why he is pictured without the Roman collar), however, he remained a practicing priest saying his daily masses and hearing confessions.

Eleven months after the death of Fr. Malachi Martin, Rome reveals what they say, is the contents of the Third Secret, claiming it was about John Paul II and the attempt on his life in 1981. (11)

Since the world was told that it would better understand the meaning of the Third Secret in 1960, we know that what Rome revealed in 2000 and their conclusion was a complete fabrication concocted to deflect the real Secret and its meaning.

Not only that but what modernist Rome revealed was not shocking, would not fill any confessional as it didn't, nor would there be any reason for John XXIII not to reveal what Rome actually revealed 40 years later, not to mention the fact that it was conveniently revealed after the death of Fr. Malachi Martin, the one man who could have and would have refuted their lie.

With this information, lets again look at the three initial questions:

1. Since Our Lady foreknew the chastisements of the wars, how is it she didn't foresee her Third Secret not being revealed in and by 1960?

   Answer: She was fully aware that it would not be revealed and there is no reason to believe She didn't know.

2. Why did Our Lady say the pope of 1960 was to reveal the Secret if She knew that the pope of 1960 would not do so?

   Answer: Either as a warning to beware of this man who claimed to be pope or simply that there would be no true pope to reveal it.

3. If She did foresee that it wouldn't be revealed, why did She say that it would be best understood by 1960?

Answer: This is the crux of the issue. Pope Pius XII had already stated that after him would come the deluge. (12)

The 1958 conclave elects a known modernist and Mason.

So Our Lady is pointing to the time. She already said a Great Chastisement would come between the years of 1958 and 1960.

Fr. Malachi said it was not about a war as with earlier chastisements but far worse.

What is far worse than a nuclear war? What happened between the years of 1958 to 1960?

I submit the death of Pope Pius XII and the uncanonically elected Roncalli to the papacy was it.

What is the worst thing that could ever happen to the world? Would it not be what sedevancantists hold to be true? That the papacy has been usurped and the true faith was replaced by a counterfeit version, with millions of Catholics being led astray from Truth right into hell? Was not hell and saving souls what Fatima was all about?

The Third Secret did not specifically say anything about the conclave or an election of some antipope or Fr Malachi Martin would have become a sedevacantist immediately but rather it indicated an apostasy from the top and the coming antichrist, which would initiate the Great Apostasy. How far at the top? If the very top (the pope) were actually an apostate, then he would not be a true pope. It is that simple.

Not revealing the Third Secret was in essence revealing it. It is the message but a hidden message, yet everybody seemed to miss that Our Lady would know that the Secret would not be revealed in 1960 saying it would better understood then. She was telling us what it is by not having it revealed.

If you don't believe in the approved apparition of Fatima with a verifiable miracle witnessed by over 75,000 people, then you would be viewed by the faithful as faithless. Not revealing a Secret by the Blessed Virgin Mary when asked by her to do so, is saying to all the faithful that you simply don't trust them to believe the Catholic Faith as it has always been preached. A true pope would not try to usurp the authority of Heaven and this is precisely what John XXIII did.

The truly faithful believe in Fatima because they know the miracles that have come from it could not possibly come from hell or else the Catholic Church already defected by approving it. Remember, the Church was fully aware of the contents of the Secret when She approved the apparition.

John XXIII claimed Fatima was the center of all hope and yet refused to reveal the Secret. Why? Was he truly faithless, a wicked man, or both?

One more thing as a little side note...Pope Pius XII consecrated specifically Russia to the Immaculate Heart of Mary on July 7, 1952, fulfilling Our Lady's promise. She never promised he would do it with all the bishops but that he would do it none-the-less. (13)

Consequently, Russia converted out of its Communist ways ending the persecution on her Christians and there was a certain period of peace. The nations that were annihilated into the Soviet Union have regained their sovereignty. (14)

(1.) Miracles, Signs, and Wonders, Globe Digests, p. 78, by Joanne Asala and Steven Butchart

(2.) Fatima, The Great Sign, Tan, back cover, by Francis Johnston

(3.) Controversy has surrounded this interview with Fr. Augustin Fuentes. Two years later, an anonymous note came from the episcopal curia of Coimbra denouncing the interview as fraudulent. Sr. Lucy was then silenced. Fr. Joaquin Alonso, who wrote over 5,000 documents on Fatima at the request of the bishop of Fatima, wrote in 1975 that the interview with Fr Augustine Fuentes was authentic.

(4.) Our Lady of Fatima, MacMillion, First Edition 1947, p. 211, by William Thomas Walsh, and Sermon, Third Secret of Fatima, Most Reverend Robert F. McKenna O.P.

(5.) The Dimond Brothers website of the Most Holy Family Monastery claims to have the very letter by the assassin's daughter.

(6.) Coast to Coast AM radio program, May 8, 1998, Art Bell with Fr Malachi Martin

(7.) Fr Malachi Martin referred to the opening speech at the Second Vatican Council in the 1998 interview with Art Bell

(8.) Fatima, The Great Sign, Tan, p. 12, by Francis Johnston

(9.) Coast to Coast AM radio program, May 8, 1998, Art Bell with Fr Malachi Martin

(10.) Private exchanges with his closest friends.

(11.) Inside the Vatican, Special Supplement June-July 2000, and Inside the Vatican June-July 2000

(12.) The Destruction of Christian Tradition, World Wisdom, p. 132, by Rama P. Coomaraswamy

(13.) Fatima, The Great Sign, Tan, p. 89, by Francis Johnston, states that Lucia wrote after the 1952 Consecration of Russia, "I am grieved that it has not yet been carried out as Our Lady had asked. Patience! ... Let us hope that Our Lady, as a good Mother, will be pleased to accept it." The initial quote in 1917 stated by Our Lady, "In the end, ...The Holy Father will consecrate Russia to me; it will be converted."

(14.) Our Lady of Fatima, MacMillion, First Edition 1947, p. 226, by William Thomas Walsh, indicates the conversion of Russia referred by Our Lady was conversion out of Communism since this is the error that needed to be corrected by the papal consecration before it spreads to every nation.

The Simplest Logical Argument For the Sedevacantist Position Against the Vatican 2 Church

There are two different religions that claim to be the historic Catholic Church:

The Church of Rome today that follows the teachings, practices, and leaders that followed the Second Vatican Council which we'll call "Church A", and the historic Catholic Church that is the Church of Rome just prior to the same Vatican Council rejecting those same particular teachings, practices, and leaders, which we'll call "Church B."

Which is the true Catholic Church? How can we tell?

From the objective point of view, one would have to look at all the arguments from both sides to hear how each side tries to justify their particular position. Subjectively, bias and prejudice will interfere for most people.

However, by taking Pascal's Wager to the next level, we can know for sure which church is not the true one without having to look at all of the arguments leaving the subjective to be of goodwill and follow simple logic.

Church A teaches that it has the fullness of means of salvation but that other churches, though not having the fullness of, do have a means of salvation. In other words, the Vatican 2 Church is the primary or best way of getting to heaven while all the others only provide a way.

Church B teaches that it is the only means of salvation. In other words, it is the only way to heaven while all the other churches take you to hell.

If Church B is the true Church, they have a chance to get to heaven, while the members of Church A go to hell.

If Church A is the true Church, they have the best means of getting to heaven, but members of Church B still have a means to salvation.

In other words, Church B cannot lose, when Church A can lose and indeed will lose it all because...

You would not make a wager on a horserace betting that all the horses come in first in a dead heat. You bet on one particular horse to win!

Church A wages on all the horses to win though it believes only one has the best chance of winning.

This is logically absurd.

If one were looking for the one true Church of Christ out of all of the churches of the world claiming to be truly Christian, the very first thing one should ask is which of the churches claim to be the only way to heaven and which churches don't.

Logically, the true Church of Christ must claim to be the ONLY church with the means of getting to heaven.

Christ would not leave us to decide on His Church with a 50% chance of salvation against a false church with better odds. In other words, He would not leave us a church with an impossible chance of salvation, but rather our only chance of salvation.

The Church of the Second Vatican Council cannot possibly be the true Church based on this one argument alone. Therefore, it must logically be a false church.

The historic Church has always taught that She is the ONLY Church with the means of getting to heaven, as it has been taught in every generation, which means she alone is the true Catholic Church.

Which of the two churches will you wager your soul on?

You can't lose in Church B but you will lose it all in Church A.

PAPAL ANOMALIES

Pope-sifting has been used to describe private judgment of laymen to determine what pope has taught heresy or issued some harmful law thus making the layman to freely exercise what teaching or practice he will hold or reject.

Sedevacantists are often accused of pope-sifting meaning that they will freely exercise what pope is a true pope or an antipope, thus only following what pope he believes is true.

At first glance, this accusation seems to have some merit but when you zero in on the premise, you'll find that the accusation is an excuse from having to find out or know the truth on some matter. In other words, just follow the crowd and believe everything the majority holds regardless of what the truth really is.

This writing will go much further back than 1958 to see just what can be found within the history of the papacy. The findings are interesting but the conclusions are astounding.

First Anomaly

When Liberius (reigned 352-366) was banished to Beroea by Emperor Constantius II in 355, Felix II was elected pope. Liberius was restored but the government recognized Felix as did by many supporters, including clergy. Felix is recognized in the official list of popes. He became known a courageous defender of the Nicene faith and laid his life down for it.

Liberius went down in history as a traitor to orthodoxy and a persecutor of the faithful because he had excommunicated Athanasius and accepted the ambiguous First Creed of Sirmium, which omitted the Nicene's "consubstantial with the Father."

Later, after the death of the Emperor, he recanted everything and attempted to make amends for his wrongdoing.

The Catholic Encyclopedia calls Pope Felix II as (more properly Antipope).

Comment: If not under any real duress, perhaps Liberius lost his papacy for his weakness in pleasing man rather than God thus making Felix a true pope and making Liberius an antipope after his signature to the false creed. If Liberius were under real duress when signing the false creed, he would have been a true pope making Felix an antipope the whole time. Felix could not be considered malicious or a non-Catholic for the mistake since Liberius was at least a doubtful pope. A doubtful pope is as bad as an antipope or no pope at all since there would always be a doubt to his acts. There cannot be a doubtful pope for there cannot be any doubt about any authoritative papal act.

Second Anomaly

On his deathbed in 530, Pope Felix IV had designated his archdeacon Boniface as his successor. The majority of the clergy and senate rejected the designation as an unconstitutional procedure.

The deacon Dioscorus was elected and consecrated by a large majority at the election held at the Lateran basilica.

In rejecting the election, the minority later elected Boniface in a hall of the palace and consecrated him on the same day.

There was a schism, but Dioscorus died 22 days later.

No doubt, by Canon Law at that time, Dioscorus was the legitimate pope, which would have necessarily made Boniface II an antipope. When Dioscorus died, the sixty presbyters who favored him, was made by Boniface II to retract and condemn

Dioscorus' memory. Pope Agapitus I had the document of condemnation solemnly burned in St. Peter's in 535.

Dioscorus is not named in the official list of popes but should be according to Canon Law, as at least, Pope Agapitus recognized him as a true pope.

Comment: Boniface should be considered an antipope until Dioscorus died. Boniface could have been a true pope after Dioscorus if recognized after that, although he would have been completely an illicit pope. It is possible that Boniface was never a true pope, since mere recognition of the majority doesn't necessarily make a true pope provided that no law prohibited an unlawfully elected pope to be considered a true pope.

Third Anomaly

When Pope St. Silverius (reigned 536-537) was wrongly exiled, Vigilius was consecrated pope in his place.

Pope St. Silverius was proved innocent and returned only to find Vigilius had replaced him, who in turn, exiled him again to an island where he died. Silverius was later venerated as a saint and was placed in the Roman Martyrology.

Vigilius (reigned 537-555) appears to be acknowledged by all of the clergy as the pope after St Silverius death, but his ascent to the throne was unlawful. Again, provided there was no law prohibiting recognition of an unlawfully elected person to be considered a true pope, the majority recognition may prove Vigilius a true pope.

Fourth Anomaly

Pope Honorius I was elected pope Oct. 27, 625. Later, in a reply to Sergius I, patriarch of Constantinople, he approved the heresy of monothelitism, which said Christ had only one will.

Pope St. Agatho anathematized Honorius at the Third Council of Constantinople, but died before deliberations. Pope St. Leo II confirmed St. Agatho and ratified it in 682.

Comment: The Church then recognized that a pope could become a heretic, and indeed Honorius did become one. The anathema would have meant that Honorius could have been considered a non-pope at the time of his heresy since a pope cannot be a heretic and pope at the same time.

It has been argued that Honorius was unjustly excommunicated since the dogma had not yet been defined or that he could not be present to recant, which would mean he was only a material heretic or a Catholic in error, therefore making his excommunication null.

The fact is Saints Agatho and Leo believed Honorius to be a true heretic. They also believed a pope could become a true heretic and could be anathematized as they proved with their excommunication of Honorius. They also believed that one could be a true heretic even if a dogma had not yet been defined.

Whatever the truth is about Honorius, he is, at best, a doubtful pope after his heresy, which means he might as well be considered an antipope from then on.

Fifth Anomaly

When Pope St. Martin I (reigned 649-653, died 655) was unjustly exiled in 653, St. Eugene I was consecrated pope in his place.

According to letters of St. Martin, he expressed and expected the Roman Church not to elect another pope while he was still alive. When they did despite his wishes, St. Martin relinquished the papacy for the good of the Church. He was the last pope to be venerated as a martyr.

Comment: Pope St. Eugene was unlawfully elected, but apparently must be considered a true pope since St. Martin abdicated for Eugene and the good of the Church. Apparently, there was no law prohibiting an unlawfully elected person to be considered pope.

Sixth Anomaly

The second Stephen elected died 4 days later (March 752) and was never consecrated as pope. Canon Law at that time required consecration to be considered a true pope. He was not recognized as pope until the 16th century, which now considers him a true pope despite the law at that time and despite the fact the historical Church never recognized him.

Seventh Anomaly

When Pope Formosus died in 896, he was replaced by the short 15-day reign of Boniface VI. Then Stephen VI (or the VII depending on how you view the sixth anomaly) was elected.

Over resentment of Formosus for having crowned Arnulf, and for the personal animosity he had with the pontiff, Stephen had a mock trial with the disinterred corpse of Formosus. Stephen charged Formosus with perjury, violating the canons prohibiting the translation of bishops, and coveting the papacy.

Stephen declared all acts of Formosus null and void including his ordinations. This resulted in the cancellation of his own consecration as bishop of Anagni thus under canon law, no objections could be raised against his papacy.

He had the three fingers of Formosus' right hand cut off and his body thrown in the Tiber. It was secretly retrieved by a hermit and buried.

When Stephen died, Romanus was elected. Because he did not do enough to restore the dignity of Formosus, he was deposed. His death is unknown.

Pope Theodore II, the next pope, restored Formosus, condemned the actions of Stephen, and declared all acts of Formosus valid including those ordinations. The next pope, John IX, confirmed Theodore's actions and again restored Formosus. John called Formosus' crowing of Arnulf as barbaric which was forced upon him. The translation of bishops was confirmed but in the case of Formosus, it was considered an exceptional.

Comment: The conclusion of this anomaly means that a pope's declaration of nullity of orders is not a guarantee unless Stephen's unstable mental capacity kept him from truly obtaining the papacy. This would mean he was actually an antipope.

Eighth Anomaly

Pope John X was deposed by popular demand in May 928. Leo VI was elected to succeed John. Leo died Dec. 928 and John X died in prison in 929. Stephen VII or VIII was elected in Dec. 928 in place of Leo while John X was still alive in prison.

All three are considered true popes on the official list.

Comment: Unless John consented in giving up the papacy or believed he no longer was the true pope, then Leo and Stephen are really antipopes.

Ninth Anomaly

Agapitus II was the pope from 946 to 955. He owed his promotion to the throne to Alberic II, prince of Rome. As Alberic lay dying in 954, he forced the leading Romans, with Pope Agapitus in attendance to declare his son Octavian, as the next pope as he would also be the prince of Rome.

This violated the decree of Pope St. Symmachus (3-1-499) forbidding agreements during a pope's lifetime about the choice of his successor.

Octavian was elected at the age of 18 and took the name John XII. He changed churches into brothels, and even toasted the devil at the High Altar. While John was indulging in unnatural sexual relations with a married woman, the husband murdered him in the act in 964.

Due to John's debauched behavior, the Roman Synod presided by Emperor Otto I deposed John on Dec. 4, 963 and elected Leo VIII in his place.

Leo was an experience Lateran official but only a layman. He was rushed through the lower orders, and consecrated bishop on Dec. 6.

At the synod in St. Peter's on Feb. 26, 964, John deposed and excommunicated Leo as a usurper of the Holy See, for being uncanonically ordained, and guilty of perfidy to his lawful pope. Anyone who was ordained by Leo was forced to confess that his orders were null and void.

After John's death, the Romans elected Benedict V as successor to John XII. Otto restored Leo to the throne on June 23. Days later, Leo held another synod to depose and degrade Benedict as a usurper to the Holy See.

Benedict humbly accepted and died a holy man in 966. He never tried to regain the papacy after Leo's death in 965.

All three, John XII, Leo VIII, and Benedict V, are listed as true popes in the official list.

Comment: John should not be considered a true pope because his election violated the decree that forbade such an election. However, if he were true pope then Leo is doubtful unless

John initially consented to give up the papacy. If this were so, then John would have become the antipope after trying to retake the papacy while Leo was the true pope after the initial consent of John. It would seem Benedict should have never been considered a true pope since even Benedict recognized Leo, unless his recognition only came after Otto restored him. If John was not a true pope because of the violated decree, then Benedict would be a true pope until he abdicated wrongly believing John to be the true pope. John was at best a doubtful pope. If Leo were uncanonically ordained, then he would not be a true pope either.

Tenth Anomaly

In 974, when Pope Benedict VI was imprisoned in Castel Saint'-Angelo, Boniface VII was elected and consecrated as the pope, and then had a priest named Stephen murder Benedict VI.

Benedict VII was also elected and consecrated pope in 974. He held a synod and excommunicated Boniface VII.

After Benedict VII died, Boniface VII had Benedict VII's successor Pope John XIV seized, brutally assaulted, and imprisoned in the Castel Saint'-Angelo in 984 who died 4 months later.

Boniface died in 985 and his corpse was stripped of his papal vestments, and then dragged through the streets naked as people trampled on it and stabbed it with spears. His name was used in slang as "malefatius" from the normal saying of Bonifatius. He was considered a valid pope for the short period after the death of John XIV and placed in the official list of popes until 1904.

Comment: Boniface should have never been recognized and his removal from the list in 1904 was correct.

Eleventh Anomaly

Pope Benedict IX was consecrated pope in 1032. (One source says at 12 years old while others say in his twenties) He was an alleged homosexual, and practiced in the occult. His violent and dissolute life led the Romans to drive him out in 1044.

Sylvester III was elected, but Benedict expelled Sylvester. Benedict then resigned his office in 1045 and Gregory VI was elected apparently through bribery as Benedict had designated him as his successor. Benedict tried to depose Gregory, but King Henry III deposed Benedict, Sylvester and Gregory at the Council of Sutri in 1046.

The German Pope Clement II was placed on the throne after the Council and died 8 months later. Benedict returned to the throne de facto, after Clement's death, and held to the papacy until July 16, 1048.

It should be noted that Clement condemned simony in a synod. He decreed 40 days of hard penance for anyone who knowingly got ordained by simoniac bishops.

Henry forced Benedict out and had a second German Pope, Damasus II, installed. Benedict believed himself to be the true pope.

After Damasus' death, Pope St. Leo IX succeeded in Feb. 1049 and held a synod in the Lataran in 1049 condemning simony and clerical unchastity and charged Benedict of simony and then excommunicated Benedict for not appearing. St. Leo maintained Clement's rule of penance and deposed many simoniac bishops and he even reordained men who were initially ordained by simoniac bishops. This means that at least some simoniac bishops were not recognized as valid bishops or their consecrations was considered invalid.

It is said that St. Leo lifted the excommunication of Benedict IX on his deathbed hoping he would see the truth.

Leo died in 1053 and was succeeded by Victor II on April 13, 1055. Benedict IX was still alive in Sept 18, 1055 but was dead by Jan. 1056.

For the possible exception of Sylvester, all these men were considered true popes and on the official list.

Comment: If Benedict's second abdication were valid then Gregory would have been a legit pope.

If Gregory was legit and accepted being deposed then Clement was legit. If Benedict was a true pope and his abdication was invalid, then Gregory, Clement, Damasus and Victor were antipopes.

If Benedict were truly practicing the occult, then he would have been ipso facto no pope and Sylvester would have been true pope until he abdicated thinking he was rightly deposed.

If simony invalidates an election (as it should) then Benedict became an antipope, as did Gregory, but Clement would have been the true pope as were those that followed him.

The lifting of the excommunication of Benedict by St. Leo was for not showing up at the synod, which would seem to have made Benedict an antipope at least for the time of Clement. The official list is incorrect again.

Twelfth Anomaly

Pope Benedict X (reigned 1058-1059, died 1073) is considered to be an antipope by the Catholic Encyclopedia but he functioned as a pope for 9 months and was considered pope by many of the faithful. He was forced to the papacy but resigned.

Thirteenth Anomaly

Anacletus II was elected Feb. 14, 1130 despite the fact that Innocent II was reigning as pope at the time.

Anacletus gained control of Rome and the majority of cardinals recognized him as the true pope.

St. Bernard of Clairvaux sided with Innocent and convinced the faithful to join him.

The two popes debated their cases before Roger at Salerno in Nov through Dec of 1137, but Innocent gained the upper hand. Anacletus died Jan 25, 1138 and his successor Victor IV submitted to Innocent thus ending the schism.

Comment: The majority doesn't always mean right.

Fourteenth Anomaly

The era of the late 14th century was a mess of unprecedented measure. Popes Urban VI, Boniface IX, Innocent VII, Gregory XII, Clement VII, Benedict XIII, Clement VIII are all highly disputed.

Pope Urban VI (Bartolomeo Prignano) was elected on April 8, 1378 by 15 of the 16 cardinals, but a rioting crowd kept him from consenting. The next day 12 cardinals confirmed the election and enthroned him on April 18. On August 2, the French cardinals who were of the majority of the conclave declared the April election invalid "as having been made, not freely, but under fear" of mob violence, and invited Urban to abdicate. On August 9, the French cardinals informed the whole Catholic world that Urban was deposed as an intruder.

The French cardinals elected Robert of Geneva as Pope Clement VII on Oct. 31. This was the beginning of the Great

Schism, which lasted from 1378 to 1417 or 1429 depending on how one views it.

Europe had to decide between the "popes" who excommunicated each other.

Urban had to create a new curia because the old one sided with Clement. Urban was mentally unstable and worked not to heal the schism but help a worthless nephew gain control of the kingdom of Naples. He died on Oct 15, 1389 and was rejected by the majority of the Church (however, St. Catherine of Sienna did recognize him) and is considered the legitimate pope in the official list.

Clement VII was recognized as the true pope by the majority of the original cardinals and by many if not most Catholics in general. Charles V also recognized him, as did many of the monarchies around Europe except Germany and the eastern and Nordic countries. He with his line is considered invalid making them all antipopes on the official list.

Clement made 16 yr old Peter of Luxemburg bishop at Metz and then cardinal in 1384. Peter later was beatified in 1527 adding credibility to his pontificate.

He excommunicated the successor of Urban, Boniface IX who was elected on Nov. 2, 1389. Boniface also excommunicated Clement but had offered Clement a chance to become legate to Spain and France if he would abdicate, but he refused.

Clement died on Sept. 16, 1394. He was never recognized as a true pope in the official list.

Boniface was notorious for his nepotism and made money by auctioning offices to the highest bidder, selling indulgences, and created jubilees by charging pilgrims for the journey and seeing of shrines. The future antipope John XXIII (Baldassare Cossa) helped Boniface finance the scandalous practices.

Benedict XIII (Pedro de Luna) was elected Sept 28 to succeed Clement. He offered to meet Boniface to settle the schism but Boniface was not interested who used health issues as an excuse not to meet. Before Boniface died in 1404, he had canonized Bridget of Sweden on Oct 7, 1391.

Benedict was a good man who wanted to end the schism. His friend St. Vincent Ferrer, the greatest miracle worker the Catholic Church ever had, was at his side while acting as pope. Benedict tried to heal the schism with negotiations with Innocent VII who succeeded Boniface on Oct. 17 1404. Innocent's election was opposed by the majority of Rome, but was admired for his strict spiritual life. He died on Nov. 6, 1406.

Gregory XII succeeded Innocent on Nov. 30, 1406. Both he and Benedict wanted an end to the schism but both strongly believed each was the true pope. Negotiations were never made and the cardinals went to Pisa (without Benedict or Gregory because they refused to attend) and elected Alexander V on June 26 1409. Alexander rightly condemned John Wycliffe and he died suddenly 5 months later on May 3, 1410. He is considered an antipope.

John XXIII was elected May 17, 1410, and was considered as true pope by the majority of the faithful. He called a Council at Pisa, which condemned Wycliffe and Huss in 1413. He called another council at Constance in Nov. 1414 but was deposed by the council on May 29, 1415, and died Nov 22, 1919. He is considered an antipope but his grave site says that he was once the pope.

Gregory XII abdicated during the council on July 4, 1415.

The council deposed Benedict XIII July 26, 1417, and who later died May 23, 1423. Benedict always believed he was the true pope and is considered the true pope by some today. His crosier and chalice are displayed in the local Church and is remembered as Papa Luna. He is not on the official list of popes.

Martin V was elected to succeed Gregory on Nov 11, 1417. Clement VIII was elected June 10, 1423 to replace Benedict. He later abdicated on July 26, 1429 and recognized Martin V, thus ending the Great Schism. Some believe the schism last after Benedict XIII was deposed and Martin was elected.

Comment: If the French cardinals are correct that they were not fully compliant in electing Urban due to fear, then his election should be considered null as with his successors Boniface, Innocent, and Gregory.

This would mean the official list got it backwards and should have placed the Avignon line as the true line of papal succession, which were Clement VII, Benedict XIII and Clement VIII. Martin V would have been an antipope until Clement abdicated only then to be a true pope.

However, this is not how history has viewed it wanting a true Roman line regardless of the situation instead of seeing a valid Avignon line.

It is also possible that none of them were true popes until Martin V. Be that as it may, all of them are at least doubtful popes except Martin V after Clement VIII abdicated and joined Martin.

Fifteenth Anomaly

Alexander VI (Rodrigo de Borgia) being the second richest cardinal bought out the papacy with outright bribery and promised riches in Aug 11, 1492. He had previously father several children and perhaps, practiced incest with one of his daughters. He was notorious for his debauched life as pope, which involved concubines. He also reframed from correcting the many of the same abuses of priests and bishops.

Dominican priest and staunch defender of orthodoxy and holiness, Girolamo Savonarola denounced Alexander for simony, which according to Savonarola, invalidated the election of Alexander thus making him an antipope.

Alexander excommunicated Savonarola on May 12, 1497 in the bull *Cum saepenumero*, but the Dominican rejected the bull as invalid since Alexander didn't have the power to do so. Savonarola, along with two other priests, were imprisoned, tortured, and finally hanged on May 23, 1498. They were burned completely and their ashes dumped into the river Arno to prevent relics to be collected.

Pope Julius II condemned simony in his bull *Cum tam divino* in 1513. He said that any ecclesial office, including the papacy, would be null and void if obtained by simony.

Savonarola, with miracles attributed to his name, was venerated by later great saints such as: St. Philip Neri, St. Catherine Ricci, St. John Fisher, Pope St. Pius V, and Pope St. Pius X.

Although Alexander is considered a true pope and listed as such on the official list, perhaps Savonarola was correct since the bull of Pope Julius II would have been true from the time of Peter himself by divine law.

In the Book of Acts we read, "And when Simon saw that, by the imposition of the hands of the apostles, the Holy Ghost was given, he offered them money, Saying: Give me also this power, that on whomsoever I shall lay my hands, he may receive the Holy Ghost. But Peter said to him: Keep thy money to thyself, to perish with thee: because thou hast thought that the gift of God may be purchased with money. Thou hast no part or lot in this matter. For thy heart is not right in the sight of God."

It would appear that all claimants to the papacy under simony should be considered null and void, not merely because of the bull of Pope Julius who perhaps obtained the papacy the same way, but by the divine law of God.

The case of Benedict IX and Gregory VI (who were addressed in the 11th anomaly) most certainly falls under this law.

The great poet Dante placed Nicholas III in hell buried upside down, the soles of his feet burning with oil mocking baptism. Nicholas tells Dante that both Pope Boniface VIII and Pope Clement V were in hell for the sin of simony.

If what Dante alludes in his poem is true, then those particular men should not have any real right to the papacy by divine law.

Again, it should be noted that Pope St. Leo IX would reordain men who were previously ordained by known simoniac bishops. This was either because St. Leo didn't believe simoniac bishops to be true bishops or they were true bishops but had no power to exercise any authority.

Regardless of how history may view Alexander VI (the whole Church seems to recognize him as a true pope but a bad one), I submit that he was at least a doubtful pope and Savonarola was right in declaring him as having no right to the papacy.

Conclusions from the official papal list and history:

1. The list recognizes true popes as antipopes.

2. The list recognizes antipopes or doubtful popes as true popes.

3. The list recognizes popes who were unlawfully elected.

4. The list demonstrates that throughout history, the list changes and may recognize a pope at one time but not now or vice versa.

5. The list doesn't always recognize Canon law.

6. True popes have falsely believed in antipopes.

7. True popes have falsely condemned other true popes.

8. True popes have falsely nullified orders.

9. Antipopes are sometimes recognized as true popes from the majority of the faithful.

10. Simony has not always been recognized as a nullifying factor in the election of popes as it should be.

11. The majority of the Church has at one time followed all the previous conclusions.

12. The Church has recognized that a true pope can become a heretic making him an antipope.

13. The Church can go many years (over 40) not knowing who the true pope is thus demonstrating that the Church can function to some extent (if not correctly or completely)

indefinitely without a pope since doubtful popes is as bad as no pope at all.

14. It is possible to have another true pope outside of any law since it has happened already in history.

Our Lady of Guadalupe

We'll end this book with a story of Our Lady of Guadalupe.

When the Blessed Virgin Mary appeared to Juan Diego in 1531, in the Aztec language, she called herself, *"Te Coatlaxopeuh,"* meaning "She who crushes the head of the stone serpent."

The Spaniards misunderstood Juan Diego and Juan Bernardino thinking they were saying Guadalupe, a famous shrine of Our Lady in Spain from an apparition in the 13th century.

In the Spanish apparition, Our Lady instructed a man named "Gil" where to find a buried statue of her, known as the

Immaculate Conception, hidden during the 8th century Moslem invasion.

Our Lady of Guadalupe or *Te Coatlaxopeuh* can be seen in Holy Scripture.

In Genesis 3:15, the first prophecy of Our Lord and Lady is told. From this Scripture passage, we see several things relating to the famous image of Our Lady of Guadalupe.

The "woman" crushes the head of Satan, just as Our Lady titled herself.

All bibles but one says "HE" will crush the head. However, this is a false translation.

The historic rendering of this Hebrew pronoun "hu" has always and should be rendered "SHE," because the "woman" and not the "seed" is the antecedent of "hu."

This follows the context, because Gen 3:15 says the enmity is between the "woman" and "Satan", then it says, between her "seed" and Satan's "seed."

If you read the Hebrew pronoun as "he" crushing the head of "Satan" then you have misplaced the context of who has enmity with whom. "She" will crush the head since she was the object that follows and the one who was said to have enmity with "Satan." We know of course that it is because of her "seed" that she does this.

St. Jerome got it right making the Douay Rheims Version of the Bible the only accurate English translation on this verse.

"He," Jesus may also have enmity with the devil, but within the context of Gen. 3:15, it is "She" that will crush the head of Satan. Thus, the Catholic Church has always been right by showing statues of Mary stepping on the serpent.

This same verse also follows the fall of Adam and Eve, which gives us Original Sin. (This means, because of Adam and Eve's disobedience, we are conceived without Sanctifying Grace and in union with the devil.)

After they disobeyed, we are told there will be a "woman" who will not be like them or us. This "woman" will have enmity with Satan, which means she will be conceived with Sanctifying Grace, hence, the Immaculate Conception.

This is what the Spaniards believed about Our Lady of Guadalupe of Spain. Now they think she is appearing under the same name but in reality, she was appearing under a different name that not only refers to her as one with enmity with the devil, but as one who actually crushes his head.

The Aztecs worshipped the stone serpent, or the devil, identified in picture writing as a crescent moon as they made human sacrifices to this god.

Just as our statues show Our Lady standing on the serpent represented as a snake, now the Aztecs see Our Lady in the image standing on their stone serpent god represented as a crescent moon.

Our Lady of Guadalupe is with child (Christ) as the ribbon belt around her waist indicates under the tradition of the Aztecs. This, of course, being the "seed" demonstrated from the verse of Holy Scripture.

In 1509, Montezuma's sister, Princess Papantzin, lying in a coffin thought to have died, had a vision of ships with large black crosses on the sails. She was let go after she woke and banged on the coffin. She said men on these ships would bring a new religion of the one true God, and 10 years later the prophecy came true with the arrival of Cortez.

The same Franciscan cross as the vision of the princess is shown around the neck of Our Lady of Guadalupe.

In the Apocalypse 12:1, we see a woman clothed with the sun with a moon under her feet, with a crown of twelve stars.

The image of Our Lady of Guadalupe shows a woman clothed with the sun with a moon under her feet. The turquoise mantle with gold stars indicated the woman was a heavenly queen, as those particular colors were reserved for Aztec royalty.

On October 12, 1895, Pope Leo XIII authorized the first crowning of Our Lady of Guadalupe.

On October 12, 1945, Pope Pius XII said from his radio message, "We are certain that while you are recognized as Queen and mother, the Americas and Mexico will have been saved."

The stars on her tilma indicate literally a heavenly apparition as those stars fit the constellations seen on that night of 1531.

The constellations, Hydra (the dragon), Scorpio (the scorpion is the sign of Lucifer), and Draco (the serpent) surround the holy image as some kind of anti-trinity. No doubt, this ought to remind us that a terrible war is being waged on us by all of hell itself.

Based on the configuration of these constellations, we know that the constellation Leo (the lion) fits perfectly within the abdomen section of the image. Christ is known as the "Lion of the tribe of Juda, the root of David."

Our Lady once said she would save the world by the Brown Scapular and the Holy Rosary.

She is the woman mentioned in the beginning of the Bible crushing Satan with her seed (Jesus Christ Our Lord and Savior,) and she is mentioned at the end of the Bible, with Jesus Christ, where the victory over Death and Hell is won.

Pray the most Holy Rosary of the Blessed Virgin Mary, Our Lady of Guadalupe and wear devotedly her precious garment, the Brown Scapular.

Hold fast the historic Catholic Faith found only in the underground Catholic Church, the real rock on which Christ built. Fight the greatest of all attacks from hell by rejecting the new modernist Masonic religion of Rome, which usurped the Catholic name.

In the end, the Immaculate Heart of Mary will triumph!

APPENDIX I

Cardinal Franzelin, translated by James Larrabee.

VACANCY OF THE APOSTOLIC SEE

15. "Hence the distinction arises between the seat [*sedes*, See] and the one sitting in it [*sedens*], by reason of perpetuity. The seat, that is the perpetual right of the primacy, never ceases, on the part of God in His unchangeable law and supernatural providence, and on the part of the Church in her right and duty of forever keeping as a deposit the power divinely instituted on behalf of the individual successors of Peter, and of securing their succession by a fixed law; but the individual heirs or those sitting [*sedentes*] in the Apostolic seat are mortal men; and therefore the seat can never fail, but it can be *vacant* and often is vacant. Then indeed the divine law and institution of perpetuity remains, and by the same reason the right and duty in the Church of procuring the succession according to the established law; there remain also the participations in the powers [of the papacy] to the extent they are communicable to others [e.g. to the Cardinals or bishops], and have been communicated by the successor of Peter while still alive, or have been lawfully established and not abrogated [thus the jurisdiction of bishops, granted by the Pope, does not cease when he dies]; but the highest power itself, together with its rights and prerogatives, which can in no way exist except in the one individual heir of Peter, now actually belong to no one while the See is vacant.

"From this can be understood the distinction in the condition of the Church herself in the time of the *vacancy of the See* and the time of the *occupation of the See* [*sedis plenae*], namely that in the former time, a successor of Peter, the visible rock and visible head of the Church, *is owed* to the vacant Apostolic See by divine right or law but *does not yet exist*; in the time of the occupation of the See he now *actually sits* by divine right. It is most important to consider the very root of the whole life of the

Church, by which I mean the indefectibility and infallible custody of the deposit of the faith. Certainly there remains in the Church not only indefectibility *in believing* (called passive infallibility) but also infallibility *in proclaiming* the truth already revealed and already sufficiently proposed for Catholic belief, even while she is for a time bereaved of her visible head, so that neither the whole body of the Church in its belief, nor the whole Episcopate in its teaching, can depart from the faith handed down and fall into heresy, because this permanence of the Spirit of truth in the Church, the kingdom and spouse and body of Christ, is included in the very promise and institution of the indefectibility of the Church *for all days* even to the consummation of the world. The same is to be said, by the same reasoning, for the unity of communion against a universal schism, as for the truth of the faith against heresy. For the divine law and promise of perpetual succession in the See of Peter, as the root and center of Catholic unity, remains; and to this law and promise correspond, on the part of the Church, not only the right and duty of, but also indefectibility in, legitimately procuring and receiving the succession and in keeping the unity of communion with the Petrine See even when vacant, in view of the successor who is awaited and will indefectibly come ... " (Franzelin, op. cit., p. 221-223)

Pope Pius IX elevates Father Franzelin, who was teaching this doctrine publicly under his nose at the Roman College, to the ranks of Cardinal in 1876.

APPENDIX II

Divine and Canon Laws and their Applications

Pope Pius XII, Mystici Corporis Christi (# 23), June 29, 1943: "*For not every sin, however grave it may be, is such as of its own nature to sever a man from the Body of the Church, as does schism or heresy or apostasy.*"

Censure and Vindictive Penalties

It's false to hold that only Church (authorities) can determine if a manifest heretic is a manifest heretic and therefore, outside the Church. Canon 2314.1 can't be skipped over for Canon 2314.2 with the argument, *"While canon 188.4 says the office becomes vacant when one publicly defects from the Faith, canon 2314.2 requires formal warnings followed by the obstinate refusal to heed the warnings before the public defection can be established."*

Canon 2314.1 states that all heretics incur ipso facto excommunication. An explanation of canonical penalties by Professor of Canon Law, Rev. P. Charles Augustine, O.S.B., D.D., shows why the above assertion is erroneous:

"2) The penalties here enunciated are twofold: censure and vindictive penalties; besides, a distinction is drawn, according to can. 2207, n. 1, by reason of dignity, between laymen and clerics.

a) The censure inflicted is excommunication incurred ipso facto, which per se requires not even a declaratory sentence... Note that the term moniti [warnings] *(2314 Â§1, n. 2) does not refer to the incurring of the censure. Consequently, no canonical warning or admonition is required."* (A COMMENTARY ON THE NEW CODE OF CANON LAW, Volume VIII, Book V, Penal Code, Canon 2314, pp. 275-276; B. Herder Book Company, Imprimatur by John J. Glennon, Archbishop of Saint Louis, Friday, August 25, 1922)

As far as the papacy is concerned, not one of the three canons (1939.1, 2223.4, 2314.2) could possibly apply. Another Professor of Canon Law, R. P. Udalricus Beste, O.S.B., I.C.D., explains why not:

"Not a few canonists teach that, outside of death and abdication, the pontifical dignity can also be lost by falling into certain insanity, which is legally equivalent to death, as well as through manifest and notorious heresy. In the latter case, a pope would automatically fall from his power, and this indeed without the issuance of any sentence, for the first See [i.e., the See of Peter] is judged by no one.

"The reason is that, by falling into heresy, the pope ceases to be a member of the Church. He who is not a member of a society, obviously, cannot be its head. We can find no example of this in history." (Introductio in Codicem. 3rd ed. Collegeville: St. John's Abbey Press, 1946)

In addition to Augustine's explanation of Canon 2314, Augustine also explains in Canon 2315 that there are three types of suspicion for heretics.

*"Violent suspicion amounts to morally certain proof...*and *is to be considered as a positive proof and therefore rather falls under can. 2314.*

Interestingly, under Canon 2315, repeated warnings are to be given to suspected heretic clerics, and if they don't amend themselves, shall be deemed heretics and liable to the penalties thereof. Heretics wouldn't have to be warned again and again to fulfill Canon 2314.2.

Using Ecclesiastical Law to Trump Divine Law

Vatican 2 apologists enjoy using arguments that make Ecclesiastical Law trump Divine Law. An example was given in Objection 9 p. 291.

They'll say, *"While, according to Divine Law, formal heresy results in self-expulsion from the Church without the need for a declaratory sentence, ecclesiastical law (can 2223.4) requires a declaratory sentence (sententia declaratoria dari debet) of said heresy if the common good of the Church requires it."*

Apparently, they didn't read that Canon 2223.4 referred to a superior making the declaratory sentence. The pope has no superiors and therefore the law can't apply mentioned earlier. All the expert canonists teach that a heretic pope automatically loses his office *"without any declaratory sentence."* The pope is judged and warned by no one.

However, Vatican 2 apologists don't stop there. They also state, *"Popes St. Pius X and Pius XII's legislation is clear that 'by reason of any excommunication 'whatsoever' a Cardinal is not excluded from being elected to the papacy. 'Any excommunication...whatsoever' necessarily includes a Cardinal's excommunication for heresy. This means the governing ecclesiastical law – which Sedevacantists agree applies to the question at hand – presumes the validity of papal elections, until there is a determination by the Church of whether or not Divine Law has been violated. Ecclesiastical law, then, requires this formal determination to be made by the Church after the election."*

In other words, despite the Divine Law that heretics are outside of the Church (top quote from Pope Pius XII), Vatican 2 apologists think two popes have legislated the permission for a known heretical non-member of the Church, while still in heresy, to be elected to the head of the Church only to be determined later by church authorities if the newly elected pope is, indeed, a heretic, and therefore not a true pope. Yet, no one can judge the pope to be a heretic, anyway. Someone might argue that since the election wouldn't have been valid to begin with because of an election of a heretic, then no one would be judging a true pope. However, if this were the case, then the papal legislation would simply be stupid, because it would be a complete waste of time, not to mention, dangerous. Why would the popes legislate the permission of a formal heretic to be elected at all? The answer is they wouldn't.

Since Vatican 2 apologists misinterpret Canon 188.4, 2314, and others, their error leads them to misapply Popes St. Pius X and XII's legislation. Heretics lose all jurisdiction of authority therefore any cardinal who becomes a heretic ceases to be a cardinal. The cardinals being referred to in the papal legislation of Popes Pius X, and XII, are those that fall under different penalties. The experts in Canon Law such as, Maroto, Coronata, Werbz-Vidal, and Marietti explain that heretics and schismatics are barred from the papacy by Divine Law.

Anti-sedevacanters like to create their own novel interpretations, and in the end, their interpretations violate the Divine Law.

It Gets Comical

Vatican 2 apologists have said, *"Sedevacantists are schismatic and hence automatically excommunicated from the Church under both Divine and ecclesiastical law (canon 1325, par. 2)."*

So what? According to their own argument, we (sedevacantists) could still be validly elected pope with jurisdiction over the whole Church. Yet, they contradict themselves here, because they argued using Canons 1939, 2223.4, and 2324.2 that it takes investigations, warnings, and perhaps a trial before someone could be considered schismatic and automatically excommunicated. Vatican 2 apologists are applying the very argument which they condemn as invalid. What baffoonery!

Lastly

A couple of more commentaries that bury such arguments against sedevacantism:

Canon 2200.2, 1917 Code of Canon Law: *"When an external violation of the law has been committed, malice is presumed in the external forum until the contrary is proven."*

"The very commission of any act which signifies heresy, e.g., the statement of some doctrine contrary or contradictory to a revealed and defined dogma, gives sufficient ground for juridical presumption of heretical depravity... Excusing circumstances have to be proved in the external forum, and the burden of proof is on the person whose action has given rise to the imputation of heresy. In the absence of such proof, all such excuses are presumed not to exist." (Eric F. Mackenzie, A.M., S.T.L., J.C.L. Rev., *The Delict of Heresy,* Washington, D.C.: The Catholic Univ. of America, 1932, p. 35. (Cf. Canon 2200.2)

Rev. P. Charles Augustine goes into more detail as he explains Canon 2216-2217 and the different penalties:

"Why can the Church, unlike the State, inflict a penalty latae sententiae? It appears unjust and unworthy of a perfect society to condemn one before he is heard. But we must not forget that the Church is a peculiar society, with a religious character that does not remain on the surface, but penetrates and encompasses the whole man. She reaches into the court of conscience. Besides, the most sacred offices might be neglected and abused without punishment because of lack of witnesses and plaintiffs, and the fear of penalty and final exposure may check malice and carelessness. Therefore the first traces of censures latae sententiae coincide with the spread of evil influences in the sixth and seventh century. In order to protect ecclesiastical discipline more efficaciously, this quasi self-executory remedy was found most efficient and secure. (pp. 74-75 Book Vol. VIII, book V)

Appendix III

Evangelium vitae and the Death Penalty

In the past, the Catholic Church promoted the practice of the death penalty for sodomites as a just punishment because the Church considers sodomy an abominable crime against God and society.

At the Council of Nabluse, 1120 AD, under the Patriarch of Jerusalem Garmond of Picquigny and King Baldwin II, three canons [8-10] were issued that called for death by the stake sodomites who participated either actively or passively, unless it was a child or an elderly person acting against his will.

Four centuries later, the Fifth Lateran Council decreed that sodomites be executed by secular authorities.

In one of his very first acts as pope, St. Pius V in *Cum Primum* on April 1, 1566 ordered that sodomites be executed by the secular authorities.

Two years later, he declared in a Constitution:

"That horrible crime, on account of which corrupt and obscene cities were destroyed by fire through divine condemnation, causes us most bitter sorrow and shocks our mind, impelling us to repress such a crime with the greatest possible zeal.

Quite opportunely the Fifth Lateran Council [1512-1517] issued this decree: "Let any member of the clergy caught in that vice against nature, given that the wrath of God falls over the sons of perfidy, be removed from the clerical order or forced to do penance in a monastery" (chap. 4, X, V, 31).

So that the contagion of such a grave offense may not advance with greater audacity by taking advantage of impunity, which is the greatest incitement to sin, and so as to more severely punish the clerics who are guilty of this nefarious crime and who are not frightened by the death of their souls, we determine that they should be handed over to the severity of the secular authority, which enforces civil law.

Therefore, wishing to pursue with greater rigor than we have exerted since the beginning of our pontificate, we establish that any priest or member of the clergy, either secular or regular, who commits such an execrable crime, by force of the present law be deprived of every clerical privilege, of every post, dignity and ecclesiastical benefit, and having been degraded by an ecclesiastical judge, let him be immediately delivered to the secular authority to be put to death, as mandated by law as the fitting punishment for laymen who have sunk into this abyss." (Constitution *Horrendum illud scelus*, August 30, 1568, in *Bullarium Romanum*, Rome: *Typographia Reverendae Camerae Apostolicae*, Mainardi, 1738, chap. 3, p. 33)

Catholics must recognize that the Catholic Church's teaching and practice of the death penalty for such crimes as sodomy is moral and just or else the Gates of Hell have prevailed against the Catholic Church for teaching and practicing an unjust and immoral act.

In John Paul II's hallmark encyclical, *Evangelium vitae*, 1995, he implies that the historic teaching and practice of executing sodomites was immoral and unjust.

He writes…

27. Modern society in fact has the means of effectively suppressing crime by rendering criminals harmless without definitively denying them the chance to reform.

40. Of course we must recognize that in the Old Testament this sense of the value of life, though already quite marked, does not yet reach the refinement found in the Sermon on the Mount. This is apparent in some aspects of the current penal legislation, which provided for severe forms of corporal punishment and even the death penalty. But the overall message, which the New Testament will bring to perfection, is a forceful appeal for respect for the inviolability of physical life and the integrity of the person. It culminates in the positive commandment which obliges us to be responsible for our neighbour as for ourselves: "You shall love your neighbour as yourself" (Lev 19:18).

41. The commandment "You shall not kill", included and more fully expressed in the positive command of love for one's neighbour, is reaffirmed in all its force by the Lord Jesus. To the rich young man who asks him: "Teacher, what good deed must I do, to have eternal life?", Jesus replies: "If you would enter life, keep the commandments" (Mt 19:16,17). And he quotes, as the first of these: "You shall not kill" (Mt 19:18). In the Sermon on the Mount, Jesus demands from his disciples a righteousness which surpasses that of the Scribes and Pharisees, also with regard to respect for life: "You have heard that it was said to the men of old, ?You shall not kill; and whoever kills shall be liable to judgment'. But I say to you that every one who is angry with his brother shall be liable to judgment" (Mt 5:21-22).

Notice that John Paul II ignores the fact that the death penalty is also a punishment, not merely a deterrent for future crimes.

In his misrepresentation of the New Testament, he actually implies that the love of neighbor is equal to God. If one commits a crime against God deserving of death, then he shall be put to death. Love of neighbor should not be used to justify the life of man over the due punishment to God's justice. John Paul is saying that man should be given the type of respect that his life is inviolable which would necessarily place man's dignity on equal status with God. The love of God is first and the love of neighbor is second. You will find that Vatican 2 does not make this distinction when it stated, *"This is why the first and greatest commandment is love of God and of neighbor." Gaudium et Spes* #24 This is an outrageous lie!

While love of neighbor does reflect love for God, it does not mean that love of neighbor is the same as love for God.

John Paul made the argument that the death penalty goes against Christ and the Commandment *"You shall not kill."*

John Paul II continues...

56. This is the context in which to place the problem of the death penalty. On this matter there is a growing tendency, both in the Church and in civil society, to demand that it be applied in a very limited way or even that it be abolished completely. The problem must be viewed in the context of a system of penal justice ever more in line with human dignity and thus, in the end, with God's plan for man and society. The primary purpose of the punishment which society inflicts is "to redress the disorder caused by the offence". [Catechism of the Catholic Church, No. 2266.] Public authority must redress the violation of personal and social rights by imposing on the offender an adequate punishment for the crime, as a condition for the offender to regain the exercise of his or her freedom. In this way authority also fulfils the purpose of defending public order and ensuring people's safety, while at the same time offering the offender an incentive and help to change his or her behaviour and be rehabilitated. [Cf. ibid.]

It is clear that, for these purposes to be achieved, the nature and extent of the punishment must be carefully evaluated and decided upon, and ought not go to the extreme of executing the offender except in cases of absolute necessity: in other words, when it would not be possible otherwise to defend society. Today however, as a result of steady improvements in the organization of the penal system, such cases are very rare, if not practically non-existent.

According to John Paul II, the death penalty is justified only when it defends public order and ensuring people's safety. Such cases where men cannot be kept from being a threat to society are, of course, practically non-existent. Maximum security would take care of any real problems.

In the past, sodomites were a threat to society as St. Pius V implied, but even though they could have been locked away and given time to reform, the historic Catholic Church didn't do so.

The new religion of Rome raised the level of man's dignity equal to God with the teaching that the love of God and neighbor are one and the same.

Modernist Rome has necessarily rejected the historic teaching and practice of the Catholic Church of putting sodomites to death thus undercutting the very foundation of their own religion.

Evangelium vitae is a typical modernist document since truth yesterday is not truth today.

One might argue that it is not an infallible document and therefore no doctrine has been infringed.

Regardless, John Paul II has personally rejected Catholic doctrine and practice and his document will now be accepted by millions leading them astray.

ABOUT THE AUTHOR

Steven Brian Speray resides in Versailles, Kentucky with his wife and three children.

His training was in Strategic Weapons Systems (Submarine Ballistic Missiles) of the U.S. Navy.

He has worked as a Catholic apologist writing, teaching, and giving lectures on the Catholic Faith.

Steven has authored several books on the Catholic Church, such as:

- Baptism of Desire or Blood (A Defense in Brief, *Ad Majorem Dei Gloriam*)
- Catholicism in a Nutshell
- The Key to the Apocalypse
- Papal Anomalies and their Implications
- Rome's Great Heresy – The Popes of Vatican 2 Reject a Catholic Dogma
- Rome's Great Apostasy –The Popes of Vatican 2 Reject a Divine Law

Steven is an avid weightlifter and swimmer, and a retired boxer (undefeated). You may find him playing tennis with his brothers, or chopping wood for the winter.

www.ingramcontent.com/pod-product-compliance
Lightning Source LLC
Chambersburg PA
CBHW021753230426
43669CB00006B/65

* 9 7 8 0 5 7 8 0 3 5 7 4 1 *